Open Spaces for Interactions and Learning Diversities

Open Spaces for Interactions and Learning Diversities

Edited by

Alessio Surian
University of Padova, Italy

SENSE PUBLISHERS
ROTTERDAM/BOSTON/TAIPEI

A C.I.P. record for this book is available from the Library of Congress.

ISBN: 978-94-6300-338-4 (paperback)
ISBN: 978-94-6300-339-1 (hardback)
ISBN: 978-94-6300-340-7 (e-book)

Published by: Sense Publishers,
P.O. Box 21858,
3001 AW Rotterdam,
The Netherlands
https://www.sensepublishers.com/

All chapters in this book have undergone peer review.

Printed on acid-free paper

TABLE OF CONTENTS

PART 1

THE SPACE AND TIME OF LEARNING INTERACTIONS

ALESSIO SURIAN

1. LEARNING WITH PASSION AND COMPASSION

INTRODUCTION

As the conference that brought together the authors of the following chapters was approaching, one spring morning poet Maya Angelou passed away. One of the conference and of this book key word is "open". What is an open attitude? Suddenly I went back to one of her facebook posts dated July 5th 2011. She wrote:

> *My mission in life is not merely to survive, but to thrive; and to do so with some passion, some compassion, some humor, and some style.*

Likewise, as scholars focusing from a sociocultural perspective on learning and educational relations in order to take into account passions and compassions in what we experience and reflect upon we are adopting an emerging orientation towards multidisciplinary research work in the field of learning interactions (Grossen, 2009).

In this spirit, such affective dimension was enhanced in our conference by opening each day by listening to live music performed by some of the best travelled musicians that Padova would offer: Wilson Columbus, Luca Manneschi, Alberto Vedovato, Andrea Ferlini, and Luca Xodo who also contributed this book's cover photo. In a similar way songs were helping Mediterranean people to act to support and to welcome refugees crossing the Mare Nostrum, and to mourn those who lost their lives while moving across borders. As Gang sing "*Mare ti prego stanotte, falli passare, mare nostro mare – Tonight I am praying you sea, let them cross, be our sea*". In this spirit the first key-note speech was delivered by Gianfranco Bonesso (Venice Municipality) who skilfully placed participants' studies on learning, interactions and multicultural contexts in relation to the actual challenges of public policies promoting diversity as a social advantage.

Unlikely previous SIGs publications in this field, this book presents a broader spectrum of contents to offer glimpses into some of the variety of current research fields. To provide a common thread the authors were invited to respond to the following question:

> What are the challenges that global movements and cross-cultural communication continue to pose to many areas of teaching, learning and education?

The conference organisers assumption was that with increasing dynamics and diversity in most societies (i.e., offline and online mobility, inter-institutional

A. Surian (Ed.), Open Spaces for Interactions and Learning Diversities, 3–12.

collaborations, migrations and intercultural encounters as well as individual transitions) this area of research becomes even more important in learning research. While changes related to cultural diversity are visible and at work in social, cultural and political contexts, cultural diversity as such is being ignored or rejected across many countries in Europe. It is the denial or hidden nature of diversity in educational settings and learning processes, reflected in the marginalisation of this topic that the conference wanted to address.

Therefore, the following chapters are intended to open up spaces to talk, promote and struggle for the relevance of addressing learning diversities. This includes current and new directions for theoretical and methodological discussions. They concern spaces of interaction and diversity research across single and multiple moments, different contexts and various time scales. They also explore the diversity of theories used to address these issues and how we theorize the relationship between centres and margins in understanding the idea of opening spaces for dialogue.

A MEETING OF SPECIAL INTEREST GROUPS IN 2014

The following chapters offer diverse approaches to studying learning interactions and discourses. They follow up previous research exploring the potential and challenges that each strand of research can bring to understanding the psychological, social and cultural life of educational relations and how they mediate the situated practice of learning in today's contexts (Kumpulainen, Hmelo-Silver, & César, 2009).

The book is one of the results of a conference with the same title held at the University of Padova, 27–30 August 2014. It was organised by a scientific committee including Sanne Akkerman, Aleksandar Baucal, Gert Biesta, Sarah Crafter, Giuseppe Ritella, Alessio Surian, Rupert Wegerif. The members of the committee were participating in and representing three Special Interest Groups (SIG) of the European Association for Research on Learning and Instruction (EARLI). The three SIGs addressed Social Interaction in Learning and Instruction (SIG 10), Learning and Teaching in Culturally Diverse Settings (SIG 21), and Educational Theories (SIG 25). Therefore this book continues a series of publications that came out after SIGs meetings in these fields of research, beginning with 'Social Interaction in Learning and Instruction. The Meaning of Discourse for the Construction of Knowledge' edited in 2000 by Helen Cowie and Geerdina van der Aalsvoort which was based on papers that had been presented at the meeting in Leiden 1998 of SIG Social Interaction in Learning and Instruction. Two publications followed up in 2009 as the result of meetings of SIG members, mainly the Lisbon conference that in 2004 joined forces of members of SIG Social Interaction in Learning and Instruction, and SIG Special Educational needs. Kristiina Kumpulainen, Cindy Hmelo-Silver, and Margarida Cesar edited 'Investigating classroom interaction. Methodologies in action' which reviews diverse approaches to investigate classroom practice. Margarida Cesar and Kristiina Kumpulainen also edited 'Social Interactions in Multicultural Settings' which offers the results of studies focusing on the multilingual and multicultural dimension of formal education. In 2012, Eva Hjörne, Geerdina van der Aalsvoort, and Guida De Abreu edited 'Learning, Social Interaction and Diversity – Exploring Identities' which is based on studies presented during the Gothenburg, May 2008 conference organised by three SIGs: Social Interaction in Learning and Instruction, Learning and Teaching in Culturally Diverse Settings, and Special Educational Needs.

SIGs 10 and 21 continued the reflection in Utrecht 2010, at the 'Moving through cultures of learning' conference, and at the 'Patchwork: Learning Diversities' conference held in Belgrade in 2012. The 2013 London EARLI Advanced Studies Colloquium on Educational Theories triggered SIG 25 on the same theme and this Special Interest Group collaboration with SIG 10 and 21.

THE SPACE AND TIME OF LEARNING INTERACTIONS

The focus of the next chapters is to examine the role of interactions and diversity within practices of learning and the way such interactions and ideas of diversity co-evolve. Following the "open" spirit of the conference, authors were free to choose the format and length of their chapters. As a result the various contributions offer a variety of choices to text length and to writing approaches depending on the available data and core research methods and content focus. The inter-textual fabric is visible in the socio-cultural framework adopted by the authors, exploring learning as occurring through participation and collaboration within and across social groups. In an implicit or explicit way most chapters discuss issues of intersubjectivity, the ability to expand one's own perception in order to include other perceptions and ways of thinking (Moro, Müller Mirza, & Roman, 2014). Special attention is being paid to the role of conversation and dialogues in social interaction across different contexts (Baucal, Arcidiacono, & Budjevac, 2011). Spaces and places are a key focus and they are the specific subject of the second and the third chapter.

In the second chapter Peter Renshaw and Ron Tooth take the reader to Queensland Australia in order to go back to Vygotsky's notion of *perezhivanie*. They present Storythread a narrative-based and place-responsive pedagogy that enables them to explore deep learning and significant changes to self as reported by students that experienced such learning activity. In turn, this enables them to explore Lev Vygotsky's notion of *perezhivanie*, an understanding of learning as a transformative process based on dialogue involving intellectual and deep emotional insights that leads to reflection on oneself and one's future. To facilitate such process they avoid enhancing precision in the pedagogical design in order to favour richness and openness of the learning environment, as a way to offer deep learning opportunities to as many students as possible. This implies visiting natural places through excursion that are "inherently unpredictable".

Along with Vygotsky's, Mikhail Bakhtin's ideas offer a remarkable canvas for exploring learning interactions from a dialogical perspective. In the third chapter, Giuseppe Ritella and Beatrice Ligorio focus on the ways space and time are negotiated in dialogical interactions and on the social process that embeds such interactions. A technology rich environment hosting a media design project course offers them the opportunity to use Bakhtin's concept of chronotope to investigate how a group of students constructs space and time while designing their project. They identify three aspects of space-time negotiation, and they conduct three studies to explore them.

Stefano Oliverio contributes a fourth chapter that builds bridges across educational theories and diversity issues by exploring the hyphenation practices from a philosophical perspective, beginning with the Italian philosopher Gianni Vattimo. In investigating our contemporary existential condition, Vattimo saw one of its chief features as the liberation of differences and of what could be generally called "dialect." Vattimo explicitly opposes this trait to the project of the humanistic Bildung as it was articulated in German tradition and found its culmination in Hegel's idea of the self-transparency of consciousness. To this idea of an "educated society" understood as an "enlightened" and therefore "transparent" society, Vattimo counters the project of a valorisation of the pluralisation of history and culture as it is/may be promoted thanks to the proliferation of communication. Vattimo seems to champion the passage from a dialectic to a dialectal Bildung. On the one hand, Oliverio's chapter intends to emphasize the educational significance of this project; on the other, though, it raises the question whether a 'dialectal Bildung' is sufficient to cope with contemporary scenarios. If the role that the liberation of 'dialects' has in breaking the grip of monological and ultimately diversity-erasing approaches in education is not objectionable, what can be discussed is whether it can represent a final option. In particular, the contribution engages with this question by drawing upon some ingenious ideas of Horace Kallen on hyphenation. In the heat of the polemics on the hyphenated America (the derogatory phrase used to attack the immigrants who were not considered true Americans, but only Italian-American, Irish-American etc. because they did not belong to the English stock of the first settlers) Kallen countered that 'culture is spiritual hyphenation.' Oliverio's chapter suggests that the educational engagement aimed at valorising plurality should consist not so much in a 'dialectal Bildung' as in the cultivation of the awareness of our constitutive 'hyphenated condition.' To achieve this end, a reinterpretation of the Matthew Lipman community of philosophical inquiry (CPI) is appealed to in the light of Hansen's idea of educational cosmopolitanism and Delanty's critical cosmopolitanism. The CPI will be presented as a 'space of borders' and re-interpreted against the backdrop of a reading of the Bakhtin's notions of getting into shape and borders.

NARRATIVE APPROACHES, KNOWLEDGE CO-CONSTRUCTION,
AND SOCIAL INTERACTION

The role of narrative in relation to social inclusion in educational and research practice is addressed in the fifth chapter by Colette Daiute and Philip Kreniske who address two relevant questions:

How might narrating be useful for participants' evaluation of higher education institutions claiming to be inclusive?

How might those complex uses of narrating serve meaning making by diverse groups, in this case immigrant and native-born students in higher education?

Daiute and Kreniske' study of narrating in the rapidly changing institution of the community college in the United States illustrates a dynamic theory of narrative, that narrating is an activity and means of making sense of experience, how one fits, and what might be important to change. They argue that research focused on social inclusion in education must design for complexity of meaning, as individuals' participation in institutions is likely to involve critique, as well as connection, and dilemmas that can usefully be raised toward improved social integration. After briefly discussing the foundational theory of narrating, their chapter presents the design and results of a study asking community college students to narrate their best ad worst experiences in college. Analyses of the 546 narratives revealed 4 major and 20 supporting categories of values students emphasized with their narratives. Results show that participants used the different narrative genres to express different meanings of the college and that U.S.-born and immigrant students oriented in some different ways to their colleges. Their findings illustrate why researchers must approach narrating as a social process for interacting in the relevant world.

The sixth chapter on dialogic interactions and collective writing in primary years involves the collaboration among seven colleagues:

Sylvia Rojas-Drummond, Ana María Márquez, Riikka Hofmann, Fiona Maine, Ana Luisa Rubio, José Hernández, Kissy Guzmán.

They extensively report an investigation into the development of children's literacy as a result of their involvement in a Learning Together programme focused on dialogic and text production strategies. The year-long study included 120 grade-six (11–12 year olds) children from two (experimental and control) Mexican elementary schools. Both groups engaged in individual and group pre- and post- intervention Tests of Textual Production in which they were required to produce a written text as a result of collaboratively synthesising and transforming information about a topic from different written sources. In addition to the gathering of quantitative data, the dialogic interactions of two 'focal triads' of children engaging in the pre- and post- Tests of Textual Production were analysed using the Ethnography of Communication in combination with a socio-cultural Scheme for Educational Dialogue Analysis which is provided at the end of the chapter. Findings show that children who participated in the Learning Together programme, employed styles of communication that were more dialogic when collaborating in triads during the post-test than in the pre-test. They also produced higher quality written texts. The statistically significant results suggest that Learning Together participants appropriated and transferred the dialogic and text production strategies promoted, so that they could apply these effectively not only in collaborative contexts but also independently, in a self-regulated and autonomous fashion.

The analysis of the communication process in peer learning and knowledge co-construction is also at the core of the study by Susanne Jurkowski and Martin Hänze. Their seventh chapter analyses students' discourse within the framework of transactive communication, i.e. communication that refers to and builds on a learning partner's idea such as critique, extension, and integration. Their results are based on an experiment involving eighty university students. According to their results trained students outperform control students in extending their partner's ideas. Training also has a positive effect on students' knowledge acquisition which was partially mediated by students' improved transactive communication.

The eighth chapter is devoted by Anikó Zsolnai, László Kasik to the social and personal features that play a key role in the development of social problem solving and coping strategies in adolescence. Their focus is on Hungarian students. Their study suggests four main conclusions, namely that (a) negative problem orientation, rational problem solving and avoidance show increasing tendency with age; (b) overt aggression, impulsivity and avoidance as coping strategies were used by older children in a significantly higher proportion than by younger children; (c) family characteristics (family type, mothers' educational level) play a major role in the development of social problem solving and coping strategies; (d) school success shows positive correlation with social problem solving and coping strategies, and these values increase with age.

ADDRESSING CULTURAL DIVERSITY

The next four chapters deal with linguistic and cultural diversity in formal education. In the ninth chapter Ksenija Krstić, Ljiljana B. Lazarević, Ivana Stepanovic Ilić address the following question: Why some children dropout from schools in Serbia before they earned a secondary education diploma? It must be noted that Serbia has a major problem with high school dropout rate. In 2013, in Serbia 25.3% of young people between 18 and 24 years were not in education, employment or training system. Dropout rates are even higher for children from marginalised groups. According to 2014 data dropout rate is over 78% for children from Roma community. This work is a part of the larger study aiming at studying the factors causing dropout from Serbian educational system. The study focuses on the analysis of educational system and school context from the perspective of students who left school. The main aim is to analyse case studies of early school leavers in order to get better understanding of factors influencing dropout, to describe the risks and barriers in educational system which increase a chances for dropout, and to indicate the causes and dynamics that cause dropping-out.

Teuta Mehmeti and Anne-Nelly Perret-Clermont devote the tenth chapter to inquire further in three directions: (a) to better understand what are the pedagogical designs that favour success of pupils from migrant (Albanian) families within the Swiss school system; (b) to reconsider more attentively the cognitive processes that are afforded or required by these pedagogical designs; and (c) to better understand the communication dynamics between students and teachers. Albanian-speaking children in Switzerland are often subject to failure in school within a context where negative social representations are conveyed by the media and through political discourse about Albanian migrants. Nonetheless, recent studies suggest that it is the very structure and functioning of the Swiss school system that might be a relevant obstacle for these children's school success. Mehmeti's and Perret-Clermont's study shows that in conditions where children are explicitly invited to be active and to develop their own thinking and confront their peers with it, they show significant involvement, are active, and they present remarkable argumentations. They defend their standpoints and provide arguments. The chapter also discusses teachers' negative representations due to a supposedly sociocultural distance between them and the children.

An introductory Finnish L2 programme for seven-year-old Swedish-speaking children is the subject of the study that Fredrik Rusk, Michaela Pörn, and Fritjof Sahlström present in the eleventh chapter. Using conversation analysis, they analyse participants' management of L2 knowledge in interaction when solving the problems of understanding the L2, and how children negotiate rights and primacy to own and others L2 knowledge. In their study learning is understood as a social action: as something participants demonstrably and explicitly do in the contingency of social interaction. They analyse "Doing learning" from a participant's perspective and by considering the learning object as something that participants actively orient to and co-construct in social interaction. The study suggests that the management of L2 knowledge is facilitated by a choice of task and/or content that is partially familiar to the children.

Classroom practices in relation to teachers beliefs and practices, and to inclusive education are also at the core of the twelfth chapter. In the final chapter in this section Jelena Radišić and Aleksander Baucal practice their "critical eye" on the teaching of language and math in Serbia. Inclusive practices in the Serbian education system have been recognised as one of the major pillars in changing the country's teaching system. In that sense inclusiveness is not only discussed from the perspective of special needs education, but provides a perspective on different socio-economic backgrounds, differences between local communities, etc. However despite the efforts over the past decade or so, very little seems to have been achieved in changing teachers' practices inclining them towards a more inclusive approach. In this chapter we focus on practices of teaching and learning in language and mathematics classrooms taking into account how teachers cater for the diverse needs of the students with whom they work. Data are drawn from a mixed method study exploring teacher beliefs on teaching and learning and their associated classroom practices. A sample of 96 upper secondary teachers teaching Serbian language and literature (L1) and mathematics participated in the study. For the purpose of this chapter exemplary episodes were chosen in order to examine the topic in focus. After identifying four groups of teachers: 'traditional', 'traditional stressing atmosphere', 'laissez faire' and 'modern' types, the practices of each type where examined from the perspective of their catering for different students' needs. All teacher types except the "modern" one provide little space for students' voices and personal understandings regardless of the subject they teach. While the "traditional" type teachers maintain a distance between themselves and the students, this is not the case for other teacher types. Only in case of the "modern" type teacher there is a clear focus on catering for different students' ideas and solutions thus providing equal amounts of space and time for everyone in the classroom. Taking into account the country's current practices in teachers' initial education and professional development, the preconditions that facilitate teachers embracing more inclusive approach are discussed.

FROM RESEARCH TO TEACHING

The thirteenth chapter by Jane Hughes still focuses on diversity and takes a sociocultural perspective in exploring a teaching curriculum in a business school. It explores how students come to 'figure' out who they are as they participate in an educational world constructed by a teacher. Accounting education research, taking a social constructivist perspective, has highlighted the difficulties in teaching accounting, a discipline derived from a professional business practice, in a university setting. The dominance of procedural knowledge (problem-solving that focuses on an algorithmic aspect), rather than conceptual knowledge, in accounting education has been noted. The tendency of university students to rely on a procedural knowledge of accounting, such as memorisation and rote learning, is unsatisfactory for entry to a professional world of accounting or business, due to the complex accounting issues arising for professionals in the twenty-first century. The chapter explores the figured worlds of academic accounting, in a university business school, to assess how students participated in and made sense of their accounting studies.

The learning trajectories and identity development of three students, selected due to the diversity of their backgrounds, prior study and work experiences, are explored. Students' figured worlds are dominated by the "pedagogical authority" of the examination, as communicated in the lectures and seminars (in the teaching and tasks). Students positioned themselves as examination strategists, seen in their classroom behaviour (tasks and relationships). All three students' learning trajectories showed how they used examination strategies, developed using accounting processes, to bridge the gap between actual and designate identity and achieve their career investment aim. One student was able to find a conceptual understanding of accounting, as he was able to position himself in a figured world of professional business management (evidenced in his narrative), as well as a figured world of examination strategies. Other students remained in a figured world of examination strategies and their understanding was limited to examination techniques and associated study skills. The three student trajectories showed how different worlds and identities might develop from participation in the same educational setting. The sociocultural perspective of figured worlds and identity development suggests a further way to make sense of student success and failure in accounting. In particular, the sociocultural perspective in this chapter considers how to explore the heterogeneity in student study behaviours, noted by both higher education and accounting education researchers.

Values education is addressed by Alfred Weinberger, Jean-Luc Patry in the fourteenth chapter devoted to V*a*KE (Values *and* Knowledge Education). Empirical evidence suggests that teachers neglect values education due to the high amount of subject matter they have to teach and the lack of knowledge and methods to get involved with values education. To overcome these problems the authors developed a teaching method that allows integrating values education with curricular subject matter goals: the constructivist teaching method V*a*KE. The approach emphasizes solving moral dilemmas as a source to trigger moral questions as well as questions related to content. The chapter describes the theoretical and practical framework of V*a*KE as well as main results of empirical studies that test the validity of the theory, and problems and difficulties that can arise during the implementation process.

In the last and fifteenth chapter Christian Tarchi and Alessio Surian describe ways to use critical incidents and the use of higher education students' video-logs as ways to both research and promote learning about intercultural abilities. They note how the increase of internationalization initiatives promoted by higher education institutions from all over the world, does not necessarily lead to greater intercultural sensitivity and how students with different acculturation strategies, might have different needs, and different sources of cultural stress. The chapter focuses on ways to provide teachers and practitioners working in cross-cultural educational settings with tools to reflect on students' development of intercultural sensitivity and awareness. To this aim, and to foster theoretical advances about the nature of diversity understandings and strategies, the chapter proposes the combined use of video-logs to foster reflection on intercultural sensitivity, and acculturation scales to foster reflection on intercultural awareness.

Finally, I would like to express my gratitude to EARLI for supporting the SIGs meeting activities and to the reviewers and the colleagues that made the conference and this publication possible. Heartfelt thanks to the scholars who opened the Padova conference with dialogues across the various research fields that inspired further discussions during the conference sessions that contributed to the above mentioned chapters: Gert Biesta, David Clarke, Michèle Grossen, Rupert Wegerif, Sangeeta Bagga-Gupta.

REFERENCES

Baucal, A., Arcidiacono, F., & Budjevac, N. (Eds.). (2011). *Studying interaction in different contexts: A qualitative view.* Belgrade: Institute of Psychology.

César, M., & Kumpulainen, M. (Eds.). (2009). *Social interactions in multicultural settings.* Rotterdam, The Netherlands: Sense Publishers.

Cowie, H., & van der Aalsvoort, G. (Eds.). (2000). *Social interaction in learning and instruction. The meaning of discourse for the construction of knowledge.* Amsterdam, The Netherlands: Pergamon Press.

Grossen, M. (2009). Social interaction, discourse and learning: Methodological challenges of an emergent transdisciplinary field. In K. Kumpulainen, C. E. Hmelo-Silver, & M. Cesar (Eds.), *Investigating classroom interaction* (pp. 263–275). Rotterdam, The Netherlands: Sense Publishers.

Hjörne, E., van der Aalsvoort, G., & De Abreu, G. (Eds.). (2012). *Learning, social interaction and diversity – Exploring identities.* Rotterdam, The Netherlands: Sense Publishers.

Kumpulainen, M., Hmelo-Silver, C. E., & César, M. (Eds.). (2009). *Investigating classroom interaction. Methodologies in action.* Rotterdam, The Netherlands: Sense Publishers.

Moro, C., Müller Mirza, N., & Roman, P. (Eds.). (2014). *L'intersubjectivit Mirza, N., raction. Methodologies in actionng: Methodological challenges o* Lausanne:Actualités psychologiques 1, Antipodes.

Alessio Surian
University of Padova

PETER RENSHAW AND RON TOOTH

2. PEREZHIVANIE MEDIATED THROUGH NARRATIVE PLACE-RESPONSIVE PEDAGOGY

INTRODUCTION

We explore in this chapter episodes of deep learning and significant changes to self that students report after experiencing a narrative-based and place-responsive pedagogy called *Storythread*. To theorise this kind of learning we deploy Vygotsky's notion of *perezhivanie* because it treats learning as an amalgam of intellectual and emotional insights that leads to reflection on oneself and one's future. Vygotsky wrote only sparingly about *perezhivanie* towards the end of his life (Vygotsky, 1934/1994). He sketched a view of development that situated emotional experiences as central to the trajectory and direction of a person's life. Given the fragmentary and unfinished nature of Vygotsky's exploration, the interpretation of *perezhivanie* is contested, but most scholars accept the phrase "emotional experience in a social situation" as a starting definition (Blunden, 2014; Gonzales Rey, 2011; Smagorinsky, 2011; Vadeboncoeur & Collie, 2013). *Perezhivanie* provides a unit of analysis where there is re-organisation of aspects of the *self* and ones plans for the future. It is not the external situation or environment per se that is crucial but the subjective and emotional sense that individuals make of their experiences and this will vary across individuals depending on their interests and personal histories.

Storythread is a pedagogy that seems to engage students intellectually and emotionally. It connects students' first-hand and emotional experiences in a natural place (in this case, in Karawatha forest), with learning about the ecology of the place, and the story of a local environmental advocate (in this case, Bernice Volz) who worked hard to preserve the forest for future generations. The current design of *Storythread* evolved across three decades. In the 1980s Ron Tooth, an environmental educator, began adapting drama and arts-based methods for engaging children in first-hand learning experiences beyond the classroom. Over time these methods were extended to foreground the competing motives of characters and protagonists in the narrative (real and imaginary) who faced dilemmas about how to achieve a personal goal while relating in an ethical and caring way to a natural environment. Students were invited to enter imaginatively into these narratives about place and conflicting motivations in order to dialogue with the protagonists (actual or role-played) and amongst themselves about how to resolve the dilemmas. In this process they needed to articulate reasoned arguments, express their values and be critically reflective in the light of their knowledge of the environment and the perspectives of

A. Surian (Ed.), Open Spaces for Interactions and Learning Diversities, 13–23.

others. In the late 1990s as educational research focussed more on the importance of children's domain-specific knowledge, *Storythread* gave more explicit attention to scaffolding children's scientific concepts and methods of inquiry. Finally in the past 5 years, *Storythread* has been conceived as a place-responsive pedagogy that weaves together the unique learning affordances of specific places, with opportunities to develop new identities for oneself and connect to other people as environmental advocates. The current approach to *Storythread* is an amalgam of these diverse influences. It offers students different "hooks" to engage them in learning, whether the hook is attentiveness and quiet contemplation; or interest in science per se; or the beauty of the place; or the inspiration of the characters such as Bernice Votz, or the physicality of engaging first-hand in the natural environment.

Feedback on the effectiveness of *Storythread* has been collected over many years from the staff at the environmental education centre, from visiting teachers, parents and from students. Methods of collecting feedback have included professional diaries kept by the centre staff and teachers, surveys collected from students, and more recently interviews with students, written reflections from students on their experiences, and measures of students' conceptual learning and values. This feedback was used to inform the on-going iterative design and modification of the pedagogy and in addition it provided vivid instances of how the programme had changed particular children or led to a broader change in students' behaviour at school such as avoiding littering, or showing interest in and respect for animals around the school such as birds, lizards and ants in the playground. The emotional responsiveness of students to the *Storythread* excursions was mentioned quite often by teachers and parents who accompanied the students. Many students expressed a new understanding of themselves, a new sense of their possible futures and new resolutions about advocating for the environment. To explore this type of emotional and subjective learning, we deploy below the Vygotskian concept of *perezhivanie* (Vygotsky, 1934/1994) in analysing students' interviews, written responses and drawings after their excursion.

RESEARCH CONTEXT AND PEDAGOGY

Design-Based Approach

The present chapter draws upon data from a project that investigated place-responsive pedagogies in seven environmental and outdoor education centres across different regions of Queensland Australia. The project was guided by a design-based approach that Wang and Hannafin (2005) define as a "systematic but flexible methodology aimed to improve educational practices through iterative analysis, design, development, and implementation, based on collaboration among researchers and practitioners in real-world settings, and leading to contextually-sensitive design principles and theories" (p. 6). The data and analyses presented below were collected from one of the seven environmental education centres, namely, Pullenvale

Environmental Education Centre, and arose from an excursion to Karawatha forest. To provide the setting and context for the research we describe below key features of the excursion. We turn first to the actual forest and its unique affordances for influencing students' learning.

Karawatha

Karawatha is a preserved forest remnant of 1000 hectares located in the southern suburbs of Brisbane. It includes wetlands, a diversity of forest types and micro-climate zones, as well as multiple threatened frog species and birds. It was preserved in the 1990s through the advocacy of a local community action group led by a resident and self-taught naturalist, Bernice Volz. Students prepare prior to the excursion for about 6 weeks by thinking about how they might become environmental advocates, reading about Bernice, practicing how to listen and observe in natural settings (see *dadarri* below), and learning about the ecology and micro-climates of Karawatha. After the excursion they continue to work on the records of their visit to Karawatha, write personal responses and reflect on their experiences and learning as environmental advocates guided by their classroom teachers.

Local/Global Environmental Advocacy

Part of the place-responsive pedagogy employed at Karawatha foregrounds the life and values of Bernice as an environmental advocate. Prior to the excursion they are given background information about her life and her connection to Karawatha. During the excursion they have the opportunity to talk to Bernice via mobile phone, and to imaginatively enter into the role of 'environmental advocates.' They learn that Bernice had documented Karawatha's flora and fauna via an international data network called *PPBIO*, which is coordinated in Manaus, Brazil by Dr William Magnusson (http://ppbio.inpa.gov.br/en/home) and in Brisbane, Australia by Dr Mark Hero (http://ppbio.inpa.gov.br/ppbiointer). Multiple *PPBIO* sites are monitored in Brazil, Nepal as well as Australia to record the local fauna and flora in specific habitats, and to provide longitudinal data to determine the effects of human activities as well climate change. Students learn, through their excursion to Karawatha, about the connection between this global knowledge network and their local environment. In this way the place-responsive pedagogy enacted at Karawatha links environmental advocacy to personal commitments and civic action, as well as to the development of scientific understandings and inquiry regarding diverse eco-systems.

Blanket Role

In preparation at school for their excursion to Karawatha students are invited to take on the *blanket role* of 'environmental advocates.' A *blanket role* is a convention in drama where all the participants take the same role within a whole-group role-play or process drama. It is often used with younger students because it is a highly engaging way for them to connect imaginatively and actively with others and with place. At Karawatha students move beyond the traditional fictional roles of drama practice into a new space where they are invited to see themselves as a new kind of person who is growing and developing the values and skills of the environmental advocate and discovering their own voice and sense of agency in their daily life. Through the blanket role of environmental advocate students focus on Bernice's local knowledge, values, and community actions and consider why she so willingly committed herself to preserve Karawatha from development. During the excursion, students develop their knowledge and skills as environmental advocates by exploring the wetlands area for themselves, attentively and mindfully observing and recording the life of the forest, and visiting significant places that were important to Bernice. Together with the teachers they traverse Karawatha from one side to the other, passing through diverse ecological zones, noting the sudden changes in the forest zones, and imagining themselves walking in Bernice's shoes as well as walking in the presence of the Indigenous custodians of the land who have lived and walked in Karawatha for thousands of years. In summary, students are scaffolded at their schools and then at Karawatha to experience and explore the multiple aspects of the blanket role of environmental advocacy, that includes scientific understanding and knowledge, aesthetic appreciation of the natural environment, and the capacity to communicate to others what they have learned so that they can become agents of change in their school and community.

Dadirri

A key learning activity that is designed to connect the students to place is called dadirri. It means inner, deep listening and quiet, still awareness. It is a 'tuning in' experience with the specific aim to come to a deeper understanding of nature. Dadirri is an Australian Indigenous practice shared by the Indigenous elder, Miriam-Rose Ungunmerr-Baumann of the Ngangikurungkurr people from Daly River in the Northern Territory, Australia. Students are introduced to the concept and then asked to practice dadirri by sitting quietly alone in the forest for approximately fifteen minutes, trying to relax as they observe, listen to, and feel the natural place around them.

ANALYSIS AND FINDINGS

The extracts from students discussed below were collected either from in-depth interviews conducted in 2013 with a group of grade six students after their Karawatha excursion, or were collected in 2014 from the letters written by grade seven students to Bernice Votz about their Karawatha excursion. One hundred letters were sampled from students who attended three different schools, each on separate excursions to Karawatha. Extracts from these letters are explored below for evidence of deep emotional learning and changes to self.

Our initial examination of the students' interviews and letters revealed deep and eloquent responses from many students. For example, one student reported:

> Before I did this program I just saw myself as someone who is passionate about nature and, yeah, someone who cares about wildlife but after I'd done this program I see myself as a wildlife warrior and I feel more confident in myself and I've become more alert and observant with my surroundings and it has given me a new confidence to go out and see the environment, instead of – just sitting and think oh I like the environment, I like nature, but not actually doing anything about what's happening. (Year 6 Student)

The extract highlights the student's heightened sense of herself across time. In the past she had been passionate and caring about wildlife, but now in the present she has become a wildlife warrior who is more alert and observant. In the future she imagines herself as more confident to engage and do something about what's happening. This reflection on herself across time and the emotional tone of her response suggests that the Karawatha experience could be a defining moment in her developmental trajectory.

Another student realised she had begun to relate to Karawatha through an entirely new mode, that is, through "feelings" rather than through "seeing". She reported that the *dadirri* activity of quiet contemplation alone in the forest had moved her into a different kind of learning that allowed her to view herself in a completely new way.

> Before I saw the environment through visuals and now I see it through feelings. (Year 7 Student)

It was accounts such as this that led us to consider the relevance of *perezhivanie* for analysing the changes reported by students following the Karawatha excursion.

Our deployment of *perezhivanie* in this chapter is exploratory and illustrative. The analytical use of *perezhivanie* in empirical research is quite limited at this stage. It has been used recently to investigate early childhood play (Fleer & Hammer, 2013) and storyworlds (Ferholt, 2015) created by young children with assistance from adults as they step into and out of various roles during episodes of imaginative play. In these studies, *perezhivanie* draws attention to episodes of heightened emotional engagement within a role. These episodes become topics of conversation and reflection between children and adults as they revisit the stories they have created and enacted. It's *as if* they are floating above the experience and learning from the episode as they recall and evaluate the emotional experiences within and beyond the stories. The child is both acting imaginatively (*as if* somebody else) but also able to shift to consider the "as-if self" from the perspective of their past and present self. In these moments they are learning about emotions and themselves simultaneously.

Ferholt (2015) has defined certain features of *perezhivanie* that emerged from her research on playworlds. She summarises the features as involving the following:

the relationship between the individual and the environment is the event; cognition and emotion are dynamically related; another person is needed for this experience; time flows in more than one direction; experiencing the self, not directly but through the medium of experiencing the others; a form of inter subjectivity in which we insert ourselves into the stories of others in order to gain the foresight that allows us to proceed (in the face of despair); an internal and subjective labour of 'entering into', which is not done by the mind alone, but rather involves the whole of life or a state of consciousness; twice-behaved behaviour. (Ferholt, 2015, p. 71)

While not adopting all these elements relevant to *perezhivanie* as expressed in playworlds, we will consider the following as indicative of *perezhivanie* in relation to the Karawatha excursion: first, description of change that seems important to the student; second expression of emotion related to an insight or new understanding; third a reference to the temporal dimension of the self in the past, present and/or the future; fourth, some sense of a changing relationship between oneself and others; and finally a reflective stance on the experience.

Explorations of Perezhivanie

Students indicated that they had changed their views of themselves at school and in the world generally. Sometimes, these were described in terms of change in relation to *personal qualities* or specific personal characteristics such as openness, confidence, alertness, attentiveness, and passion. One boy could see that because of the entire Karawatha experience his openness to others had increased:

I've noticed – I'm more open to new ideas from people because it used to be just like me, me, me but now I'm listening to others because what they say also matters and doing this program, yeah, has let me, like, open up my brain and allow other people's thoughts. (Year 7 Student)

In this extract we can identify features of *perezhivanie*. There is a report of significant change (*this program yeah has let me, like, open up my brain*), a new understanding of oneself (*it used to be just like me me me*) and a new relationship with others (*allow other people's thoughts*).

Other students summarized their new sense of self as an identity shift – as in the eloquent quotation above where the student says, '*after I'd done this program I see myself as a wildlife warrior*'. These self-identifying labels provide students with a strong well-formed schema for deciding how to act in spontaneous and proactive ways. For example, in the poetic comments following, a year seven student imagines green leaves growing inside her – representing a new more passionate and exciting self.

Well, this is a bit weird but I think that these, my inside of my body used to be dark and focused on one thing at a time. When I used to write, like, for

English and stuff it would just be so boring and I wouldn't use the same sort of expression and passion that I do now because – but now inside where it used to be all dark and nothing special about it, it's sort of got these green leaves and it's just twirling around and I think that if people keep on doing this that's what will happen to them. And so I think that I've grown more exciting and passionate and not so dull and blank that I was before and so I think that this has improved everything about me not just my nature smartness, so I think it's been really great. (Year 7 Student)

Just as in the studies of children's play by Fleer and Hammer (2013) and Fernholt (2015), the Karawatha experience has provided this student with an imaginative template to reconsider her past self and project a new more exciting and passionate self into the future. The metaphor of the growing green shoots provides the means for elaborating and communicating this new sense of self. She sees advantages for everyone in engaging in this kind of experience. (*I think that if people keep on doing this that's what will happen to them.*) So in this extract we can see the key elements of *perezhivanie* – significant change from an old self to a new self (*this has improved everything about me*), heightened emotional engagement (*it's been really great*), and the implication that her relationships with others have changed (*improved everything about me not just my nature smartness*).

The way that direct experiences of nature and place can generate a diversity of nuanced personal responses and new understandings about the self is captured in the following two quite typical responses that were sent to Bernice Volz. They were written at the time in the excursion when the whole group had spoken to Bernice on the phone. Students always want to share how much they appreciated what she had done and what they had learned. These letters to Bernice were constructed when emotion was at its highest and the motivation to speak from the heart was most intense. The authentic voice of both students is evident. Daniel has realized that his knowledge and understanding have been slowly growing over time through deep listening, and this has now allowed him to describe himself to Bernice as the kind of person who is growing closer to "the bush" and wants to spend more time in nature.

Dear Bernice. When I first started walking in Karawatha I did not know much about my surroundings. Then I noticed that being attentive and looking and listening to the environment really grew my knowledge and understanding. After a while I felt like I knew more about the bush and I grew closer to the bush and the environment and came to peace with my surroundings. Today I've learnt lots more about Karawatha and the environment. Also I learned lots about Dadirri (deep listening). As an Environmental Advocate I will now help protect the bush and care for it. Spend more time in the bush. Best wishes Bernice. Daniel. (Year 7 Student)

For Daniel there is growth in knowledge, as well as peacefulness and attentiveness in his relationship to the forest. In the future he proposes to spend more time there and become an advocate. This combination of emotional responsiveness, intellectual engagement and a sense of changing identity suggests that the excursion has been a moment of *perezhivanie* for Daniel.

For Cathy, being immersed in the beauty of Karawatha, as well as being inspired by what Bernice had achieved, affected her in a very personal and profound way. She reveals herself as a deep thinker who has used this experience to reflect on her own life and values. What is particularly moving about her response is the open willingness to share her empathy for Karawatha with Bernice and her ability to use her experience to reflect deeply on herself and what she wants to achieve. The experience has allowed her to mediate a process of self-reflection that seems new for her and is typical of what happens for many students.

Dear Bernice. When I first started walking in Karawatha I was unsure of what I was going to discover, but I was very interested in the forest and its unique beginning. Then I noticed the biodiversity was so untouched and beautiful in its own incredible way. After a while I felt confused as to why people could ever doubt the fact that this beautiful, unique place could ever be denied to the future generations. Today I've learnt the true importance of the incredible forest in an urbanizing world. Some places MUST be preserved for those in the future so they can appreciate Karawatha and other forests. As an Environmental Advocate I will now try to become dedicated to preserving that which is of the most vital importance to the Earth. I want to do what you have given us for generations to come and preserve that which is precious. You have inspired me. Best wishes Bernice. (Year 7 Student)

Cathy expresses a range of emotions including uncertainty (I was unsure…), confusion (I felt confused…) determination (some places MUST be preserved…) and inspiration (You have inspired me). These emotions are closely connected to her emerging knowledge of Karawatha as a unique place with biodiversity that is threatened in an urbanising world. In addition to these emotional and intellectual responses, Cathy sees her future *self* as dedicated to preserving the forest for future generations. Cathy locates herself in a temporal zone that stretches back to the beginning of the forest and projects forward to generations to come. These four aspects of her account of the excursion, namely, emotional responsiveness, intellectual engagement, changing self and temporality are indicative of *perezhivanie* – a significant emotional charged experience that will likely have far-reaching consequences for her developing personality.

Another student in expressing what had changed for him during the Karawatha excursion wrote the words below and drew the image (Figure 1) to express how he had connected emotionally to the natural world while using one of the key pedagogical tools, *dadirri*.

Dadirri is very important and that we are all connected in a way. The forest is a place of imagination and discovery and that everything is linked just like vines coming from you and link with the vines of trees. (Year 7 Student)

The representation of emotion in the drawing is somewhat conventional in deploying a heart for love, but in combination with the text we sense here an imaginative engagement and insight with regard to the forest – a realisation that "we are all connected in a way". Again this combination of emotion and insight suggests that the visit to Karawatha and the practice of dadirri created a *perezhivanie* for this student.

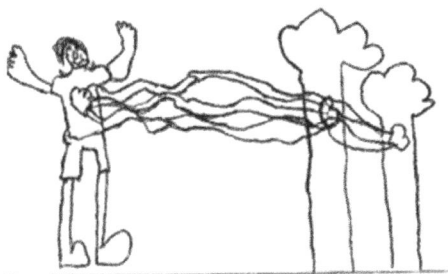

Figure 1. Year 7 Student's Drawing of Connection to the Forest

This account resonates with what Abram (1997, p. 69) called a "renewed attentiveness … through a rejuvenation of sensorial empathy with the living systems that sustain us." Abram (1997) suggests that this is what leads to a new environmental ethic that will transform how we see ourselves in the world. We have seen this ethical response in Karawatha many times, especially when students engage in *dadirri* in a deep way, and allow themselves to become connected to the many changing and interacting details of nature around them – the movement of the wind in the trees, the unexpected surprise of sudden rain, the myriad of subtle colours and textures, the different ecological zones and the calls of animals. Within *dadirri* students move through a slow and emergent process that transforms their understanding of themselves and of their relationship to the place, but often in quite different ways. The nature of the *perezhivanie* varies greatly across depending on what creates the emotional responsiveness for particular students.

CONCLUSION

In the Russian language *perezhivanie* carries a sense of suffering (Vygotsky, 1934/1994) and Russian scholars exemplify *perezhivanie* mainly with regard to insights arising from overcoming personal trauma and dealing with crises rather than in the context of more positive emotional experiences and associated learning (Blunden, 2014). However, contemporary scholars (Ferholt, 2015; Fleer & Hammer, 2013) are deploying *perezhivanie* more broadly to describe positive and expanding learning arising from episodes of deep emotional engagement. It is this positive sense that we have deployed *perezhivanie* to describe the complex learning arising from *Storythread* pedagogy.

Perezhivanie has been explored here as a unit of analysis to describe students' learning as simultaneously emotional, intellectual, and ontological. As our extracts and examples have illustrated, students report changes in their knowledge, their sense of self and their plans for the future using emotive and reflective language and drawings. They link these changes directly to aspects of the *Storythread* pedagogy such as the practice of *dadirri*, or the awareness of Karawatha's ecosystems, or the aesthetic beauty of the forest, or the character of Bernice Votz. We suggest that the multifaceted activities and experiences included in *Storythread* offer a variety of 'hooks' that capture the interest of different students. Rather than attempting to design a highly technical differentiated pedagogy targeted to specific individual differences, the design of *Storythread* was open to diverse pedagogical approaches, including narrative strategies, inquiry science methods, drama through the blanket role, and authentic models of advocacy, such as Bernice Volz. We reported on how these diverse features of *Storythread* captured the interest of different students so that multiple entry points and pathways were provided for students to learn from their experiences. This is consistent with the notion of *perezhivanie* that foregrounds the subjective dimension of learning and the personal sense that each student makes of their experiences. Rather than seeking precision of pedagogical design we seek richness and openness so that deep learning opportunities are offered to as many students as possible.

Natural places are inherently unpredictable, so during the Karawatha excursion students can be exposed to sudden changes in the weather, the appearance and disappearance of birds, insects and amphibians, and moments of heightened sensory awareness. These experiences contrast with the predictability of habitual classroom practices where students rarely have to take risks or work outside their comfort zones. It is not surprising, therefore, that many parents (who accompany groups of students on the excursion) report that they still vividly remember their childhood excursions to nature reserves and forests. It is also commonly reported by teachers that normally distracted and disengaged students in classroom learning, are sometimes transformed into leaders and enthusiastic participants at Karawatha. This highlights the affordance of learning through first-hand experiences, and the opportunity it provides some students to move beyond their established identity as resistant learners. *Perezhivanie* cannot be engineered or predicted in particular cases, but the combination of a multifaceted narrative based pedagogy such as *Storythread* linked to sensorial and unpredictable experiences in a natural environment seem to provide the conditions for memorable and transformative learning for many students.

REFERENCES

Abram, D. (1997). *The spell of the sensuous: Perception and language in a more-than-human world.* New York, NY: Pantheon.
Blunden, A. (2014). *Notes on perezhivanie.* Retrieved October 28, 2015, from http://www.ethicalpolitics.org/seminars/perezhivanie.htm

Ferholt, B. (2015). *Perezhivanie* in researching playworlds: Applying the concept of *perezhivanie* in the study of play. In S. Davis, B. Ferholt, H. G. Clemson, S.-M. Jansson, & A. Marjanovic-Shane (Eds.), *Dramatic interactions in education: Vygotskian and sociocultural approaches to drama, education and research* (pp. 57–75). London: Bloomsbury Academic.

Fleer, M., & Hammer, M. (2013). 'Perezhivanie' in group settings: A cultural-historical reading of emotion regulation. *Australasian Journal of Early Childhood, 38*(3), 127–134.

González Rey, F. (2011). A re-examination of defining moments in Vygotsky's work and their implications for his continuing legacy. *Mind, Culture, and Activity, 18*(3), 257–275.

Smagorinsky, P. (2011). Vygotsky's stage theory: The psychology of art and the actor under the direction of perezhivanie. *Mind, Culture, and Activity, 18*(4), 319–341.

Tooth, R. (2007). *Growing a sense of place: Storythread and the transformation of a school* (PhD Thesis). The University of Queensland, Brisbane.

Tooth, R., & Renshaw, P. (2012). *Storythread* pedagogy for environmental education. In T. Wrigley, P. Thomson, & B. Lingard (Eds.), *Changing schools: Alternative ways to make a world of difference* (pp. 113–127). London, UK: Routledge.

Tooth, R., Wager, L., & Proellocks, T. (1988). Story, setting and drama – A new look at environmental education. *Australian Journal of Environmental Education, 4*, 31–34.

Wang, F., & Hannafin, M. (2005). Design-based research and technology-enhanced learning environments. *Educational Technology, Research and Development, 53*(4), 5–23.

Vadeboncoeur, J., & Collie, R. J. (2013). Locating social and emotional learning in schooled environments: A Vygotskian perspective on learning as unified. *Mind, Culture, and Activity, 20*, 201–225.

Vygotsky, L. S. (1934/1994). The problem of the environment. In R. van der Veer & J. Valsiner (Eds.), *The Vygotsky reader* (pp. 338–354). Oxford, UK: Blackwell.

Peter Renshaw
School of Education
University of Queensland

Ron Tooth
School of Education
University of Queensland
Pullenvale Environmental Education Centre
Queensland

GIUSEPPE RITELLA AND BEATRICE LIGORIO

3. INVESTIGATING CHRONOTOPES IN A MEDIA DESIGN COURSE

INTRODUCTION

Space and time are fundamental aspects of educational practices, but their analysis has occupied a marginal place in literature on the subject. A few authors claim that investigating space and time is crucial for contemporary educational theory because we are living in an era of profound change, where the space-time of schooling is transformed both by policy makers (Renshaw, 2014) and by the advent of digital technology (Kumpulainen et al., 2013).

In order to discuss the social construction of space and time, scholars often refer to Bakhtin's concept of chronotope, which literally means space-time. By means of this concept, Bakhtin intended to rethink the Kantian categories of space and time from a social perspective (Holquist, 1982). For Bakhtin, the way in which space and time relations are artistically expressed in the novel specifies the meaning of texts and defines literary genres. From this perspective, space and time are not independent given realities: they are interdependent social constructions that can be expressed in texts, and can change under the pressure of cultural historical transformations.

This chapter is aimed at discussing a case study in which we have used the concept of chronotope to investigate how a group of students constructs space and time during a media design project course, in a technology rich environment. We focus on the social process through which space and time are negotiated in dialogical interactions. In a first exploration of the data, we have identified three aspects of space-time negotiation, and then conducted three studies to explore them. While the detailed results of each study will be published in separate articles (Ritella, Ligorio & Hakkarainen, in preparation; forthcoming), here we describe and discuss the design of the whole research project, as well as summarising the preliminary interpretation of the data.

THE RELEVANCE OF CHRONOTOPES IN TECHNOLOGY-ENHANCED LEARNING

When referring to educational situations enriched by technology, the term chronotope refers to the arrangement of space and time emerging during the development of shared practices, both in terms of material arrangements of bodies and objects, and semiotic construction of space and time in and through discourse. To understand

A. Surian (Ed.), Open Spaces for Interactions and Learning Diversities, 25–36.

chronotopes in education, material and discursive aspects should be integrated. The interconnection between semiotic and material processes is evident when one analyses the impact of technology on educational practices. Indeed, technology generates new media with its own specific material features (Goody, 1977; McLuhan & Lapham, 1964; Olson, 1994), which trigger transformations of semiotic processes in terms of perceptual features, workability and the sharing of semiotic arrays. For example, word-processor software permits one to easily revise texts without re-writing them (workability), or to visualise them in different sizes, colours, brightness levels, and so on (perceptual features), as well as sharing documents with anyone in real time (sharing) (Ritella & Hakkarainen, 2012).

Technological instruments are both medium and sign (Cole, 1996). The features of the medium (material relations) and those of signs and symbols (semiotic relations) are both relevant in defining space-time relations. Writing with pen and paper, or discussing in a web forum, or building a collaborative concept map in virtual space, or carrying out all of these activities together in the classroom triggers a transformation of the arrangement of the spaces of learning, as well as how time is perceived and organised.

Furthermore, space and time can be considered as material manifestations of ideology and power relations that also have the potential for subverting given realities (Foucault, 1977). On the one hand, space-time frames in education are concrete manifestations of pedagogical regimes embedded in the everyday life of schools and classrooms (Matusov, 2009; Renshaw, 2014). On the other hand, within these historically developing routine time-space matrices, students and teachers can exert their agency, transform their environments and cultivate their identities in dialogue with others (Brown & Renshaw, 2006).

In the following sections, we briefly summarise the main aspects of the chronotopes that have been analysed in educational literature and discuss the theoretical ideas that have informed our conceptualisation of chronotope.

DEFINITIONS OF CHRONOTOPES AND CONNECTED IDEAS

Building on Bakhtin's (1981) idea that chronotopes shape the meaning of narratives, a few authors (Leander, 2001; Bloome et al., 2009) have emphasised that space and time are constantly renegotiated in social interaction. In line with this claim, chronotopes can be defined as emergent, dynamic configurations of space-time that are iteratively negotiated by participants through discourse, in interaction with the material world. To use a visual metaphor, chronotopes can be thought of as evolving trajectories that actors depict while moving through different kinds of semiotic, social and material spaces (Lemke, 2004; Ligorio & Ritella, 2010).

Such an understanding of chronotopes is built on the assumption that our thinking and learning entail the use of external artefacts and participation in social relations, and are intrinsically distributed in space and time. This claim, extensively expressed in the field of distributed cognition (Hollan et al., 2000; Kirsh, 1995), has been elaborated in connection to Vygotsky's ideas (1981) about the development of the higher mental functions. In his efforts to understand development, Vygotsky claimed that the external world, especially social interactions and symbols, plays a relevant role in the genesis of higher mental functions. In this process the external world cannot be considered as composed of a set of isolated objects but rather as a connected whole (Bateson, 1972; Cole, 1996). Important parts of this complex net are the artefacts – i.e. parts of the environment transformed by people in order to be used as tools. Artefacts, through the process of appropriation, become instruments mediating activities in different ways (Beguin & Rabardel, 2005). Educational environments are becoming more and more complex systems, allowing students and teachers to use, build, and manipulate many different types of artefacts. Understanding how they affect the framing of space-time in education is relevant to improve the efficacy of rich educational environments.

OUR CONCEPTUALISATION OF CHRONOTOPE

Following the definition of chronotope as the emergent configuration of temporal and spatial relations, we are interested in understanding chronotopes in relation to knowledge creation practices supported by digital technology. In our work (Ritella, Ligorio & Hakkarainen, submitted), we are developing an integrated conceptualisation of chronotope, where both discursive and material aspects of space-time relations are considered at different levels of analysis. We claim that, when analysing the micro-genesis of chronotopes through situated interaction, four interconnected social processes are involved:

• Negotiation of the meanings associated with the perceived space-time of an activity. This aspect becomes visible mostly when discussing constraints and opportunities related to the resources available and the given time-structure of the activity (perceiving chronotopes);
• Discursive organisation of an activity, in a future-oriented process, involving the selection of tools and workspaces, and the organisation of a schedule (envisioning chronotopes). This aspect is especially important when multiple physical, social and virtual spaces may function as resources for an activity, and a complex orchestration is needed;
• Material organisation of bodies and objects during an activity (enacting chronotopes): participants engage in embodied actions aimed at arranging the space-time of their activity by means of dynamic configurations of body orientation, gaze, disposition of artefacts in space. This process is intrinsically connected with the envisioning of chronotopes;
• Emergence of patterns of interaction that can be detected by the external observer (emerging chronotopes). For example, at the micro-level, participants can cyclically dispose their bodies and the relevant resources in specific

configurations that have an impact on how the collaborative processes unfold, what kind of outcomes will emerge and how fast (or slow) the activity will be conducted (Ligorio & Ritella, 2010; Ritella, Ligorio & Hakkarainen, 2015).

In the analysis of these processes we also take into account the views and cultural models used by individuals to make sense of the situation, including expectations and assumptions about how the space and time of activities 'should' be framed. These cultural models are intrinsically connected with students' world views and dominant discourses within their cultural environment.

In the following section we briefly summarise the research design and the main results of the studies we have conducted

THE RESEARCH PROJECT

Our research project involves the investigation of chronotopes as they are negotiated by groups of students collaborating on a design task. The investigation involves an interdisciplinary media design course held at Metropolia University, in Helsinki. The students worked in teams of four to five participants to develop a media design project.

At the start of the course, representatives of companies presented project topics. The groups had to choose one of these topics and try to develop a product or service based on that topic. As intermediate tasks, they had to develop certain artefacts (business plan, sales pitch, etc.) that would be assessed by teachers. The course lasted 16 weeks and the students worked together for two days per week for a total of ten hours per week. They could use a technologically-rich environment involving smart-boards, tablets, and notebooks. Groups were free to negotiate and select the tools they considered appropriate at the different stages of the course, which would give them a relatively high degree of autonomy in managing the collaboration.

With the approval and the support of teachers, the researcher introduced the aims of the investigation to the students, and asked two groups to volunteer as participants in the study. Nine students volunteered, allowing the researcher to video their teamwork and participation in stimulated-recall group interviews. The students filled in a survey about background information and signed an informed consent form about the research aims and the use of the data.

We collected data through participant observation, involving the collection of audio and video records, which allowed the documentation of multi-level activity processes taking place while participants were engaged in technology-mediated learning (Goodwin, 2000; Roth, 2005; Sawyer & DeZutter, 2009). Twelve sessions were selected and before each of them, the first author asked participants about the schedule for that session. In order to reduce the risk of something interesting remaining unintelligible (Kivelä & Myllari, 2008) two cameras and two audio recorders were used to document spatio-temporal patterns, each focusing on one-group interaction. Generally, the observers did not intervene in the interaction, but just observed, when possible standing/sitting near the camera and changing the focus of the camera when the participants moved. Furthermore, any impressions about the ongoing collaboration were documented using field notes, which are source of rich information about the context of interactions.

Moreover, because of the importance of what was taking place in the virtual space, screen records of smart-board-mediated activity complemented the data. These records were synchronised with the video-audio record of the interaction for a co-ordinated analysis. The software package Transana was used to transcribe, categorise and comment on video clips.

Finally, we had access to the intranet, whereby both teachers and students could insert and update artefacts related to the course, including the diary where students could describe their activities related to the course. The researcher had access to a Dropbox folder containing one of the group's up-loaded relevant artefacts and he was also invited to join a private Facebook group. These data were considered as secondary and used to clarify the interpretation of ambiguous speech or actions from the video.

Our general research question concerned how the negotiation of emergent chronotopes influenced the building of a shared understanding of the collaborative task by students. During the initial exploration of the data we developed three specific research questions concerning chronotopes:

a. How did the students arrange the physical space-time?
b. How do the students negotiate envisioned chronotopes while discussing and performing the task? And how are these envisioned chronotopes characterized?
c. What cultural models of the task emerged when students engaged in post-hoc reflection on the task, through stimulated recall group interviews and how were these connected to the emerging chronotopes?

The data were analysed through a qualitative ethnographic methodology (Goodwin, 1994, 2000) that required many cycles of reviewing the videos searching for episodes relevant for addressing the questions listed above. Two researchers first worked independently to select the pertinent episodes, and then compared and agreed on the significance and interpretation of each selected episode, involving a third researcher in case of discrepancies.

The in-depth qualitative analysis of the discursive and video data allowed us to better understand the features of chronotopes.

THE FEATURES OF CHRONOTOPES

As already suggested by the short review reported above, chronotopes are complex and require a multidimensional analysis (Ritella & Ligorio, in press). Based on our research questions we could single out three different dimensions of the emerging chronotopes: (a) the actually enacted movement of bodies and objects; (b) the envisioning of space-time through discourse; (c) the cultural models involved in the process of envisioning the chronotopes. In the following sections we briefly summarize our preliminary findings by means of some anecdotal evidence, consisting of short excerpts from the data. A full analysis of each of these studies will be presented in separate articles.

Enacted Chronotopes and Technology

Enacted chronotopes are arrangements of bodies and artefacts in space and time performed by participants during the activity. The analysis of this aspect of chronotope allows to examine the embodied nature of learning.

In our case, we observed the enactment of different arrangements of bodies and tools in the three phases of the course. The way the workspace was arranged changed when comparing the beginning of the course with halfway and thereafter it stabilised (Figures 1–3).

Figures 1–3: The three pictures represent the typical configurations of participation across the three phases of the course. At the beginning of the course, the students mainly worked sitting in circles using the smartboard or the screen of a laptop as shared focus of attention (Figure 1). During the second (Figure 2) and third (Figure 3) phase of the course, the students worked most of the time on individual tasks, using their laptops or the computers at the computer laboratory. During these phases, joint discussion was still present but was a secondary layer of activity relevant only occasionally.

The different patterns of organization of bodies and objects could be related to the strong need to create a shared understanding of the task and discuss the organisation of the activity at the outset of the course. Indeed, during the initial phase the students were often involved in such discussion, supported by the use of shared artefacts. However, from the middle to the end of the course, the professional competences of

Figure 1. A configuration of participation at the beginning of the course

Figure 2. A configuration of participation during the second phase of the course

Figure 3. A configuration of participation at the end of the course

the students were required to finalise the project, therefore the spaces relevant for the activity became mostly the personal computers at the computer laboratory and the students' own laptops.

The organisation of the virtual space was set according to the same rationale: at the beginning of the course generic software (such as word processor, concept map tools) was mostly used, but halfway and at the end of the course professional software loaded on the computers (e.g. programming software, Photoshop, etc) became crucial for the activity. The different types of activities carried out in the different phases of the course, affected the arrangement of the social and semiotic spaces available.

31

Furthermore, Dropbox was a fundamental means of co-ordinating individual efforts. All of the artefacts used and produced by students were stored in a Dropbox folder, which was used by each student for sharing the results of their work and monitoring the work of their colleagues. The importance of Dropbox was amplified by the lack of a stable physical workspace. Every week students had to book rooms to work in and were not able to use a permanent physical space to store their shared artefacts. Moreover, computers and tablets provided by the university were also used by other students, so they did not save documents on the local hard drives because of the risk of other students deleting them.

Envisioned Chronotopes and Task Interpretation

We defined the envisioning of chronotopes as the discursive negotiation of space-time while participants accomplish a task. This is particularly interesting in courses – such as the one we analysed – where students have a high degree of freedom regarding the organisation of the collaboration. Indeed, in this type of context students have to reach a shared understanding of the situation and negotiate the relevant space-time frames of their participation. We found students constantly negotiating the envisioned chronotopes to make sense of the current task: the discussion about what the task involved and how it could be accomplished was strictly connected to the negotiation of chronotopes.

In particular, students defined the temporal development of the activity according to the current interpretation of the task. This temporal framing of the activity was crucial for anticipating and evaluating the potential developments of the task in the future, and it was ultimately used to regulate both individual and collaborative efforts. In the following, we present an utterance in which a student clearly define the time-structure of their activity. The excerpt is taken from the third session of collaboration, when the students decided the target group for the product to be developed during the course. Interpreting the task (i.e. "defining the user group"), involved the use of markers of time (e.g., now [...] then) to define a temporally ordered sequence of subtasks. The understanding of the meaning and the scope of the task, implied the definition of its temporal development.

"We need to actually get the whole list now and then and actually choose the most important group to focus on"

In this process, an important role was played by the perception of chronotopic constraints and opportunities: the students' performance and their decision-making were framed into the perceived opportunities and constraints of the envisioned time-space. For example, while defining the scope of the activity, the students evaluated the feasibility of the sub-task that they were planning to undertake. At times, as in the following example, they ponder the interpretation of the task considering the space-time of the course:

if we were working every single day for six months on this project then we could do this but so little time.

In the excerpt above, a student assesses the current interpretation of the task against the perceived time constraints of the course.

In sum, we have found that the negotiation of a shared understanding of the task is interdependent with the envisioning of chronotopes: grounding the "envisioned", potential development of the task in space and time is an integral part of students' sensemaking.

Cultural Models and Chronotopes

This aspect concerns the role that cultural models – the implicit assumptions and expectations developed during the life experience of participants in similar contexts – play in the process of space-time framing. This is very relevant for educational practices because, usually, the educational context is a sort of symbolic place where activities, knowledge and social processes are strongly connected to different space-times, such as the space-time of professional practice that students are moving toward. What is happening in the 'here' and 'now' of the educational context makes sense in the light of what will happen in other contexts, such as the professional context or in life in general. In psychology, it is well known that in reasoning and decision-making people tend to focus on a limited number of mental models of the situation and neglect to explore alternative ways to frame it (Legrenzi et al., 1993).

In our data, students framed the situation mainly by using two types of cultural model: (a) the model concerning the design of a real product meant to be actually used by the target group, (b) the model concerning the participation in a media design course.

As follows, we show an excerpt taken from the interviews, where a student clarifies that he has participated in similar courses in the past, and that his previous experience gave him some cues for making sense of the current course. In other words, the student acknowledges that through previous experience he had developed a "cultural model" of this type of courses.

Excerpt 3
Jack (a student from the Netherlands): for my, for my point you just, you have the project, and you have to start it, and happen... well not... two years or three years of projects like this in Holland, we do this project this kind of projects all the time. So it's just like you start and then you have to begin with something, and you just begin with the thing you do... all the time just get your ideas on paper, get some things right written down, and start ... start thinking about it.

In the excerpt above, the student states that he has already developed some knowledge regarding the processes involved in this type of courses. In particular, he describes – based on his experience – the initial phase of a project, using many markers of time ("start", "begin", "then", etc.), and mentioning also some spatial elements (e.g. "get your ideas on paper").

Cultural models, such as the one described by this student, were used both to frame the interpretation of the task and to negotiate the relevant space-time frames for the activity. In this way, cultural models worked as the interface between the discursive construction of chronotopes and the reaching of a shared understanding of the task.

CONCLUSIONS

The research presented here was prompted by Bakthin's concept of chronotope. Our aim was to understand the role played by the space-time configurations – chronotopes – during a collaborative task involving the use of technology. We qualitatively analysed videos and interviews collected in a university media design course. We can claim that the already complex definition given by Bakhtin became even more articulated when applied in this context. Looking at chronotopes allowed us to recognise the strong interdependency between the collaborative framing of time-space and the sense-making concerning the task. We found that chronotopes are characterised by: (a) how material elements – including the physical bodies of participants and the tools composing the physical space – are organised; (b) how space and time is discursively framed, in a future-oriented process; (c) the underlying cultural models. We call these features: envisioning of chronotopes, enactment of chronotopes, and chronotopic attributes of cultural models.

These three aspects describe a very articulated vision of chronotopes. We believe that this vision enables chronotopes to be used as methodological and semiotic tools with which to make an in-depth inquiry into collaborative processes. Understanding such processes offers advantages for both educational and professional contexts.

REFERENCES

Bakhtin, M. (1981). *The dialogic imagination. Four essays by M. M. Bakhtin*. Austin, TX: University of Texas Press.
Bateson, G. (1972). *Steps to an ecology of mind: Collected essays in anthropology, psychiatry, evolution, and epistemology*. Chicago, IL: The Chicago University Press.
Bloome, D., Beierle, M., Grigorenko, M., & Goldman, S. (2009). Learning over time: Uses of intercontextuality, collective memories, and classroom chronotopes in the construction of learning opportunities in a ninth-grade language arts classroom. *Language and Education, 23*(4), 313–334.
Brown, R., & Renshaw, P. (2006). Positioning students as actors and authors: A chronotopic analysis of collaborative learning activities. *Mind, Culture and Activity, 13*(3), 247–259.
Cole, M. (1996). *Cultural psychology: A once and future discipline*. Cambridge, MA: Harvard University Press.

Foucault, M. (1977). *Discipline and punish: The birth of the prison.* New York, NY: Vintage.

Goodwin, C. (2000). Practices of color classification. *Mind, Culture, and Activity, 7*(1 & 2), 19–36.

Goody, J. (1977). *The domestication of the savage mind.* Cambridge: Cambridge University Press.

Hollan, J., Hutchins, E., & Kirsh, D. (2000). Distributed cognition: Toward a new foundation for human-computer interaction research. *ACM Transactions on Computer-Human Interaction, 7,* 174–196.

Holquist, M. (1982). Bakhtin and Rabelais: Theory as praxis. *Boundary 2, 11,* 5–19

Kirsh, D. (1995). The intelligent use of space. *Artificial Intelligence, 73*(1), 31–68.

Kivelä, M., & Mylläri, J. (2008). *Making sense of content creation in the physical and virtual in Primary School.* The second international DREAM conference, University of Southern Denmark, Odense.

Kumpulainen K., Mikkola A., & Jaatinen A. (2013). The chronotopes of technology-mediated creative learning practices in an elementary school community. *Learning, Media and Technology, 39*(1), 53–74.

Leander, K. M. (2001). 'This is our freedom bus going home right now': Producing and hybridizing space-time contexts in pedagogical discourse. *Journal of Literacy Research, 33*(4), 637–679.

Legrenzi, P., Girotto, V., & Johnson-Laird, P.N. (1993). Focussing in reasoning and decision-making. *Cognition, 49*(1), 37–66.

Lemke, J. L. (2004). *Learning across multiple places and their chronotopes.* Contribution to the symposium: Spaces and boundaries of learning, San Diego, CA. Retrieved from http://www.personal.umich.edu/~jaylemke/papers/aera_2004.htm

Ligorio, M. B., & Ritella, G. (2010). The collaborative construction of chronotopes during computer-supported collaborative professional tasks. *International Journal of Computer-Supported Collaborative Learning, 5*(4), 433–452.

Matusov, E. (2009). *Journey into dialogic pedagogy.* New York, NY: Nova Science Publishers.

McLuhan, M., & Lapham, L. H. (1964). *Understanding media: The extensions of man.* Cambridge, MA: MIT Press.

Olson, D. (1994). *The world on paper: The conceptual and cognitive implications of writing and reading.* Cambridge: Cambridge University Press.

Renshaw, P. D. (2014). Classroom chronotopes privileged by contemporary educational policy. In S. Phillipson, Y. L. Ku Kelly, & N. Phillipson Shane (Eds.), *Constructing educational achievement: A sociocultural perspective.* Abingdon, OX: Routledge

Ritella, G., & Hakkarainen, K. (2012). Instrumental genesis in technology-mediated learning: From double stimulation to expansive knowledge practices. *International Journal of Computer-Supported Collaborative Learning, 7*(2), 239–258.

Ritella, G., & Ligorio, M. B. (in press). Investigating chronotopes to advance a dialogical theory of collaborative sensemaking. *Culture & Psychology.*

Ritella, G., Ligorio, M. B., & Hakkarainen, K. (2015). The role of context in a collaborative problem-solving task during professional development. *Technology, Pedagogy and Education,* 1–18.

Ritella, G., Ligorio, M. B., & Hakkarainen, K. (submitted). Theorizing space-time relations in education: The concept of chronotope.

Ritella, G., Ligorio, M. B., & Hakkarainen, K. (in preparation). Interconnections between the envisioning of chronotopes and the interpretation of a collaborative task.

Ritella, G., Ligorio, M. B., & Hakkarainen, K. (forthcoming). Chronotopes and cultural models: Making sense of the task in a media design course.

Roth, W. M. (2005). *Doing qualitative research: Praxis of method.* Rotterdam, The Netherlands: Sense Publishers.

Sawyer, R. K., & DeZutter, S. (2009, May). Distributed creativity: How collective creations emerge from collaboration. *Psychology of Aesthetics, Creativity, and the Arts, 3*(2), 81–92.

Vygotsky, L. S. (1978). *Mind in society.* Cambridge, MA: Harvard University Press.

Vygotsky, L. S. (1981). The genesis of higher mental functions. In J. V. Wertsch (Ed.), *The concept of activity in Soviet psychology* (pp. 144–188). Armonk, NY: Sharpe.

Giuseppe Ritella
University of Helsinki

Beatrice Ligorio
University of Bari

STEFANO OLIVERIO

4. HYPHENATED SUBJECTS, BEYOND THE 'DIALECTAL' BILDUNG

The 'Cosmopolitan' Community of Inquiry as an Intermediate Space[1]

INTRODUCTION

Investigating our contemporary existential condition, the Italian philosopher Gianni Vattimo saw one of its chief features as the liberation of differences and of what could be generally called "dialect." Vattimo explicitly opposes this trait to the project of the humanistic *Bildung* as it was articulated in German tradition and found its culmination in Hegel's idea of the self-transparency of consciousness. To this idea of an "educated society" understood as an "enlightened" and therefore "transparent" society, Vattimo counters the project of a valorization of the pluralization of history and culture as it is/may be promoted thanks to the proliferation of communication. We could say that Vattimo seems to champion the passage from a dialectic to a dialectal *Bildung*. On the one hand, the paper intends to emphasize the educational significance of this project; on the other, though, it raises the question whether a 'dialectal *Bildung*' is sufficient to cope with contemporary scenarios. If the role that the liberation of 'dialects' has in breaking the grip of monological and ultimately diversity-erasing approaches in education is not objectionable, what can be discussed is whether it can represent a final option. In particular, the contribution will engage with this question through drawing upon some ingenious ideas of Horace Kallen on *hyphenation*. In the heat of the polemics on the *hyphenated America* (the derogatory phrase used to attack the immigrants who were not considered true Americans, but only Italo-American, Irish-American etc. because they did not belong to the English stock of the first settlers) Kallen countered that 'culture is spiritual hyphenation.' In the perspective the present chapter endeavours to work out, the educational engagement aimed at valorising plurality should consist not so much in a 'dialectal *Bildung*' as in the cultivation of the awareness of our constitutive 'hyphenated condition.' To achieve this end, a reinterpretation of the Matthew Lipman community of philosophical inquiry (CPI) is appealed to in the light of Hansen's idea of *educational cosmopolitanism* and Delanty's *critical cosmopolitanism*. The CPI will be presented as a 'space of

A. Surian (Ed.), Open Spaces for Interactions and Learning Diversities, 37–49.

borders' and re-interpreted against the backdrop of a reading of the Bakhtin's notions of getting into shape and borders.

FROM DIALECTIC TO 'DIALECTAL' BILDUNG?

In *La società trasparente* [The Transparent Society], the Italian philosopher Gianni Vattimo establishes a peculiar connection between what he considers as the emancipative role of the media and their challenge to modern *Bildung*. The model of *Bildung* was that of "human history as an ongoing process of emancipation, as if it were the perfection of the ideal man [*sic*] (the essay *On the Education of the Human Race* by Lessing, 1780, is the typical expression of this perspective)" (p. 8).[2] By contrast, according to Vattimo, the goal of the *transparent society*—understood as a "more enlightened, more 'educated' society" (p. 13)—is done away with by virtue of the media which promote a "giddy proliferation of communication" so that "more and more subcultures 'have their say'" (*Ibidem*). This pluralization produces the dissolution of the idea of a unilinear development of history and of a final re-appropriation by a universal subject.

Vattimo draws significant inferences from this cultural constellation which encourages us, in his opinion, to go beyond modern *Bildung*. In particular, he suggests that a new ideal of emancipation emerges which is based upon "the oscillation [and] the plurality" (p. 15):

> Here emancipation consists rather in the disorientation, which is, also and at the same time, the liberation of differences, of the local elements, of what could be generally called dialect. [...] The liberation of differences is an act through which *they 'find their voice,' come into presence, and therefore they 'get into shape'* for recognition [...]. If, in a world of dialects, I speak my own dialect, I shall be conscious that it is not the only 'language,' but that it is precisely one amongst many [...]. (pp. 17–18. Italics added)

To make a (serious) pun, we can state that Vattimo is inviting us to go beyond the dialectic *Bildung* towards a 'dialectal *Bildung*,' the former being the one which postulates an incessant going through differences to attain a final self-reappropriation within the transparency of self-consciousness, the latter, instead, thriving on plurality and on "a continual oscillation between belonging and disorientation" (p. 19).

In his argumentation Vattimo introduces a key notion—that of *Bildung*—which is one of most pivotal concepts of German philosophical and educational tradition, especially in the works of Herder, Goethe, Humboldt and Hegel. *Bildung* combines and unites the ideas of culture and education and refers to a kind of self-cultivation in which the individual, by participating in the institutions and social practices of his/her own culture and familiarizing him/herself with its greatest achievements, develops his/her potential and 'forms' his/her humanity. *Bildung* is at the same time 'culture' and 'formative education,' as Carlyle suggested translating it.

As an innovative reader and interpreter of Gadamer, Vattimo builds and elaborates on his revisitation of the idea of *Bildung*. On the one hand, Gadamer, in the wake of Hegel, highlights that culture [*Bildung*] is a "rising to the universal" (Gadamer, 2004, p. 11) in that "[i]t is the universal nature of human Bildung to constitute itself as a universal intellectual being. Whoever abandons himself to his particularity is ungebildet ('unformed') [...]" (*Ibidem*). This rising to the universal realizes itself through "recogniz[ing] one's own in the stranger, to become at home in it [...] Thus what constitutes the essence of Bildung is clearly not estrangement as such, but the return to oneself—which presupposes estrangement to be sure" (Ibid., p. 13).[3] On the other hand, Gadamer specifies that we can gain important insights from Hegel's notion of Bildung "without being tied to Hegel's philosophy of absolute spirit" (*Ibidem*). The outcome of this re-appropriation of a Hegel purged of the ideas of the finality and closure of the System is that the

> general characteristic of Bildung [is] keeping oneself open to what is other— to other, more universal points of view. It embraces a sense of proportion and distance in relation to itself, and hence consists in rising above itself to universality. To distance oneself from oneself and from one's private purposes means to look at these in the way the others see them. The universality is by no means a universality of the concept or understanding. This is not a case of a particular being determined by a universal; nothing is proved conclusively. The universal viewpoints to which the cultivated man [sic] (gelbildet) keeps himself open are not a fixed applicable yardstick, but are present to him only as the viewpoints of possible others. (Ibid., pp. 15–16)

In my reading there is, however, an important difference between Gadamer's treatment of *Bildung* and Vattimo's cultural pluralism and 'dialectalism.' Although both take their leave of Hegel's absolutism and the fatal conceit of a final synthesis, that is, of the final self-appropriation on the part of a universal subject, the former seems to preserve the demand for a *Bildung* tensionally directed to universality, in which universality emerges through the dialogue between the plurality of the viewpoints; the latter, instead, frightened by the monologism of Hegel's Absolute and excited by the possibilities of emancipation linked with the liberation of differences, seems to dismiss any 'discourse of universality' as inevitably homogenizing and/or as exposing us to the danger of forms of discourse that delete plurality.

To put it differently: Vattimo endorses completely Gadamer's emphasis on *Bildung* and his misgivings about Hegel's dialectics, insofar as it pretends to attain an absolute knowledge, but he thinks that, in order to release the emancipative potential of the discourse of *Bildung*, this has to be 'dialectally' (not dialectically!) inflected, in the sense that it has to abandon any demand for universality by fully championing the recognition of the diversity of dialects that find their voices.

While the significance of the fact that 'dialects' have their say cannot be gainsaid, it is moot whether the mere proliferation of the plurality of cultures, without promoting at the same time the possibility not only of their encounter but of the construction of shared and 'universal' horizons, can be sufficient in our age, marked, as it risks being, by the resistance of different cultures to converge on a humanly and historically possible universality by mutually recognizing each one's differences.

Vattimo links together the 'finding of a voice' on the part of 'other cultures,' their 'coming into presence' and their 'getting into shape': is his version of this link educationally promising or should we seek a different kind of connection? In what sense should we interpret what he calls 'oscillation between belonging and disorientation' and in what kind of spaces can it *take place*?

I have taken my cue from Vattimo's tenets because they epitomize brilliantly a specific mindset and even a sensibility, usually known as postmodernism, which has contributed to emphasizing the importance of freeing differences from the grip of monologism, which, during modernity, was translated—at the level of societal and political practices—into strategies of the *anthropophagic assimilation* or *anthropoemic exclusion of strangers* (Bauman, 1997, pp. 18 ff.). Vattimo's insistence on the plurality of subcultures which 'have their say' should not, however, be taken as a quasi-communitarian appeal: the pluralization should not work in the direction of the proliferation of self-enclosed identities but rather in that of weakened and lightened ones.

The question is whether this is sufficient in contemporary scenarios: can weakened and lightened cultural identities help us to ward off the 'clash of civilizations' or should we think also of new forms of universality, without fearing that any 'discourse of universality' is doomed to reproduce the totalizing drawbacks and the insensitivity to the differences that were typical of a specific inflection of the project of modernity. In the next section I will endeavour to point to a possible (educational) framework—and to one possible pedagogical strategy—that can respond to the need for a new kind of universality, while recognizing the rights of the dialects.

As aforementioned Vattimo elaborates his proposal of what I have called his 'dialectal *Bildung*' by valorizing the (possible) emancipative role of the media. Through this move he encounters Echeverría's (1994) idea that the emergence of the 'Telepolis' has been creating the conditions of a kind of cosmopolitanism which goes beyond the Enlightenment-, State-oriented cosmopolitanism and brings to the fore "cosmopolitan individual[s], who link up by going beyond the territorial borders which define the existence of the States" (Echeverría, 1999, p. 165).

Can Vattimo's proposal be construed, accordingly, in terms of a form of new cosmopolitanism made possible by the new media? In the following I will argue that we need a form of cosmopolitanism that goes partly beyond Vattimo's 'dialectal *Bildung*' and engages educationally with the contemporary challenges. Moreover, I will point to an educational space where cosmopolitanism can *take place* and where a specific movement between belonging and "disembedding,"[4] between 'getting into shape' and 'coming into presence' happens.

THE 'OTHER COMMUNITY' AND/OR THE CRITICAL
COSMOPOLITAN COMMUNITY

Vattimo's highlighting of the values of dialectal plurality as a weakening of modern, unilinear and homogenizing rationality can be put profitably in relation with Adolpho Lingis' reflections on the rational community. It is interesting that, in order to sketch the profile of the rational community by tracing it back to its Greek sources, Lingis emphasizes how the rational community emerges as a way of disempowering the strangeness of the stranger:

> In the mercantile port cities of Greece, strangers arrive who ask the Greeks, Why do you do as you do? In all societies where groups of humans elaborate their distinctness, the answer was and is, Because our fathers have taught us to do so, because our gods have decreed that it be so. Something new begins when the Greeks begin to give a reason that the stranger, who does not have these fathers and these gods, can accept. […] The one who so answers commits himself to his statement, commits himself to supply a reason and a reason for the reason […]. (Lingis, 1994, pp. 3–4)

As a consequence of this shift, the rational community 'imposes' a new regime of discourse:

> The rational community produces, and is produced by, a common discourse in a much stronger sense. The insights of individuals are formulated in universal categories, such that they are detached from the here-now index of the one who first formulated them. […] Then, when any rational agent speaks, he speaks as a representative of the common discourse. (Ibid., pp. 109–110)

To this kind of community Lingis opposes 'the other community:'

> Before the rational community, there was the encounter with the other, the intruder. The encounter begins with the one who exposes himself to the demand and contestation of the other. Beneath the rational community […] is another community, the community that demands that the one who has his own communal identity, who produces his own nature, expose himself to the one with whom he has nothing in common, the stranger. (Ibid., p. 10)

Biesta (2006, pp. 57 ff.) relates Lingis' rational community to the modern community in the sense of Bauman (1997) and highlights how the modern school system has chiefly aimed at building rational communities both in Lingis' sense ("It will not be too difficult to recognize the role of education—the role of schools and other educational institutions—in the constitution and reproduction of rational communities. […] Schools provide students with a very specific voice, namely, with the voice of the rational communities it represents through the curriculum" [Biesta, 2006, pp. 56–57]) and in Bauman's ("Indeed, the ideal of modern education […] is to 'release' children and students from their local, historical and cultural situations and bring them into contact with a general, rational point of view" [Ibid., p. 58]). In Biesta's words,

> [a]s educators we should neither deny nor forget that we live in a world of rational communities, that these communities are important for specific purposes, and that the main reason why we have schools, at least from a historical point of view, is in order to reproduce the world of rational communities. But we also shouldn't forget that this is not all that matters in life – and that it is perhaps even the case that what ultimately matters is not the reproduction of rational communities but the possibility for the other community to come and stay into existence. (Ibid., p. 68)

The notion of 'the other community' is closely related, as aforementioned, with the exposure to "the one with whom [we have] nothing in common, the stranger." By weaving together Lingis, Bauman—in particular the latter's idea of the new role of strangers in the postmodern constellation—and Biesta's educational reading of this thematic plexus, we could imagine—as a way of engaging with the intercultural challenges of the present—the transformation of our multi-ethnic schools into spaces where strangers can come into presence in their strangeness, without being merely assimilated.

This could trigger off a process of 'estrangement' also in the members of the hosting community, starting from the teachers, usually considered as those who usher in pupils—and all the more foreign pupils—into the dominant culture. As the Italian educationalist Davide Zoletto has finely highlighted, the teacher who really welcomes the stranger "feels strange, not because s/he is *outside* her/his own territory or her/his own time but precisely for the opposite reason: exactly because s/he is *inside* her/his territory and her/his time. But s/he perceives them in a different way. In this sense, in order to be more welcoming, s/he has to learn to become a *stranger in the classroom*" (Zoletto, 2007, p. 26).

The view briefly elaborated thus far endeavours to cluster together Bauman's disembedding, Vattimo's disorienting pluralization and Echeverría's cosmopolitan individual (without accepting, though, the latter's optimism about the 'Telepolis') by comprehending (in all meanings of the word) them within the horizon of Biesta's (2010, 2013) notion of subjectification.[5]

While Biesta's educational re-appropriation of the construct of "the other community" could be highly profitable to 'open spaces for interaction and learning diversities' and it can contribute to giving educational substance to Bauman's disembedding, insofar as it can be connected to the idea of the cosmopolitan individual (in a non-individualistic meaning), I would like to elaborate on another version of the cosmopolitan option which seems to be educationally promising. I will refer to Gerald Delanty (2006, 2009) who invokes what he calls "critical cosmopolitanism":[6]

Rather than see cosmopolitanism as a particular or singular condition that either exists or does not, a state or goal to be realized, it should instead be seen as a cultural medium of societal transformation that is based on the principle of world openness, which is associated with the notion of global publics. […] So against notions of globalization and universality, on the one side, and plurality and particularism on the other, the cultural dimension of cosmopolitanism consists more in the creation and articulation of communicative models of world openness in which societies undergo transformation. […] Cosmopolitan culture is one of self-problematization and while diversity will, by the pluralizing nature of cosmopolitanism, be inevitable the reflexive and critical self-understanding of cosmopolitanism cannot be neglected. (Delanty, 2006, pp. 27, 35)

In this perspective the challenge is to promote the emergence of a cosmopolitan culture, thriving upon self-problematization and reflectivity. It should be noted that the project of "a cosmopolitan culture" risks re-proposing that tendency to a kind of differences-erasing universality which Vattimo has taught us to mistrust. Indeed, speaking of "a cosmopolitan culture," do we not fall back again into the dream of a final unification? Would it not be better to speak, instead, of cosmopolitan cultures? I would suggest that we should maintain both expressions because in them the word 'culture' refers to two different dimensions (analogously to *Bildung* that means both culture and education); by 'cosmopolitan cultures' we could refer to cultures insofar as they avoid any "solipsistic locking up and intransitive autochthony," in the engaging phrase of Raúl Fornet-Betancourt (1998a, p. 15), and opens themselves up to the world. By 'cosmopolitan culture' we would mean the cultivation of habits of self-problematization that equip cultures (through a cosmopolitan education of the individuals) with the tools for a reflective stance.

Promoting cosmopolitan culture(s) requires something more similar to what Lingis calls "the rational community" or, to put it better, it requires that we do not understand any rational community along the lines Lingis draws.

Cosmopolitan cultures are cultures that do not recoil from and even cultivate what I will call 'hyphenation.' I am drawing upon Horace Kallen's response to the chauvinism of the British Americans who disparaged immigrants as not belonging to the English stock, by hyphenating them (Irish-American, Afro-American, Italo-American and so on):

Hyphenation as such is a fact which permeates all levels of life. A man is at once a son and a husband, a brother and a friend, a man of affairs and a student, a citizen of a state and a member of a church, one in an ethnic and social group and the citizen of a nation. […] it is absurd to lose sight of the truth that the hyphen unites very much more than it separates, and that in point of fact, *the greater the hyphenation, the greater the unanimity.* […] *culture is nothing more than spiritual hyphenation – it is humanism in the best sense of the term.* (Kallen, 1916, pp. 62–64. Italics added)

There are some aspects that I would consider to be worthwhile in Kallen's perspective, as far as I understand it. First of all, while the primacy of the individual is fully recognized, her/his need for belonging is not overlooked. By criticizing the ways in which American schools attempted to integrate the new Americans (I would not speak of inclusion in this case: see Oliverio, 2010, p. 58 ff.)—through notions of history, geography, civic education etc.—Kallen notes that "as the public school imparts it, or as the social settlement imparts it, it is not really a *life*; it [=this kind of 'culture'] is an abstraction, an arrangement of words" (Kallen, 1915, p. 95). As a consequence, the new Americans tended to recover their nationalities, which Kallen read etymologically as "*natio*, the inwardness of [their] nativity" (*Ibidem*). The net outcome of refusing hyphenation is, therefore, the risk of perpetuating self-enclosure in one's own culture, which can go hand in hand with a superficial homogenization through the media (also on this Kallen has prophetic pages). What we need, instead, is *hyphenation*, that is, "a multiplicity in a unity, an orchestration of mankind" (Ibid., p. 124).

While recognizing the need for Vattimo's oscillation between belonging and disorientation, this orchestration requires something different from a merely 'dialectal *Bildung*,' which risks sanctioning the separation without creating forms of unity. Furthermore, it would be attained by creating spaces of self-problematization and reflectivity where a movement of dis- and re-embedding takes place and where cosmopolitan culture can flourish. Can we imagine educational settings and/or pedagogical strategies that enable us to cultivate this kind of cosmopolitanism and to activate and/or recognize the dynamics of hyphenation?

THE COMMUNITY OF PHILOSOPHICAL INQUIRY AND THE REFLECTIVE IN-BETWEEN

Against the backdrop of the reflections developed, I would suggest that Matthew Lipman's (2003) community of philosophical inquiry (CPI) can represent that space through which critical cosmopolitanism can take place in educational settings (see also Oliverio, 2012). Obviously, the CPI is a kind of rational community but it should not be imagined as a space of diversities-erasing universalization. On the contrary, it should be considered as that device that allows us to operationalize David Hansen's idea of *educational cosmopolitanism*. Hansen (2011) distinguishes socialization and education, the former being "the time-honored process of drawing the young into a way of life and equipping them to sustain it. [...] Through it, the young learn ways of understanding, communicating, and interacting, along with a body of evolving cultural knowledge, that together are constitutive of their way of life" (Hansen, 2011, p. 93). Education, instead, "has to do with new forms of understanding, undergoing, and moving in the world. These modes may be in accord with processes of socialization but they do not simply replicate them" (*Ibidem*). In this sense, education is constitutively inhabited by a cosmopolitan tension.

I would like to hint at how Hansen's view, according to which cosmopolitanism implies a movement between a *reflective loyalty to the known* and a *reflective openness to the new*, could be mobilized within the CPI. We should understand the peculiar tenor of this movement: on the one hand, without the openness to the new, without a dis-embedding, no loyalty to the known would be reflective and we would have a loyalty to the *had* (to cultures as they are immediately experienced and, due to the immediacy of this experience, constantly running the risk of turning into ingrained, deep-seated and even encrusted habits) rather than to the *known* (I am idiosyncratically drawing upon Dewey's [1925] distinction). We get to know our culture, and to have a reflective loyalty to it, insofar as we open ourselves to the new, insofar as we 'estrange' ourselves. On the other hand, there is no openness onto the new if it is not an openness against the backdrop of the known.

This shuttling between the dimensions of the reflective loyalty and the reflective openness could be also interpreted as a constant *hyphenation*. In multicultural classes children from different nationalities can find in the CPI a reflectively cosmopolitan space where, through philosophical inquiry, they can investigate (and get to reflectively know) their own beliefs in comparison with those of others and go visiting (in a quasi Arendtian [1982] sense: see also Glaser, 1998) the set of ideas which contribute to underpinning the worlds of experience of their school-mates.

The sessions of philosophical inquiry could be the domain where a 'borders-getting into shape' dynamics—in reference to one's own culture and to that of others—takes place in an eminent way. By the couple borders-'getting into shape' I am referring to the re-interpretation of some of Bakhtin's tenets on the part of the Italian educationalist Daniela Manno. There is

> an equivalence between the idea of 'shape' and that of 'border.' […] If the shape [implies] border[s] and border[s] are an inter-mediate space, it is the interstitial nature of this space – a space which, by separating, and therefore giving shape, creates the possibility of the contact between the differences which emerge from it itself – which founds the temporariness of the shape and, then, the need for an incessant redefinition of it. […] inhabiting this inter-mediate space, being in-between, means being engaged in a relation by recognizing the substantial importance of alterity in order that subjectivity is given [to us]. (Manno, 2010, pp. 32–33)

By engaging in a cosmopolitan philosophical dialogue children can be involved in the interwoven processes of 'getting into shape' (= a reflective loyalty to the known, a re-embedding, a belonging, that is, a re-cognition[7] of one's own cultural allegiances) and borders-crossing (= a reflective openness to the new, a dis-embedding, a disorientation due to the plurality of dialects, that is, a recognizing of the temporariness of one's own cultural shape and the need for its constant re-definition through the encounter with other cultures, a "going visiting them," in Arendt's [1982] charming phrase). At the same time, within a CPI, by exploring commonalities along with differences new shared horizons are explored, which can represent the embryos of possible universal discourses, with the proviso that universality is always in the making and does not aspire to any final synthesis.

These processes take place within a kind of rational community where children/ people could have, though, the possibility of finding their own voice at multiple levels: their dialectal voice (dialects being understood as systems of beliefs), which is *known* as dialectal, insofar as children/people with other dialects are the partners in the cosmopolitan philosophical dialogue; their 'hyphenated voice,' insofar as children/people learn to cultivate "their shared human capacities to think, to speak, to listen, to tell and follow stories [...]" (Hansen, 2011, p. 9); and even their 'rebel voice,' insofar as the dialogue can open up the (mental) space for what Fornet-Betancourt has beautifully called "cultural disobedience" (Fornet-Betancourt, 1998a, pp. 17 ff.).

CONCLUDING REMARKS

In this chapter I have endeavoured to start exploring the question of what *Bildung* could look like in an age in which more and more cultures have their say and come into presence. While agreeing with Gianni Vattimo's idea that this flourishing of diversities ('dialects') has a genuine emancipative dimension, in that it breaks the grip of a homogenizing view of universality and of the connected idea of *Bildung* as a final self-appropriation and knowledge of a universal subject associated with a unilinear view of history, I have raised some misgivings about whether a 'dialectal *Bildung*' is an adequate response to contemporary challenges. In particular, I have insisted on the need to identify new ways of universality understood as an orchestration of differences through the promotion of an attitude of reflective and self-problematizing world openness, which does not deny, though, and even fosters the re-cognition of one's own cultural allegiances. Referring to some contemporary scholars I have referred to the need for a cosmopolitan *Bildung* and proposed the community of philosophical inquiry (CPI) as the educational setting and the pedagogical strategy through which to cultivate this cosmopolitan stance.

The CPI is a space where the participants, while experiencing the encounter with others, get to know their own cultures. In this sense, there is a shuttling between getting into a cultural shape and borders-crossing understood as a kind of going visiting others. At the same time, through philosophical dialogue people can inquire into the web of beliefs and notions that constitute their 'dialects' by discovering commonalities (and not only differences) and, therefore, they can operate in favour of the identification/construction of more universal horizons.

In the perspective here presented, the CPI as animated by a cosmopolitan tensionality is a kind of rational community that aspires to be out of the reach of the Lingis indictment according to which the rational community inaugurated by the Greek philosophical discourse erases the actual encounter with the other (the stranger) because it establishes a common and universal discourse deleting any reference to the existential pluralities. And, though, from another point of view, the challenge of Lingis cannot be underrated: by calling for philosophical inquiry as a way of fostering the cosmopolitan dialogue within classrooms is not a typically cultural-specific, Western resource (= philosophy) mobilized? Is not the universality of philosophy taken for granted? Fornet-Betancourt (1998b) has raised the question of "how we can be sure that, when we appeal to intercultural dialogue, we do not address the question of the philosophical premises of intercultural dialogue in a unilateral way or starting from a mono-cultural understanding of philosophy" (p. 160). The educational undertaking of a cosmopolitan *Bildung* through Lipman's CPI cannot evade these questions and should engage with the task of a cosmopolitan re-visitation of what doing philosophy means.

It could be expected (or, at least, hoped) that a virtuous circuit could be activated and that the educational experiences of the CPI in a cosmopolitan perspective within multicultural classrooms will help us to enrich our (= Western) view of philosophy and, on the other hand, that a theoretical work on what a cosmopolitan (or intercultural, as Fornet-Betancourt prefers to call it) philosophy could look like will give new insights into how to deploy philosophical inquiry in schools (and other educational settings) to cultivate a cosmopolitan mindset and sensibility.

NOTES

[1] The present chapter falls within the framework of the project PEACE (Philosophical Enquiry Advancing Cosmopolitan Engagement) – EU Lifelong Learning Comenius project, reference number 527659-LLP-1-2012-1-IT-COMENIUS-CMP. This project has been funded with support from the European Commission. This article reflects the views only of the author, and the Commission cannot be held responsible for any use which may be made of the information contained therein.

[2] All translations in this chapter are the author's unless otherwise specified.

[3] On the basis of the original German text I have slightly modified the quoted English edition, by translating 'estrangement' and 'the stranger' instead of 'alienation' and 'the alien.'

[4] In the wake of Giddens Bauman (1997, p. 20) means by "disembedding" the process through which the individuals are given "the benefit of an absolute beginning [and] set […] free to choose the kind of life they wish to live […]." The disembedding is originally activated by the modern State that "set about discrediting, disavowing and uprooting *les pouvoirs intermediares* of communities and traditions" (*Ibidem*). Bauman seems to see the "bringing to its conclusion the work of 'disembedding' of modernity" (p. 33) as a genuine possibility of emancipation in postmodernity, by avoiding the short cuts of overhasty re-embeddings (= the self-enclosure in monolithic and impermeable cultural identities and the cultivation of 'tribal' mindsets) that aim only to 'escape from freedom,' to use Erich Fromm's phrase.

[5] It is appropriate to specify that my use of Biesta's notion of subjectification is somewhat idiosyncratic in the present context and represents even a hermeneutical twisting. Indeed, it could be plausibly argued that the valorization of 'dialects' continues to fall within the scope of the logic of what Biesta calls 'socialization'—and therefore, of 'identity'—and does not meet the demands of subjectification and the related "educational responsibility as a responsibility for the singularity and uniqueness of *each* individual human being" (Biesta, 2006, p. 106).

[6] The notion of cosmopolitanism has been one of the concepts most explored over the last decade and it would be helpful to compare Delanty's view with other perspectives. This, however, cannot be undertaken in this chapter due to the restraints of space. Delanty speaks of a "critical cosmopolitanism" because he sees it as "relevant to the renewal of the critical theory in its traditional concern with the critique of social reality and the search for immanent transcendence […]" (Delanty, 2006, p. 2).

47

⁷ I hyphenate the word in order to express that this kind of recognition happens through a reflective stance, which brings one to the cognition of what would otherwise remain only taken for granted. Obviously by using the word re-cognition I want also to note that this 'reflective cognition' of one's own allegiances can occur only within the framework of a dialogue in which also the others' are recognized (= appreciated in their singularity).

REFERENCES

Arendt, H. (1982). *Lectures on Kant's political philosophy*. Chicago, IL: University of Chicago Press.

Bauman, Z. (1997). *Postmodernity and its discontents*. Cambridge: Polity Press.

Biesta, G. J. J. (2006). *Beyond learning. Democratic education for a human future*. Boulder, CO & London: Paradigm Publishers.

Biesta, G. J. J. (2010). *Good education in an age of measurement. Ethics, politics, democracy*. Boulder, CO & London: Paradigm Publishers.

Biesta, G. J. J. (2013). *The beautiful risk of education*. Boulder, CO & London: Paradigm Publishers.

Delanty, G. (2006). The cosmopolitan imagination: Critical cosmopolitanism and social theory. *The British Journal of Sociology, 57*(1), 25–47.

Delanty, G. (2009). *The cosmopolitan imagination. The renewal of critical social theory*. Cambridge: Cambridge University Press.

Dewey, J. (1925). *Experience and nature*. In J.A. Boydston (Ed.), *John Dewey, The later works, 1925–1953* (Vol. 1). Carbondale, IL: Southern Illinois University Press, 1981.

Echeverría, J. (1994). *Telépolis*. Barcelona: Destino Ediciónes.

Echeverría, J. (1999). *Cosmopolitas domésticos*. Barcelona: Anagrama.

Fornet-Betancourt, R. (1998a). Einführung. Lernen zu philosophieren ausgehend vom Kontext des Dialogs der Kulturen. In R. Fornet-Betancourt (Ed.), *Unterwegs zur interkulturellen Philosophie*. Frankfurt am Main: IKO Verlag.

Fornet-Betancourt, R. (1998b). Philosophische Voraussetzungen des interkulturellen Dialogs. In R. Fornet-Betancourt (Ed.), *Unterwegs zur interkulturellen Philosophie*. Frankfurt am Main: IKO Verlag.

Gadamer, H.-G. (2004). *Truth and method* (2nd ed., J. Weinsheimer & D. G. Marshall, Trans.). London & New York, NY: Continuum.

Glaser, J. (1998). Thinking together: Arendt's visiting imagination and Nussbaum's judicial spectatorship as models for a community of inquiry. *Thinking, The Journal of Philosophy for Children, 14*(1), 17–23.

Hansen, D. T. (2011). *The teacher and the world. A study of cosmopolitanism as education*. London & New York, NY: Routledge.

Kallen, H. (1915). Democracy *versus* the melting pot. In H. Kallen (Ed.), *Culture and democracy in the United States*. New York, NY: Arno Press & The New York Times, 1970.

Kallen, H. (1916). A meaning of Americanism. In H. Kallen (Ed.), *Culture and democracy in the United States*. New York, NY: Arno Press & The New York Times, 1970.

Lingis, A. (1994). *The community of those who have nothing in common*. Bloomington, IN: Indiana University Press.

Lipman, M. (2003). *Thinking in education* (2nd ed.). Cambridge: Cambridge University Press.

Manno, D. (2010). Confini da riconoscere, attraversare, creare. Un obiettivo pedagogico. *Pedagogika. it, 14*(4), 28–35.

Oliverio, S. (2010). L'inclusione interculturale come frontiera educativa. In M. Striano (Ed.), *Pratiche educative per l'inclusione sociale*. Milano: FrancoAngeli.

Oliverio, S. (2012). Complex thinking as cosmopolitanism and the drift of 'Learnification': P4C and some contemporary challenger. In M. Santi & S. Oliverio (Eds.), *Educating for complex thinking through philosophical inquiry. Models, advances, and proposals for the new millennium*. Napoli: Liguori.

Vattimo G. (2000). *La società trasparente* (2nd ed.). Milano: Garzanti.
Zoletto, D. (2007). *Straniero in classe. Una pedagogia dell'ospitalità*. Milano: Raffaello Cortina editore.

Stefano Oliverio
SInAPSi Centre
University of Naples Federico II

PART 2

NARRATIVE APPROACHES, KNOWLEDGE CO-CONSTRUCTION, AND SOCIAL INTERACTION

COLETTE DAIUTE AND PHILIP KRENISKE

5. HOPES, MISUNDERSTANDINGS AND POSSIBILITIES OF NARRATING FOR INCLUSIVE EDUCATION

INTRODUCTION

Narrating can be a means of social inclusion, but educators and researchers seeking this result must address the social relational nature of the narrative process. This chapter explains narrating as a social relational process in the context of a contemporary social inclusion project in the United States – the community college. After briefly presenting the dynamic theory of narrating (Daiute, 2014), we explain how the community college is involved in social inclusion practice and policy. We then present a study that invited students to share their interpretations of the college experience with a range of narratives as a way to evaluate the community college project and the complexity involved in gaining critical as well as supportive student perspectives.

NARRATING IS A SOCIAL PROCESS

For social inclusion, educators and researchers must extend hope with theory. Some common assumptions about narrative in education include that it is mostly valuable for sharing authentic personal experience (Graves, 1983), that it is a way to include and empower voices of minority students (Ghorashi & Ponzoni, 2014), and that it is expressive more than reflective (Bruner, 1986). A misunderstanding is that narratives are welded to persons and groups in authentic, singular, essential ways. A full analysis of that approach is beyond the scope of this article (see Daiute, 2014 for a fuller discussion), but the major difference of that typical approach and the social definition of narrative is that one approach defines narratives as representations (of persons, their beliefs, and so on), while the other defines narratives as tools that people *use* to mediate situations, relationships, and purposes. Of course, each broad orientation to narrative inquiry is nuanced, but the general misconception we would like to point out, especially relevant to issues of diversity, is that persons do not report on firmly held views or identities but they use narratives actively to reflect on and make sense of their experiences as they recount them. In other words, a misconception is that the narrative is a vehicle for meanings residing elsewhere

A. Surian (Ed.), Open Spaces for Interactions and Learning Diversities, 53–67.

rather than that the narrative is a process that enacts meaning with the features of the narrative – *how* it is expressed – in relation to the situation, purpose, and audience.

Personal stories can be compelling and revealing, yet the promise of narrating for inclusive education is that it is a social relational process. While narrative is a means of personal expression, it is also an activity. As an activity, the narrating process applies diverse qualities of narratives – genres (such as autobiography, fiction, positive mission statements, critiques, and so on) with sensitivity to the specific situations and audiences where they occur. We know, for example, that children, adolescents, and adults use narrative genres and features – character, plot, tense, values – flexibly to express diverse meanings in relation to situations and audiences (actual and imagined) (Daiute, 2014). Interestingly, a definition of narrating as a dynamic social process is especially relevant to endeavours requiring critique and change, such as education. When designing research and practice as social, educators can create inclusive thinking spaces (Perret-Clermont, 2004).

Several theoretical premises provide a foundation for considering narrating as a social developmental process. Language is the quintessential tool to "conduct human influence on the object of activity" (Vygotsky, 1978, p. 55); Stories and other symbolic tools are "externally oriented ... aimed at mastering and triumphing over nature" (ibid). Narrating engages diversity with audiences of others and within one's self. "Any utterance is a link in a very complexly organized chain of other utterances" (Bakhtin, 1986, p. 69). "An essential (constitutive) marker of the utterance is its quality of being addressed to someone... The utterance has both an author... and an addressee" (p. 95). This insight that even seemingly individual discourse – like the novel or a narrative account of an event in daily life – is an interaction in the social and physical world has been explored by philosophers (Austin, 1962; Wittgenstein, 1953), sociolinguists (Labov & Waletzky, 1997), and psychologists (Billig, 1994; Edwards, 2014), as well as by literary theorists. In brief, individual speakers and writers interact with the circumstances where they are narrating and with others – past, present, future audiences.

Extending that theoretical perspective, we explain that narrating in research and practice can elicit complex, critical, and creative interactions with the phenomena of interest. For example, an immigrant student brought to the United States illegally by parents shares certain values in public contexts – such as the importance of attending college to obtain language and vocational skills – while narrating in more secure contexts might elicit experiences of abuse by border control agents. In contrast, an American-born student might readily share critiques in a public context, while explaining resentment about remedial courses in a more private context. Such relevance to social context occurs, in fact, for all of us while not for those with certain socio-emotional disorders. Opportunities for students with such diverse histories to narrate from different positions they occupy in public life could provide a range of opportunities for sharing varied knowledge, experience, and goals. Complex meaning making about institutions, like the community college, provides resources for the development of the institution as well as for the students and other participating individuals. Nevertheless, those with greatest insights also need support for critiquing as well as aligning with powerful institutions.

Dynamic Narrative Research Design

Consistent with the dynamic theory of narrative inquiry and practice, an emphasis on narrative shifts to narrating as a process. This shift from narrative to narrating is important as the active form – "narrating" – highlights the social, interactive, and dynamic nature of this meaning-making process. To account for the social quality of narrating, research and practice designs must at a minimum invite participants to share experiences, for example, from at least two relational perspectives, such as narrating best experiences which would understandably align with the setting and purpose and sharing worst experiences, which would open the possibility to critique or distance appropriately. Dynamic narrating designs with multiple genres have offered complex meanings – that is diverse knowledge and experience by a group of participants using different narrative genres to interact with the relevant phenomenon. These include (but are not limited to) narratives of personal experience compared to narratives focusing on others; autobiographical narratives compared to fictional narratives (Daiute, 2010; 2014); narrating with instructional media (Kreniske, 2012, 2014); re-narrating a text message among teenage peers for one's own and another cultural group (Lucic, 2013); narrating in professional development situations in Europe (Daiute, Todorova, & Kovacs-Cerovic, 2015) and South America (Daiute, Eisenberg, & Vasconcellos, 2015).

This article focuses on the context of the community college in the United States because it is at the centre of contemporary issues of migration and attendant needs to educate a population that is increasingly diverse in ways that are unique to 21st century global situation.

THE MEANING OF THE CONTEMPORARY COMMUNITY COLLEGE

The following excerpt from the website of a community college in New York City describes the student population from the institutional point of view.

> … Community College's students are increasingly diverse and non-traditional in nature. They enter with significant impediments to academic success. They are more likely to be older, educationally and economically disadvantaged, have experienced academic failure at another post-secondary institution, have a significant commute to and from school, have frequently not gone directly from high school to college, are un-or under-employed, and are caring for children and/or aged parents.

This college statement indicates the potential for social integration, yet also describes the students in deficit terms, such as "disadvantaged," "academic failure" and so on. Similar to the website excerpt, research on community colleges has focused on student demographics (Jehangir, 2009; Syed, 2010); student under-achievement, as only 30% graduate and 12% progress to four-year colleges (Brock, 2010; Porchea, Allen, Robbins, & Phelps, 2010); and remedial activities like learning communities (Browne & Minnick, 2005; Stebleton & Nownes, 2011). In the past two decades community college enrolment has skyrocketed with a high proportion of enrolees being ethnic minorities, immigrants, and students from families with low incomes (Mullin, 2011; Perlstein, 2011; Teranishi, Suarez-Orozco & Suarez-Orozco, 2001; 21st Century Commission on Community Colleges, 2012). As the number of students attending community colleges has increased, so has popular discourse about the institution. A statement by President Barack Obama previewing his 2015 State of the United States Union address is an example of that high profile of the community college.

> I think everybody understands that education is the key to success in the 21st century. But what we also understand is that it's not just for kids. We also have to make sure that everybody has the opportunity to constantly train themselves for better jobs, better wages, better benefits. ... I'm going to be announcing a proposal ... to make the first two years of community college free for everybody who's willing to work for it. ... I hope we've got a chance to make sure that Congress will get behind these efforts to ensure that even as we rebound and grow in 2015, that it benefits everybody and not just some. (President Obama Announces, 2015)

In spite of such attention, research on students' interpretations of the community college in their lives is scant. Given the demographic profiles of community colleges in the United States, country of origin seems a promising perspective for insights about the meaning of the community college and its role in human development. Gaining access to students' assessments of the colleges they are attending requires methods that foreground their perspectives.

NARRATING THE CONTEMPORARY COMMUNITY COLLEGE

The premise of our research is that the community college is a system of purposes, activities, relationships, and resources, defined by participating stakeholders who interact in their mutual development. Students' narratives of their experiences in community college are developmental in several ways. The narrating process itself is relational and, thus, students' narratives are means of making sense of surrounding physical and symbolic environments. Narrating from diverse positions in the college, when it meets their needs and does not, such as in positive and negative experiences, involves different orientations to society and one's role in it. The following narratives by a student responding to an invitation to write about a best and a worst experience in community college offer personal details but also shine a light on the institution.

I'm an international student in LG College and my best experience so far on campus was in my urban sociology classes because it helped me to understand better how America is and why America became the country it is today. I've been taking good grades in this course and I feel really motivated to watch the classes since they are about what I see in real life.[1]

This student declares a personal stance ("international student"; "taking good grades" "feel motivated"), then broadening to a class, what it offered, and the relevance of that class for participating in society. The following narrative of a worst experience seizes an opportunity for critique.

Had some Financial aid issues which caused me to miss semesters in college. Another thing is Finding books for classes in lg library. Did not Happen in L College but in other college I attended. The Books that you may need to borrow for you to do your H.W. on projects may not be found in the school library.

Such dynamic narrating raises questions about the meaning of college from the participant perspective. The next section describes a case study of social narrating by several hundred students mediating social inclusion, among other endeavours, in the community college.

RESEARCH DESIGN

Research questions guiding this inquiry include "With what shared and diverse values do participants organize narratives of their best and worst experiences at their colleges?" "How do students with diverse histories, in particular U.S.-born and immigrant students, interpret the community college?"; "How might the community college be functioning as an inclusive developmental space?" Students in the study had the opportunity to reflect from a range of positions on the college experience, thus constituting an experience-based evaluation of the institution.

Professors of English, Social Studies, and Psychology courses at four community colleges in a large urban university system responded to our email request to visit their classes, discuss the study, and invite students' participation for a class period to write narratives of their best and worst experiences in the college (in addition to completing a survey about goals and activities). Our statement of purpose to the faculty and students was that we were asking them to share their experiences at the college for a project that would eventually provide summaries of the anonymous findings to administrators and faculty for improved understandings of the purpose of the community college from students' perspectives. Narrating best and worst experiences is consistent with our theoretical orientation as this range of perspectives provides diverse opportunities for critiquing (sharing worst experiences), as well as for aligning (sharing best experiences). Students who volunteered to participate included 381 students identifying as born in the U.S. or as immigrants (61% and 39%

respectively), roughly 50% male and female, ages 18 to 42, of diverse ethnicities, and linguistic backgrounds, including 111 participants speaking 2 languages, 138 speaking 3 or more languages, many with English as their third language). Participants wrote 546 narratives, 271 of best experiences and 275 of worst experiences in their colleges, thus most writing both.

Narrative Values Analysis with Mixed Methods

This mixed methods study of the best and worst experience narratives included qualitative analyses of the values organizing each narrative and quantitative compilations of values categories for the entire data set by narrative type and by country-of-origin group. Values analysis involved identifying organizing principles, beliefs, norms guiding what to say and what not to say (Daiute, 2014). Values analysis considers narratives as interactions among individuals and contexts by examining how people narrate issues in relevant circumstances, audiences, and purposes (Daiute, 2014; Daiute et al., 2003; Kreniske, 2012, 2014; Messina, 2014; Ninkovic, 2012). The values analysis process involves at least two researchers reading each narrative several times, identifying a major guiding value of the narrative and subsequently identifying any related sub-values up to 2 sub-values. The iterative process of identifying values, applying those value categories to subsets of 20 randomly selected narratives, and after achieving 90% inter-relater reliability, coding the entire set of narratives (in this case 546) with that list of values. Throughout the process, the unit of analysis was the narrative, dependent variables were the values, and independent variables were the narrative genre (best and worst experience narratives) and groups (U.S.-born and immigrant).

Considered for the pragmatic function of whole narrative, the first student narrative above indicates the importance of developing. The analytic focus of the narrative is indicated with its expression holistically from beginning to end, clued by specific features, such as process-oriented phrases like "so far," "helped me understand," "became," "I've been...," "motivated"; causal links "because" and "since", and the sequencing of elements toward predicates "...why America became the country it is today" and "motivated to watch the classes since they are about what I see in real life". Overall, as an utterance (in Bakhtin's sense), that narrative indicates the importance of the development of the society ("... why American became the country it is today") and the individual in relation to the institution ("I've been taking good grades in this course..." and "... motivated to watch ... what I see in real life"). As in other studies, the values generated via multiple readings and applying those value codes to the data were summarized with frequencies and percentages of narratives conforming to each major and sub-value category. Patterns of values offer information about narrators' orientations in different narrative types and by the diverse relevant groups of participants.

RESULTS – THE VALUE OF THE COMMUNITY COLLEGE

The analysis of the 546 narratives yielded several findings as presented in more detail in the following sections. Four major values with 20 sub-values emerged from the analysis. Most relevant to the argument in this article, students used the two narrative genres to share different meanings of the community college. Also indicative of the context sensitivity of the narrating process are the differences in values expressed by two focal groups of students who came to the community college with different histories. Analyses of narratives revealed four major categories including "participating in academics is important" (with four sub-values), "connecting is important" (five sub-values values), "disconnecting is important to acknowledge" (six sub-values values), and "developing is important) (five sub-values values). The major value categories (doing academics, connecting, developing, disconnecting) were distributed quite evenly across the major categories, which ranged from 23% to 26% of the full narrative data set.

In addition to the major value guiding each narrative, we identified up to two sub-values, to address specific details relevant to that value. Specific values related to the importance of doing academics were "acknowledging academic struggles is important", "acknowledging struggles with academic requirements is important", "acknowledging academic success is important", and "acknowledging academic support is important". The following narrative by a student who chose the pseudonym Prince Adam is an example of a narrative emphasizing the value of doing academics, with sub-values emphasizing acknowledging academic struggles and acknowledging struggles with requirements.

> The most difficult experience for me has been repeatedly failing the CatW. Despite having over a 3.9 GPA for my entire college experience, I'm unable to take freshmen English. As a result my graduation is in limbo until I pass the CatW.

Students emphasized specific values of "connecting" in five specific ways, including the importance of "connecting with people who are different from themselves", "the importance of connecting with the institution", "the importance of connecting with the college lifestyle", "the importance of connecting with peers", and "the importance of connecting with professors and advisors". The following narrative by John Hancock[2] indicates the value of connecting, with sub-values emphasizing the importance of connecting with the college lifestyle and with peers.

> My best experience in college so far was a very simple one, it wasn't much but it made me feel like a real college student was when I stayed with a group of friends and a professor that I wish I took a class with drinking coffee till 8 pm on the college campus. We were just talking and cracking jokes.

While the best experience narrative genre provided a means of aligning with the college, the worst experience narrative provided a means for students to critique the college. Sub-values emphasizing the importance of disconnecting included "the importance of acknowledging disconnects with advisors", "…disconnects with bureaucratic aspects of college", "…disconnects with essentials like finances", "…disconnects with the college lifestyle", "…disconnects with peers", and "…disconnects with professors". The following narrative by Kimberly acknowledges disconnecting specifically with the bureaucracy and with advisors.

> The whole adjustment period. I don't feel like the financial aid office or academic advisement help us as much as they should. In my opinion, some of them are as clueless as the students. And it would be nice to not get an attitude when I ask questions. I also wish that they gave us more info on a smarter route to finish college on time.

Students emphasized the value of the community college as a developmental space with five sub-values, including "developing one's self", "developing skills", "developing transformatively (becoming someone different)", "developing independence", and "developing collectively (that is with and/or for others)". The following example by Geold emphasizes the importance of transforming himself as a thinker, with the development of critical skills like asking himself "why" and explaining in great detail.

> My best experience in L community college is taking critical thinking class. It was very helpful for me to think outside of the box. Also I feel as If that calls made me become a better writer. The reason why because now when I write papers I tend to ask myself questions like "why". I always tend to explain things in detail and I feel that this class helped me with That.

As with all the narratives, the values analysis of Geold's account relies on the expression across the text to identify the apparent purpose of the narrative as an evaluation of the college experience. This narrative mentions an academic course, because values analysis focuses on the pragmatic purpose rather than only on specific words, the role of academics in changing the student's life emerges as prominent. With that array of values having been identified with 90% reliability and the other 10% of the value coding resolved by us through discussion and consensus, we addressed the question of whether and how students used the different genres. The next section discusses those diverse uses of the two narrative genres.

Diverse Narrative Genres Afford Complex Meanings of the Community College

Students used the different narrative genres – best and worst experience narratives to express very different values. Table 1 presents percentages and frequencies of the major values across the two genres, narratives of best experiences and narratives of worst experiences in college. As shown on Table 1, a Chi-square test showed that values across the genres differed significantly.

Table 1. Percentages and frequencies of major values by genre

Genre	Doing academics is important	Connecting is important	Developing is important	Acknowledging disconnects is ...	Total % (#)
Best	17 (43)	53 (135)	29 (74)	1 (2)	100 (254)
Worst	70 (91)	1 (2)	19 (53)	68 (129)	100 (275)
Chi-Squ.	272.50				
p < .001					

Note: Numbers in parentheses are the values guiding the narratives in each genre, numbers preceding the parenthesis represent percentages of the total genre

The following narratives illustrate how participants used the different genres to address very different experience. In this narrative, a female student who chose the pseudonym Samantha and identified as Asian used the best experience narrative to emphasize importance of developing herself in several ways.

My best college experience was when I got all A's in my classes. It really motivated me to even further exceed, and helped with my self-esteem.

Samantha used the worst experience narrative to acknowledge disconnects with a bureaucracy and essentials like finances and grades.

The most difficult experience was when My GPA dropped below a 2. I lost my financial aid and had to pay $800 for 2 classes. I had no means to pay that money, I wish I could have gotten a temporary loan from the college, but they didn't really help with anything. It was really difficult for me to gather the money because I don't work because of school and a small child.

We now turn to the complexity afforded by narrating from the perspectives of different groups of students whose experiences of the community college are likely to differ.

Immigrant and U.S.-Born Students Emphasized Diverse Meanings of the Community College

Addressing the question of whether diverse narrative opportunities would be useful for students of different backgrounds, a comparison of values by immigrant and U.S.-born students was especially relevant. Because community colleges present themselves as places that support students who need additional skills before attending a four-year college or university, immigrant students are a major group, 40% in our sample. Table 2 presents percentages and frequencies of the value and sub-values emphasizing the importance of developing, which was enacted differently by immigrant and U.S.-born students in this study.

Table 2. Percentages and frequencies of "Developing is Important" values by groups

Origin	Developing: transformatively ...	Collectively ...	Myself ...	Independence ...	Skills ...	Total % (#)
Immig.	5 (9)	20 (12)	33 (20)	3 (2)	30 (18)	100 (61)
U.S.	27 (16)	14 (23)	38 (62)	18 (29)	15 (24)	100 (165)
Chi-Squ.	13.30					
$p = .01$						

Note: Numbers in parentheses are the number of sub-values guiding the narratives by each group of participants, numbers preceding the parenthesis are percentages of the total Developing sub value category

As shown in Table 2, although US-born students organized their narratives around the importance of developing more than their immigrant peers, immigrant students emphasized the importance of developing with/for others – a collective – more than U.S.-born students. Immigrant students also emphasized developing skills more than U.S.-born students. On the other hand, U.S.-born students emphasized the importance of developing self more than immigrant students and developing independence.

For example, a female immigrant student who selected the pseudonym Anex wrote the following best and worst experience narratives.

The possibility to get to study after have came to the country not long ago and be eligible to financial aid.

My most difficult experience was to get enrolled after have studied before outside the country. It took more than a year between the process of submit all the documents in the way the college wanted and for them to review it, even though I did not want those credits transferred.

An independent orientation was more prominent among American-born students. Differences had to do with their tending to emphasize the importance of developing one's self, developing independence, and transforming relatively completely as a person. The narrative above by Geold is characteristic of the way the U.S.-born students enacted developing, such as with an emphasis on transforming one's self. The following is another example emphasizing independence and self.

The independence, new people...

... wish I made it to

a fouR yeaR school.

||

X

Whether diverse groups of students used the best and worst experience narratives differently is also a relevant question in this inquiry. Given the major differences in values emphasized across the narrative genres and across the country-of-origin groups, the interaction of genre by group was an analysis we considered. Nevertheless, the sample size in this study was not large enough to compare differences between genre for the immigrant and U.S. born students.

In summary, the different narrative orientations by immigrant and by U.S.-born students reveal different purposes of the community college. Immigrants highlighted belonging to the college collective, even though the bureaucratic procedures are especially problematic for them, and American students oriented more toward social problems at the college, perhaps because they take their participation for granted. Considered together, the narratives offer complex understandings of the community college as a varied and changing institution from the perspectives of student stakeholders. Results of the values analysis indicate the potential of these community colleges for intercultural relations, as a majority of both immigrant and U.S.-born students valued their college experiences for connecting with those from different backgrounds, while also seeking to gain skills and possible employment. In addition to the importance of self-development, values guiding a majority of the narratives depicted the need for ongoing development of the institution.

Given those differences across best and worst experience narratives by immigrant and American-born students, we learn how narrating positions (aligning versus distancing, by students with longer and shorter term histories in the society) allow for complex defining of the institution and its development. In brief, the community college emerges as a system of challenges and resources that students use to mediate their participation.

THE MEANING OF COMMUNITY COLLEGE

This study has illustrated how the meaning of the community college is complex, interacting with the expressive genre and with the history and positions of stakeholders – in this case students. By asking for best and worst experiences of students with histories coming to the college, the study highlights diverse definitions of the community college – diversity both within and between groups of participants. With at least two different narrating positions, the study design distances from the assumption that any group of students would have one characteristic way of responding.

Relevant to differences of developing, we read students' value of developing – not only practically but also socially, intellectually, and politically in the society where they live. Analyses of values expressed in this relatively large database of student narratives highlight the importance of the community college as a unique space for interacting with people from different cultures, walks of life, experiences, and goals. This major social value co-occurs with valuing community college for developing skills – from "people skills" to English language skills, and strategies for engaging in democratic process. Results of such analyses of values organizing the narratives by American-born and immigrant students offer insights about social inclusion as a multi-directional process by diverse stakeholders rather than primarily a process of assimilating diverse students to a norm.

Sharing their best and worst experiences in community college, the participants in this study speak to President Obama's plan to expand American prosperity "for everyone, not just for some". Creating institutions for everyone in highly diverse and currently relatively discordant societies involves creating dialogues and taking seriously the complex and diverse values, especially by students. Even just two diverse narrating perspectives involved in the present study illustrated previously unrecognized values within and across groups of students, as well as the major shared value of the community college as an opportunity for human and institutional development. That insight wrought intensively in a large set of narratives and rigorous narrative analysis acknowledges students' alignment with stated values of some of the colleges to support skills relevant to communication, critical thinking, and vocations, not as ends in themselves or for creating a labour force, but for the intrinsic personal and collective development that tends to get lost in the often cynical public discourse. The immigrant students, in particular, narrate the hope to participate meaningfully in American public life, not only for self-development and job-related skills but also for collective understanding and development via purposeful critique.

IMPLICATIONS AND CONCLUSION

An implication of these results is that research, practice, and policy with social inclusion programmes should involve students in complex narrating about their experiences to expand the mission and activities of the college. Narrating that allows critique as well as aligning with the institution is, for example, an important interventionist strategy for inviting a range of orientations to the college, rather than only asking for one's story in a neutral way or even for narrating what you know. Other possible genres that previous research has indicated open unexpected nuances of meaning include asking students and others who are the subjects of policies to position as experts, such as by writing policies, curricula, or letters of advice to others in their role in the future, elicits additional values (Daiute et al., 2015a & 2015b; Kreniske, 2014), as does writing fictional narratives, which provides a context for narrating about issues like discrimination and counter-conforming norms (Daiute, 2010).

Another implication of this study is to continue narrative inquiry with relatively large numbers of participants whose narratives can be examined rigorously for important patterns that advance across the qualitative/quantitative binary. The present study, for example, involves theory-based qualitative inquiry into values guiding narrative expressions, examined with rigorous methods and quantitative summaries and tests of the robustness of comparisons. This mixed methods approach presents patterns for ongoing research and practice about higher education. With an even larger sample, future research could, furthermore, examine relevant interactions, such as differences in the sub values across country-of-origin groups for details about the kinds of narratives that are especially amenable to discourse of different groups.

In conclusion, analysis presented here yielded several findings about a range of values guiding basic narratives whose meanings are amplified by appearing together, as differently positioned on the object of inquiry – the community college. Most relevant to the argument in this article, students used two narrative genres to share different meanings of the community college, thereby indicating that narrating is an interactive process with the features of narratives (such as the possible negative valence of narrating worst experiences and possible positive valence of narrating best experiences). In addition to participants' uses of these diverse kinds of narratives to share very different experiences and orientations to the college, the context-sensitive quality of narrating appears in the differences in meaning-making across two groups of students who came to the community college with different histories and, thus, different interactions with their colleges.

ACKNOWLEDGMENTS

The research reported in this chapter was made possible in part by a grant from the Spencer Foundation. The views expressed are those of the authors and do not necessarily reflect the views of the Spencer Foundation. The authors also thank the faculty and students who participated in this research. In addition, thank you to Ralitsa Todorova, Yulia Gorokhovsky and Kathleen Almonte for their assistance with reliability, data entry, and coding, and David Caicedo for his contribution in the broader project.

NOTES

[1] All narrative examples maintain the original phrasing and spelling.
[2] Student names are all pseudonyms they chose.

REFERENCES

21st-Century Commission on the Future of Community Colleges. (2012). *Reclaiming the American dream: Community colleges and the nation's future*. Washington, DC: American Association of Community Colleges. Retrieved from http://www.aacc.nche.edu/AboutCC/21stcenturyreport/21stCenturyReport.pdf

Austin, J. L. (1962). *How to do things with words*. Cambridge, MA: Harvard University Press.

Bakhtin, M. M. (1986). The problem of speech genres. In C. Emerson & M. Holquist (Eds.), *Speech genres and other late essays* (pp. 60–102). Austin, TX: University of Texas Press.

Billig, M. (1995). *Banal nationalism*. Thousand Oaks, CA: Sage Publications.

Brock, T. (2010). Young adults and higher education: Barriers and breakthroughs to success. *The Future of Children, 20*, 109–132.

Browne, M. N., & Minnick, K. J. (2005). The unnecessary tension between learning communities and intellectual growth. *College Student Journal, 39*, 775–783.

Bruner, J. S. (1986). *Actual minds, possible worlds*. Cambridge, MA: Harvard University Press.

Daiute, C. (2014). *Narrative inquiry: A dynamic approach.* Thousand Oaks, CA: Sage Publications.

Daiute, C., Eisenberg, Z., & Vasconcellos, V. (2015b). Considering early childhood education teachers' perceptions of risk. *International Journal of Educational Research, 71,* 40–49. Retrieved from http://dx.doi.org/10.1016/j.ijer.2015.02.010

Daiute, C., Stern, R., & Lelutiu-Weinberger, C. (2003). Negotiating violence prevention. *Journal of Social Issues, 59,* 83–101.

Daiute, C., Todorova, R., & Kovacs-Cerovic, T. (2015a). Narrating to manage participation and power relations in an education reform program. *Language & Communication, 45,* 46–58. Retrieved from http://dx.doi.org/10.1016/j.langcom.2015.08.006

Edwards, D. (2012). Discursive and scientific psychology. *British Journal of Social Psychology, 51,* 425–435.

Ghorashi, H., & Ponzoni, E. (2014). Reviving agency: Taking time and making space for rethinking diversity and inclusion. *European Journal of Social Work, 17*(2), 161–174.

Graves, D. H. (1983). *Writing: Teachers and children at work.* Portsmouth, NH: Heinemann.

Jehangir, R. (2009). Cultivating voice: First-generation students seek full academic citizenship in multicultural learning communities. *Innovative Higher Education, 34*(1), 33–49.

Kreniske, P. (2012, October). *Middle-school students negotiate a workplace simulation with threats to authority and supportive friends.* Poster presented at the meeting "Transitions from Adolescence to Adulthood," Society for Research on Child Development, Tampa, FL.

Kreniske, P. (2014). How the San of southern Africa used digital media as educational and political tools. *Journal of Interactive Technology and Pedagogy, 6.* Retrieved from http://jitp.commons.gc.cuny.edu/how-the-san-of-southern-africa-used-digital-media-as-educational-and-political-tools/

Messina, V. (2013). *Soldiers to students: Experiences of transitions of Iraq and Afghanistan war veterans.* Unpublished manuscript, Graduate Center, City University of New York, NY.

Mullin, C. M. (2011). *The road ahead: A look at the trends in the educational attainment of community college students* (Policy Brief 2011-04PBL). Washington, DC: American Association of Community Colleges.

Ninkovic, M. (2012). *Changing the subject: Human resource management in post-socialist workplaces.* (Doctoral dissertation). Graduate Center, City University of New York, New York, NY.

Perlstein, L. (2011). *The Aspen Prize for community college excellence.* Washington, DC: Aspen Institute.

Perret-Clermont, A-N. (2004). Thinking spaces of the young. In A-N Perret-Clermont, C. Pontecorvo, L. Resnick, T. Zittoun, & B. Burge (Eds.), *Joining society: Social institutions and learning in adolescence and youth* (pp. 3–10). Cambridge/New York, NY: Cambridge University Press.

Porchea, S. F., Allen, J., Robbins, S., & Phelps, R. P. (2010). Predictors of long-term enrollment and degree outcomes for community college students: Integrating academic, psychosocial, socio-demographic, and situational factors. *Journal of Higher Education, 81,* 750–778.

President Obama Announces. (2015, January). *President Obama announces free community college plan* [White House YouTube Video]. Retrieved from http://www.whitehouse.gov/photos-and-video/video/2015/01/09/president-obama-announces-free-community-college-plan

Stebleton, M., & Nownes, N. (2011). Writing and the world of work: An integrative learning community model at a two-year institution. *Journal of College Reading and Learning, 41*(2), 76–86.

Suárez-Orozco, M. (2001). Globalization, immigration, and education. *Harvard Educational Review, 71*(3), 345–365.

Syed, M. (2010). Developing an integrated self: Academic and ethnic identities among ethnically diverse college students. *Developmental Psychology, 46,* 1590–1604.

Teranishi, R. T., Suárez-Orozco, C., & Suárez-Orozco, M. (2011). Immigrants in community colleges. *Future of Children, 21*(1), 153–169.

Vygotsky, L. S. (1978). *Mind in society: The development of higher psychological processes.* Cambridge, MA: Harvard University Press.

Wittgenstein, L. (1953). *Philosophical investigations.* Oxford: Basil Blackwell.

Colette Daiute
The Graduate Center, City University of New York

Philip Kreniske
The Graduate Center and Hunter College, City University of New York

SYLVIA ROJAS-DRUMMOND, ANA MARÍA MÁRQUEZ,
RIIKKA HOFMANN, FIONA MAINE, ANA LUISA RUBIO,
JOSÉ HERNÁNDEZ AND KISSY GUZMÁN

6. ORACY AND LITERACY IN THE MAKING

Collaborative Talk and Writing in Grade 6 Mexican Classrooms

INTRODUCTION

This chapter focuses on analysing the development of oral and written communication in Mexican elementary students, in the context of the implementation of an innovative educational programme called 'Learning Together' (LT). The programme was designed to enhance oral and written communication in the students, including dialogic interactions, as well as reading comprehension and text production strategies through a variety of collaborative learning activities (Rojas-Drummond, Littleton, Hernández, & Zúñiga, 2010). Our work follows a sociocultural perspective for conceptualizing processes of development, teaching and learning, and attempts to create bridges between conceptualizations of literacy as a social practice, and current 'dialogic approaches' to investigating learning and teaching in school settings. Contemporary studies show that dialogic styles of interaction are of great value for the development of educational processes. These types of interaction encourage children to explain their reasoning, to discuss and exchange opinions, to support each other and build knowledge together, allowing them to advance their understanding and learning (Alexander, 2001, 2008; Mercer, 2000; Mercer & Littleton, 2007). To the extent that the process of teaching-and-learning is built partly as a result of the dialogic interactions between teachers and students, it is essential to understand the interactions that have proven effective in promoting student's development and learning. Unfortunately, dialogic styles of interaction rarely occur in typical traditional Mexican elementary school classrooms (Rojas-Drummond, 2000). For this reason, researchers in the field have developed programmes that explicitly promote these styles of engagement. Such is the case of the 'Thinking Together' programme developed in the UK (Dawes, Mercer & Wegerif, 2000), and the LT programme developed in Mexico (Rojas-Drummond, Gómez & Vélez, 2008; Rojas-Drummond, Littleton, Mazón & Vélez, 2012). Both programmes seek to promote dialogic styles of interaction between teachers and students, as well as among peers, to support the processes of thinking and learning in different knowledge domains. In the case of LT, emphasis is placed on enhancing literacy abilities. In the context of the implementation of this programme, the present study

A. Surian (Ed.), Open Spaces for Interactions and Learning Diversities, 69–108.

analyses its effects on the development of the dialogic interactions of sixth grade elementary students during collaborative writing activities.

Research in this area is imperative given that functional and information illiteracy are very widespread in Mexico, as well as in other developing countries in Latin America (particularly Peru, Colombia, Argentina, Brazil, Costa Rica, and Uruguay), as evidenced by international assessments (Organisation for Economic Cooperation and Development [OECD], 2010). In the case of Mexico, the above findings have been confirmed by the National Institute of Evaluation in Education (INEE, 2006). In fact, a comprehensive report made by the INEE (2007), indicate that literacy teaching practices are carried out mainly through rote learning exercises and somewhat meaningless tasks, and that the activities tend to be focused on completing the requisites dictated by the national Spanish textbooks. Thus, the use of written language is not rendered functional since it is not related to authentic social practices. In particular relation to reading comprehension, our studies have also found that, in general, public schools do not promote explicitly students' abilities for synthesizing texts (Rojas-Drummond et al., 2012). In addition, the national evaluations carried out by the INEE (2006) have shown that elementary students' writing abilities are below the minimum expected for this educational level. LT seeks to contribute to ameliorate these problems in the Mexican educational context, and could serve as an inspiration for initiatives to address the challenges posed by high levels of illiteracy in other developing countries.

THEORETICAL FRAMEWORK

Dialogic Interactions within a Sociocultural Paradigm

Inherent in the socio-cultural approach is the notion that understanding the nature of thinking, learning and development requires acknowledging the intrinsically social and communicative nature of human activity. This theory argues that intellectual development is an interactional accomplishment rooted in communicative practices, where language plays a key role as a mediator of activity, on both social and psychological levels. Similarly, education is enacted through the interactions between novices and experts. Such interactions reflect the historical development, cultural values and social practices of the societies in which educational institutions are embedded (Cole, 1996; Daniels, 2001; Lave & Wenger, 1991; Rogoff, 1990; Wells, 1999; Wertsch, 1998). Education and development are therefore conceived as social and cultural accomplishments whereby knowledge and meanings are 'co-constructed' jointly among participants of learning communities.

Recent research in the field of educational practices has emphasised the importance of dialogic interactions to support children's development, reasoning and learning (e.g. Littleton & Howe, 2010; Mercer & Littleton, 2007). This research has explored two functional aspects of these interactions. The first is teachers' use of dialogue as a means for 'scaffolding' children's learning and development

(Mercer & Littleton, 2007; Rojas-Drummond & Mercer, 2003; Rojas-Drummond, Torreblanca, Pedraza, Vélez, & Guzmán, 2013). The second is the potential value of peer group interaction and talk as another means of supporting these processes, but in a more symmetrical environment (Alexander, 2008; Fernández, Wegerif, Mercer, & Rojas-Drummond, 2001; Howe, 2010; Rojas-Drummond et al., 2010). According to Alexander, dialogic interactions are conceived as those that 'harness the power of talk to engage children, stimulate and extend their thinking, and advance their learning and understanding' (Alexander, 2008, pp. 37). These interactions are collective, reciprocal, supportive, cumulative and purposeful. Through dialogic interactions participants can create 'dialogic spaces' (Wegerif, 2007) which maintain an open, critical and constructive posture towards the exploration, confrontation and negotiation of different ideas. When opinions differ, participants may contrast their perspectives using argumentation, seeking eventual consensus. There is also an orientation towards inquiry and the joint construction of knowledge (Hennessy, Mercer, & Warwick, 2011; Mercer & Howe, 2012; Mercer & Littleton, 2007; Rojas-Drummond et al., 2010; Rojas-Drummond et al., 2013; Wells, 1999). However, research on collaborative activity in classrooms has revealed that an important bulk of the talk observed is off-task, uncooperative and sometimes entails little educational value (e.g. Alexander, 2004; Bennett & Cass, 1989). This might partly be due to the fact that children are not explicitly inducted into ways of communicating effectively. Similarly, they are not taught dialogic strategies for thinking collectively (Mercer & Littleton, 2007; Rojas-Drummond, 2000; Rojas-Drummond & Mercer, 2003). In contrast, the quality of the dialogue among participants can be improved when children are explicitly taught strategies for participating competently in collaborative activities (Mercer, 2008; Rojas-Drummond & Peon, 2004).

Given the educational value of collaborative work, we require innovative programmes where students learn to communicate productively to enhance their learning and reasoning, to solve problems and to achieve goals. The LT programme seeks to promote effective collaborative and communication abilities, including oracy and literacy, in an integrated and meaningful fashion. These abilities are essential for successful performance in school and in the personal, social and professional lives of individuals.

Collaborative Writing as a Social Practice

In the 80's and 90's, models of writing centred mainly on explaining the cognitive and psycholinguistic processes of individuals when composing texts. One example is the seminal model developed by Flower and Hayes in 1980. This model conceives of writing as a problem that experts solve effectively by engaging in sophisticated processes such as planning, composing and revising in a reflexive fashion, while novices carry out some of these processes, but in a more rudimentary way. Similarly, Scardamalia and Bereiter (1986) argue that, when composing texts, experts use iterative 'knowledge transforming' strategies, which allows them to move back and forth from engagement to reflection continuously, establishing novel connections between their knowledge about the world and about texts. In contrast, novices use more serial 'knowledge telling' strategies, employing the last phrase as the basis for the next one, without necessarily linking ideas nor engaging in much reflection. This results in a text that lacks global coherence.

Sharples (1999) integrated some elements from the previous models and proposed that writing is a process of 'creative design' in which the author is constantly making decisions about what to do before, during and after producing a text. This model claims that the communicative situation is a key condition that frames the writing process, given that it allows the writer to establish his/her intention, taking into account the characteristics of the audience. The model further emphasizes the dynamic, interdependent and flexible relationships among three phases: planning, textualization and reviewing. At each stage, there are cycles of action-reflection in which the writer transforms his/her ideas in a text (action) and makes a critical analysis of what he/she has written (reflection).

As in the case of Sharples' model, the creative aspect of writing is also emphasised by Cassany (2000), who argues that, during text production, there is a continuous tension between interpreting and creating ideas, on the one hand, and deciding how to present them, on the other. This tension involves a content dimension (what to say), and a rhetoric one (how to say it). In the former, writers construct texts by consulting relevant sources of information, and developing new ideas by linking them to prior knowledge. In the later, authors create ideas by using discursive and grammatical abilities, taking into account the communicative functions and characteristics of texts. The above processes are closely related to those described by Hayes and Flower, and Scardamalia and Bereiter, for expert writers. Cassany's model inspired the development of the rubric used in the present study to analyse children's texts, as will be explained under 'Methodological Framework'. More recently, there has been a greater emphasis on explaining also the social processes that frame writing activities. From a sociocultural perspective, literacy – including reading and writing – is conceptualized as a situated, social and cultural practice. Furthermore, writing is conceived as a complex social, cognitive and communicative process in which authors use their experiences with texts and the contexts in which they are embedded in order to transform their ideas into a coherent written discourse, thinking about their possible audience. In this view, writing results from the interaction between an individual and his/her need to communicate ideas to members of a given community; this highlights its social and communicative nature (Scribner & Cole, 1981; Street, 2005).

This shift in focus on the social dimension of literacy has given rise to current studies that analyse specifically the relations between dialogue and collaborative writing. In our line of research in this area, we have explored these processes in elementary school children. Rojas-Drummond, Mazón, Fernández and Wegerif (2006) compared children's talk in two contexts: solving logical-mathematical problems (convergent task), versus collaborative creation of summaries after reading diverse texts (divergent task). They found that children used different styles of communication when solving the convergent versus divergent tasks. In the former, children used 'Exploratory Talk', a productive type of communication characterized by the critical but constructive engagement of participants with each other's ideas, where reasoning is made explicit and claims are grounded through argumentation (Mercer, 2000). In contrast, in the latter, children tended to use 'Co-constructive Talk', which shares many similarities with 'Exploratory Talk', except that children do not necessarily use arguments to support their ideas. More recently, Rojas-Drummond et al. (2010) explored the relations between talk and collaborative writing in children's production of two types of texts, namely emails (expressive text) and opinion articles (argumentative text). Results showed that the type of text children produced shaped the type of talk that they engaged in. In particular, when writing emails, children tended to use 'Co-constructive Talk', whereas when they produced opinion articles, they engaged in oral argumentation as part of the process of constructing and supporting the opinions they expressed in their written texts. In addition, Rojas-Drummond, Albarrán and Littleton (2008) investigated how children learned to collaborate in creative writing projects, specifically the generation of multimedia stories. Analyses qualified the communicative processes by which children coordinated efforts to co-construct their oral, written and multimodal texts, particularly in the phases of 'brainstorming'. Results indicated that, explaining contexts for collaborative creative writing, involves more than understanding how joint activity is resourced by the immediate context, given that learners' interactions are also framed by the broader institutional and cultural milieu.

Some other prominent studies in this area are those of Vass and Littleton (2008) and Fisher, Myhill, Jones and Larkin (2010). Based on the Sharples (1999) model of creative writing reviewed above, Vass et al. (2008) used an analytic tool developed for creative writing tasks, linking collaborative and discursive features to social and cognitive processes associated with writing, namely 'engagement' and 'reflection'. This tool allowed an identification of some collaborative strategies which facilitated 'sharedness' and supported joint creative writing activities, such as reliance on a commonly built 'collaborative floor' and joint reviewing. These strategies indicated a shared focus which facilitated mutual inspiration. The authors argued that creative writing involves both emotion-driven and intellect-driven thinking. The tool employed an 'episode' as the unit of analysis to account for sequences of interactions in which utterances focused around writing phases such as content generation, reflection, planning and reviewing. As will be shown under 'Results', these episodes are closely linked to some of the units of analyses used in the present study, based on the Ethnography of Communication, and particularly CE such as planning, discussion about parts of the text, writing and text reviewing. However, the combination of Communicative Events (CE) with smaller units such as Communicative Acts (CA) afforded by Scheme for Educational Dialogue Analysis (SEDA), allowed us to carry out more in-depth analysis of children's dialogues, qualifying also utterances turn-by-turn (see definitions of these analytical categories under 'Methodological Framework' below). Fisher et al. (2010) in turn, carried out a study which explored talk in the different stages of writing (planning, writing and reflecting), based on the Hayes and Flower's 1980 model. They highlighted that most previous studies of talk were concerned with peer feedback and evaluation after the writing had happened, but that there is a place for talk at all points in the writing process. They classified three activities (idea generation, write aloud and reflection) to support this process. As in the case of the Vass et al., these activities are related to the CE identified in the present study mentioned above. One of the main contributions of Fisher et al.'s investigation is the development of 38 codes that describe teacher's and children's talk when engaged in writing projects. They distributed these codes into three categories (strategic, constructive and evaluative) for further analysis of types of talk. These codes share some similarities with the 33 CA that comprise SEDA. However, their analyses centered on accounting for how oral communication was used for collaborative writing. In contrast, in the context of the present investigation, SEDA allowed us to further distil specifically talk that has a dialogic quality, which is purported to play an important role in developmental and learning processes (Alexander, 2001, 2008). Therefore, accounting specifically for dialogic processes during collaborative writing represents a novel contribution of this research to the field. In sum, the dialogic perspective reviewed above, in conjunction with the conceptualization of literacy as a social practice, are central theoretical underpinnings of the present study.

METHODOLOGICAL FRAMEWORK

In order to systematically analyse dialogic interactions within the framework of a socio-cultural paradigm, we drew on the work of Hymes (1972) and Saville-Troike (2003) who describe an Ethnography of Communication. Essentially a 'nested hierarchy' (Rojas-Drummond et al., 2006), the theory organises the unique dynamic of communication into three levels. The first, and broadest level, is the 'Communicative Situation' (CS), which describes the context in which communication is happening (perhaps within a classroom, or restaurant). Embedded within this are connected turns of dialogue, the 'Communicative Events' (CE), in which the participant structure, the participants themselves, their topic, task and purpose all remain constant. For example, in a classroom context where a small group of children are engaged in a collaborative task, their conversation may be broken down into several CE as the children move from initially assigning roles to each other, to discussing the task, completing it and evaluating it. In turn, embedded within CE are the turns of conversation. Defined by their interactional functions, these 'Communicative Acts' (CA) are the small grain-size of relevance when considering how participants communicate together.

So as to further analyse CA in a fine-grained, systematic fashion, and distil those CA which have a dialogic quality, we employed a novel tool called 'The CAM-UNAM Scheme for Educational Dialogue Analysis' (SEDA) (Hennessy, Rojas-Drummond et al., in press). This tool originated from a previous scheme developed by Rojas-Drummond et al. (2013). The production, empirical testing and refinement of SEDA is the result of a 3-year (2013–15) British Academy funded collaboration between two teams in the UK and Mexico. SEDA is composed of 33 CA which attempt to capture the essence of dialogic interactions, in terms of what participant do and say as part of these forms of communication. CA are further organized into 8 clusters. These clusters are: (1) 'Invite elaboration or reasoning', which contains six codes related to invitations to explain, justify, explore possibilities, and elaborate or reformulate own or another's contributions; (2) 'Make reasoning explicit', formed by four codes associated with providing explanations, justifications, arguments and possibility thinking; (3) 'Build on ideas', composed of two codes connected to clarifying or elaborating own or other's ideas; (4) 'Express or invite ideas', with two codes, one for inviting the expression of opinions and the other for making relevant contributions; (5) 'Positioning and coordination of ideas', that contain six codes related to taking a stance in dialogue by evaluating, offering an opinion, synthesising, challenging or agreeing on different ideas/perspectives/ arguments; (6) 'Connect', with four codes associated with making explicit links to previous contributions or knowledge beyond the immediate dialogue; (7) 'Guide direction of dialogue or activity', that contains six codes connected to taking the responsibility for shaping the dialogue or activity through scaffolding strategies or by encouraging student-student dialogue, proposing courses of action or thinking time; and (8) 'Reflect on dialogue or activity', with three codes that refer to metacognitive

Table 1. Rubric for analysing text composition

Discursive dimension	Indicators	Weighted partial score per indicator
A. Coherence	1. Title	2
Evaluates the presence of text structure and the logical progression of information	2. Organisation	3
	3. Main ideas	3
	4. Synthesis strategies	3
B. Grammar	1. Cohesion	2
Evaluates links between different parts of the text, organization of words within sentences, and use of linguistic markers to connect and establish semantic relationships between sentences	2. Linguistic markers	2
	3. Concordance	2
C. Linguistic Conventionality	1. Spelling	1
Evaluates standard uses of spelling, punctuation and segmentation within texts	2. Segmentation	1
	3. Punctuation	1
Total: 3	Total: 10	Total: 20

reflection on the purpose, processes, value and outcomes of learning. A synthesised version of SEDA is presented in Appendix A. It is important to highlight that Hennessy, Rojas-Drummond et al. coded complete transcripts of lessons using this tool and obtained acceptable inter-coder reliability indices ranging from 0.541 to 0.877 using Cohen's kappa (κ). So Lastly, we developed a Rubric for Analysing Text Composition, in order to assess the quality of the texts produced by the children, based on Cassany (2000). This tool evaluates three discursive dimensions, which contain ten indicators, each representing one of ten partial scores. A summarised version of this rubric is presented in Table 1 (see Guzmán & Rojas-Drummond, 2012 for the complete version of the rubric).

METHOD

Participants

Participants were 120 Mexican sixth graders (11–12 y.o.) from two public elementary schools. The schools were equivalent in socioeconomic status, as well as degree of schooling of parents; they were also geographically close to each other. Necessary permissions from the parents of both schools were obtained so that the children could participate in the study. Children from School 1 were assigned to an experimental condition and participated in the LT programme. Children from School 2 participated as a control group, continuing with their regular classes. For each condition, children were further organized into triads (20 experimental and 20 control; n = 40 triads in total), in order to solve a Test of Textual Production in its Group version (TTP-G). They also solved a parallel version of the same test, but in an individual bases (TTP-I; n = 120). Data from these two tests were the basis for carrying out macro-analyses. At the same time, for carrying out more micro-analyses, two 'focal triads' were randomly selected (one experimental and one control), and their performance was videotaped while they solved the TTP-G. Both triads consisted of two boys and one girl.

Setting

The educational programme LT was implemented in a multipurpose classroom within the experimental school. This was especially designed for the purposes of the programme, with modular furniture for collaborative work, computers and an equipped small library (such facilities are not typically available in state-run Mexican elementary classrooms). Both versions of the TTP were administered in the children's respective classrooms.

Materials

The TTP was designed to evaluate children's abilities to compose expository texts. The test was complex and involved children reading three authentic texts taken from different published sources, all addressing a related theme. In the group version (TTP-G), triads of children were required to read the three texts, discuss and synthesize them, and then write an original text on the topic in the form of an article to be published in a magazine. The TTP-I was similar, but children were required to do these activities on an individual basis. (Both versions of the TTP, as well as detailed procedures of administration and evaluation of this test, can be found in Guzmán & Rojas-Drummond, 2012).

Design

For macro-analyses, we used a quasi-experimental, pre/post-test design with control group. Treatment groups were intact since they were not randomly assigned to each experimental condition. In relation to the dependent variable, a set of partial and total scores was obtained from analysing the productions written by the children in each version of the TTP. Then relative gains were calculated for each set of scores. The independent variable was the 'Experimental Treatment' (experimental vs. control conditions).

Procedures

In order to evaluate the effectiveness of the LT programme, the two parallel versions of the TTP (group and individual) were administered to the whole sample of children at the beginning and end of the academic year, serving as pre and post-tests respectively. In addition, video recordings were obtained of the interaction of each of the two selected 'focal triads' while they solved the group version of the TTP. Subsequently, the videos were analysed and the conversation of each triad was transcribed verbatim, together with a description of the relevant context. This was done following established conventions and procedures developed by Edwards and Mercer (1987). Between administration of the pre and post-tests, the experimental children participated in the LT programme during school hours while control children followed their regular classroom activities. It is worth clarifying that literacy was addressed by all participating teachers from the experimental and control groups as part of the state prescribed school curriculum. Thus, for the experimental group, the LT programme was implemented in addition to these regular activities, but did not require any extra school time kappa (κ).

For the implementation of LT, each teacher, with his or her respective children (30 per group), came to the multipurpose classroom. The programme was conducted in 25 sessions of 90 minutes each, distributed over a period of seven months. During each session, the group teacher, supported by up to two researchers, promoted psycholinguistic abilities related to oral and written communication in a variety of collaborative activities. The first five sessions were designed to enhance collaborative and effective oral communication abilities in the students, and particularly dialogic styles of engagement. In the following 20 sessions, children applied these abilities to carry out team projects. These centred on developing an academic article on a topic of their choice, as well as a multimodal conference. The texts were published in a popular magazine and disseminated at the end of the school year in a 'cultural fair', with the participation of the whole learning community in which LT is embedded. Children also delivered their conferences to a live audience. These activities rendered children's work meaningful and functional, in contexts where oracy and literacy could be displayed as situated social practices.

Data Analyses

For data analyses in general, we used the 'Dynamic Inverted Pyramid' method proposed by Wegerif and Mercer (1997), which employs a combination of quantitative and qualitative analytical frameworks. Briefly, following this method, mainly qualitative data are analysed at a micro-level with small samples, and then triangulated with mostly quantitative data obtained from larger samples at a more macro-level. The combination of these types of data at different levels of analyses is used to interpret results in a recursive and comprehensive fashion (see also Wegerif, Rojas-Drummond, & Mercer, 1999).

Analyses of oral communication. The transcripts of the dialogues of the two selected 'focal triads' while they were composing their articles collectively were subject to in-depth analyses using categories from the Ethnography of Communication in conjunction with SEDA (see 'Methodological Framework'). The CS corresponded to the administration of the TTP-G as a whole. For each transcript, diverse CE were identified and the transcript was segmented accordingly. The utterances contained in each segment were identified as CA and further qualified by using the 33 dialogic codes contained in SEDA. These categories were then quantified using simple non-parametric statistics, in terms of frequencies and percentages of occurrence. These analyses sought understanding of the ways the triads used language to construct their written texts jointly (see also Rojas-Drummond et al., 2006).

Analyses of written communication. The Rubric for Analysing Text Composition (see Table 1) was used to evaluate the quality of the written articles produced by the experimental and control groups in each version of the test (individual and group), comparing their scores in the pre and post-tests. For this evaluation, a weighted, partial score, was assigned to each aspect of the text, according to each of the 10 indicators which comprise the rubric. These partial scores were added up to calculate a total score for each test (maximum total score = 20). Then, the relative gains of each individual or triad were calculated by subtracting the total scores obtained in the post-test from those obtained in the pre-test. In order to evaluate the effectiveness of LT, the relative gains of the experimental and control groups were further compared, using the t-Student test for independent samples.

RESULTS

Results are presented first at a macro and then at a micro level of analysis. The macro level centres on comparisons of the relative gains obtained by the total sample of children from the experimental and control groups for solving the TTP in its two versions: TTP-I (n = 120 children) and TTP-G (n = 40 triads). For the TTP-G, we present data for both the total scores and then the partial scores obtained, according to each of the ten indicators which comprise the Rubric for Analysing Text Composition. For the TTP-I we present relative gains for the total scores only (the data for the partial scores were very similar to those of the TTP-G; they are thus not presented to avoid redundancy). The micro level focuses on data obtained after analysing oral and written communication for the two 'focal triads' only. In relation to oral communication, we report results of applying the Ethnography of Communication in combination with SEDA to the dialogues of these two 'focal triads' as they solved the pre and post-test of the TTP-G. In relation to written communication, we then present the total and partial scores obtained by each 'focal triad' in their written texts.

Macro-Level

Figure 1 represents the mean relative gains of the total scores obtained by the experimental and control groups in the TTP-G. As can be seen, the differences between both groups were highly significant, favouring the experimental group (n = 40, t = 5.89, d.f. = 1, 38; p < 0.01). This indicates that the texts written by the experimental triads after participating in the LT programme were of better quality, in comparison with those produced by the control triads.

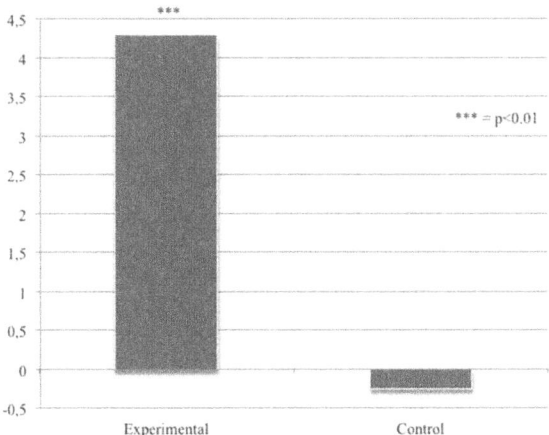

Figure 1. Mean relative gains obtained by the experimental and control groups in the TTP-G. Total score

Figure 2 illustrates the relative gains obtained by the experimental and control groups, for each of the ten partial scores which comprise the text's rubrics. The differences were significant in favour of the experimental group for six of the ten scores: organization, synthesis, cohesion, linguistic markers, punctuation, and segmentation. Even if no significant differences were found for the other four scores (title, main ideas, concordance, and spelling), the tendency of the data is in the same direction. Results reflect that the students of the experimental group, (in comparison with those of the control), structured their texts with more local and global coherence and used more sophisticated strategies for synthesising and producing their written articles, following linguistic conventionalities.

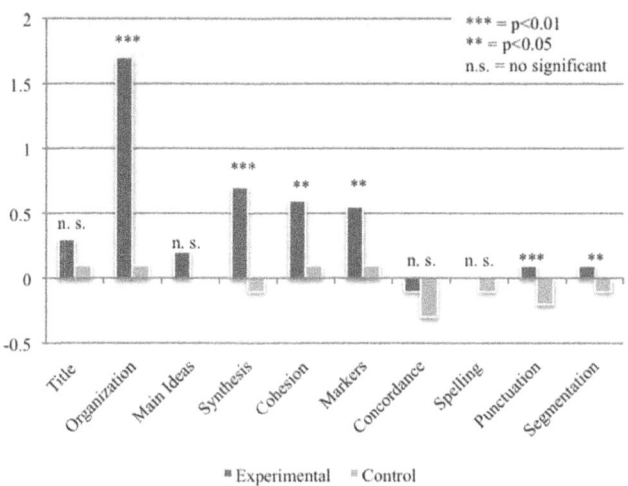

Figure 2. Mean relative gains obtained by the experimental and control groups in the TTP-G. Partial scores

The total relative gains favouring the experimental group illustrated above were not exclusive of the student's performance in the TTP-G, these gains were also reflected in the individual version of the test. As shown in Figure 3, the differences between the experimental and control groups in the TTP-I were also highly significant favouring the former (n = 120, t = 15.42, d.f = 1,118, p = < 0.01). These results indicate that the texts produced by the experimental children after participating in the LT programme were of better quality, not only when working in groups, but also individually.

Micro-Level

Results for oral communication for the two 'focal triads'. Figure 4 shows the total number of utterances produced by the experimental and control 'focal triads' while solving the TTP-G in the pre and post-test respectively.

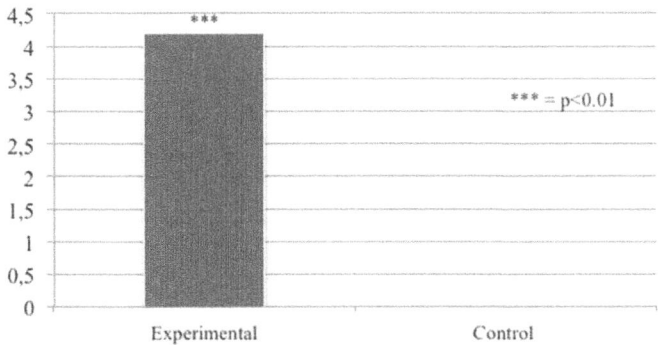

*Figure 3. Mean relative gains obtained by the experimental and
control groups in the TTP-I. Total score*

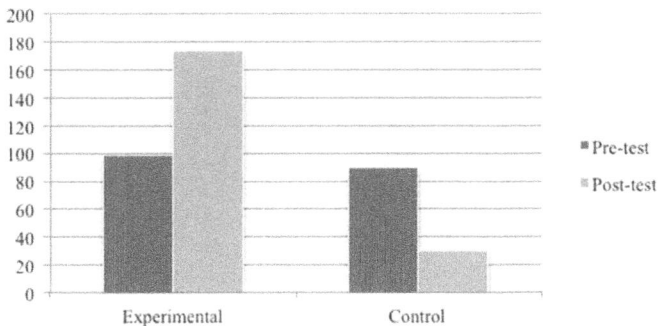

*Figure 4. Total number of utterances produced by the experimental
and control 'focal triads' in the pre and post-test*

As shown in Figure 4, the experimental and control 'focal triads' produced a similar number of utterances in the pre-test. In contrast, the experimental triad increased their utterances by 76% between tests (from 99 to 174), while the control triad decreased theirs by 67% between tests (from 90 to 30). These patterns indicate that the experimental children spoke more extensively while solving the TTP-G at the end of the year, after their participation in the LT programme, while the control children actually spoke less extensively.

Figure 5 represents the percentage of turns taken by each experimental child in the pre and post-test. Figure 6 illustrates the same data for the control triad. A comparison of these figures indicates that, in the pre-test, both triads show a similar, uneven pattern of distribution in their participation: one child took almost half of the turns. In contrast, in the post-test, the experimental children distributed their turns more evenly, while the pattern of distribution of turns in the control children was slightly more uneven than in the pre-test.

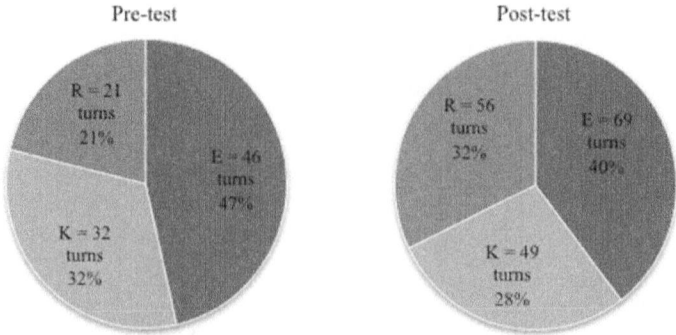

Figure 5. Distribution of turns by each participant of the experimental triad during the pre and post-test (K = Karina; E = Eduardo; and R = Roberto)

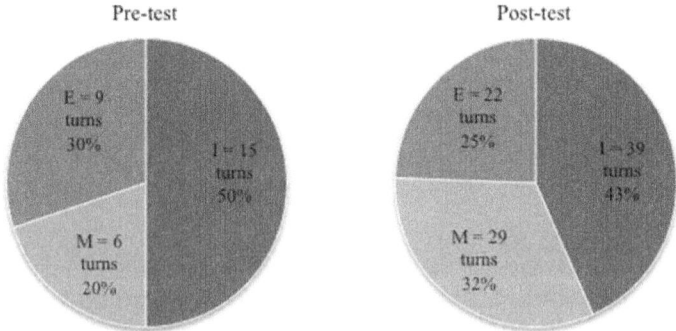

Figure 6. Distribution of turns by each participant of the control triad during the pre and post-test (I = Isabel; M = Mateo; and E = Erik)

Considering the above data, it was relevant to inquire whether the changes observed were only quantitative or also qualitative. The data presented below, analysed using the Ethnography of Communication in combination with SEDA, addressed this question.

Figures 7 and 8 represent the patterns of hierarchical distribution of levels of analyses from the Ethnography of Communication (CS, CE and CA) in terms of frequencies that occurred in the pre and post-test. Figure 7 illustrates these patterns for the experimental triad, while Figure 8 for the control triad. It is worth highlighting that each figure reports only the frequencies of CA which were coded as dialogic using SEDA, organized by cluster. Capital letters for these CA refer to the initial letter of each of the 8 clusters contained in SEDA, namely: I = Invite elaboration or reasoning; R = Make reasoning explicit; B = Build on ideas; E = Express or invite ideas; P = Positioning and Coordination; RD = Reflect on dialogue or activity; C = Connect; and G = Guide direction of dialogue or activity (see Appendix A).

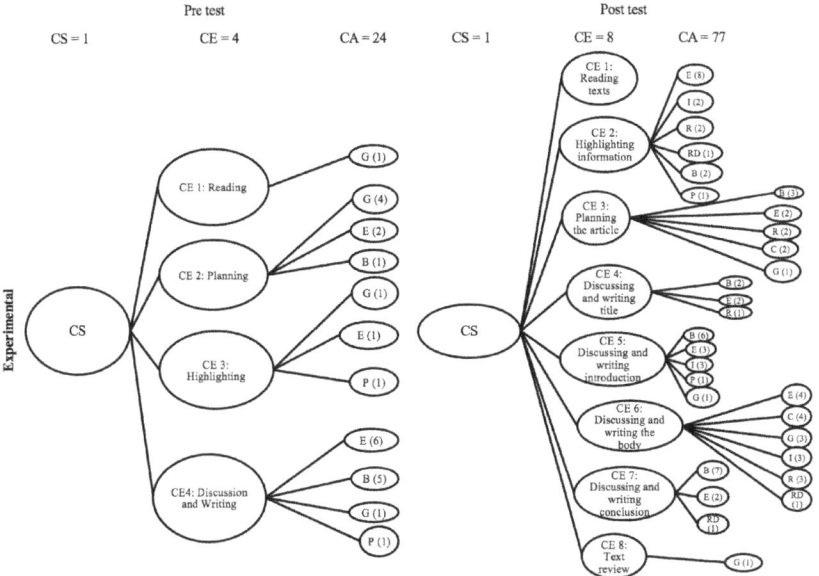

Figure 7. Patterns of hierarchical distribution of units of analyses from the Ethnography of Communication for the experimental focal triad in the pre and post-test

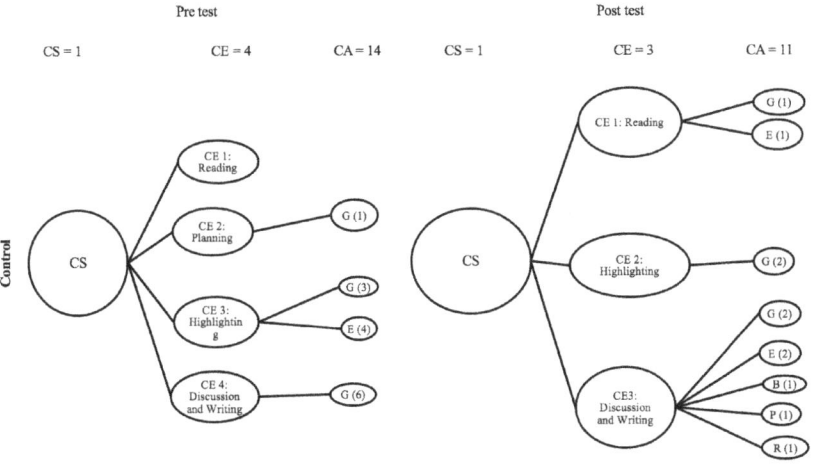

Figure 8. Patterns of hierarchical distribution of units of analyses from the Ethnography of Communication for the control focal triad in the pre and post-tes

In general, the CS for all cases is the context of solving the TTP-G by the 'focal triads'. The CE in turn correspond to the activities that the triads carried out to solve the test, including reading, planning, highlighting, writing and text revision.

83

However, the presence, order and nature of these CE vary for each triad and each test. In Figure 7, we can observe important changes in the patterns of the experimental triad between tests, where the CE double in number while the CA triple (4 CE and 24 CA in the pre-test vs. 8 CE and 77 CA in the post-test). At the same time, these patterns become more complex: in the post-test there are more intricate ramifications between CE and CA than in the pre-test (these include CE no. 2, which gives rise to 16 CA; CE no. 5, which in turn generates 14 CA; and CE no. 6, which produces 18 CA). Furthermore, in the post-test new CE arise that were not present in the pre-test, including: discussing about the title, the introduction, the body of the text and the conclusion, as well as, significantly, reviewing their text. In addition, the nature of the CE 'Planning' changes between tests. In the pre-test, this CE (no. 2) reflects a procedimental approach of mere division of labor ('who will do what'). In contrast, in the post-test, 'Planning' (CE no. 3) goes well beyond this procedimental approach, since the children also plan how they will structure their article by using technical terms (e.g. participants propose that they first have to write a title, then they must express why they were interested in the topic, then they need to compose the development section and lastly they should include a conclusion). In contrast, Figure 8 shows that the patterns of the control triad remain fairly similar between the pre and post-test (4 CE and 14 CA in the pre-test vs. 3 CE and 11 CA in the post-test). Furthermore, the CE no. 2 'Planning' which appears in the pre-test, reflects a procedimental approach of mere division of labor (similar to that of the experimental triad in the pre-test), and it doesn't even appear in the post-test, nor is there any revision of their text in either the pre or post-test.

Figures 9 and 10 illustrate the frequencies of clusters and CA in the pre and post-tests for the experimental and control 'focal triads' respectively.

In Figure 9 we can observe that, for the experimental triad, the patterns of distribution of CA within clusters change importantly between the pre and post-

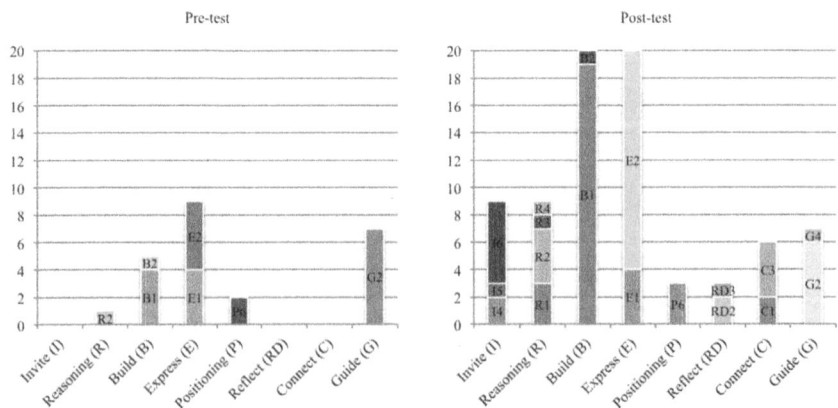

Figure 9. Frequency of clusters and D-CA for the experimental triad in the pre and post-test

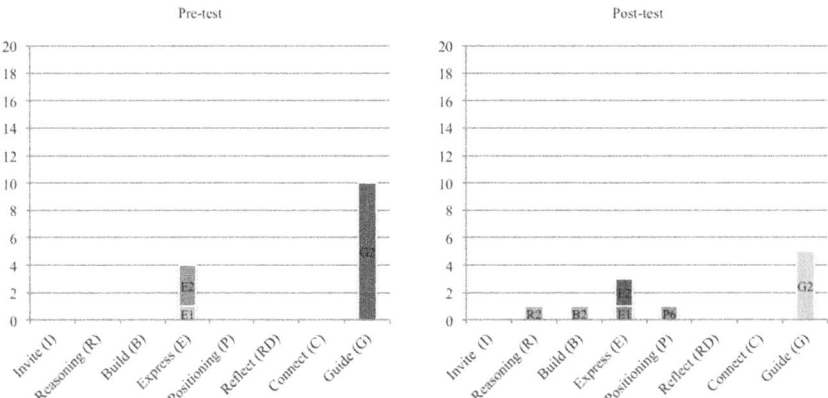

Figure 10. Frequency of clusters and D-CA for the control triad in the pre and post-test

tests. In particular, in the pre-test there is a total of 24 CA. These represent 7 dialogic codes out of the 33 contained in SEDA (21%), distributed across 5 out of the 8 clusters. In comparison with the pre-test, in the post-test these parameters increase both in number and variety: there are a total of 77 CA representing 18 dialogic codes out of the 33 (55%), and these are distributed across all 8 clusters. In contrast, Figure 10 shows that, for the control triad, there are some apparent changes between tests in the variety of CA within clusters (from 3 CA representing 2 clusters in the pre-test, to 6 CA representing 5 clusters in the post-test). However, if we look at these changes in more detail, we can appreciate that they are not very meaningful. These is because, even if in the post-test there are 3 new CA that represent 3 new clusters, their frequency is minimal (only one per category). Furthermore, the total frequency of CA does not change between tests, remaining very low in each case (14 in the pre-test vs. 11 in the post-test).

Results for written communication for the two 'focal triads'. Figure 11 shows the total scores in the TTP-G obtained by the experimental and control triads in the pre and post-tests respectively. As can be seen, the experimental triad doubled their total score between tests (an increase from 9/20 points in the pre-test to 18.5/20 in the post-test). In contrast, there were no gains in the control triad's scores between tests, and both remained quite low (7/20 points in the pre-test vs. 6.5/20 in the post-test). These differences indicate that the experimental triad, in comparison with the control, improved importantly in the quality of their written text between the beginning and end of the academic year.

Table 2 shows the ten partial scores obtained in the TTP-G by the experimental and control 'focal triads' in the pre and post-tests. The experimental triad, in comparison with the control, shows a substantial improvement in their partial scores between tests mainly in the following indicators: organization, synthesis, cohesion,

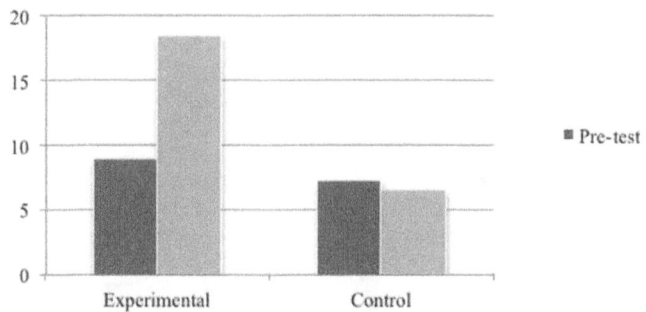

Figure 11. Total scores obtained by the experimental and control focal triads in the pre and post-test of the TTP-G

linguistic markers, concordance and spelling. These results are fairly consistent with those presented at the macro level for the whole sample of 40 triads.

Table 2. Partial scores obtained by the experimental and control 'focal triads' in the pre and post-test of the TTP-G

Indicator	Experimental triad			Control triad		
	Pre-test	*Post-test*	*Difference*	*Pre-test*	*Post-test*	*Difference*
Title	1.5	2	0.5	1.5	0.5	−1
Organisation	1	3	2	1	1	0
Main ideas	2.5	2.5	0	2	2	0
Synthesis	0.5	2	1.5	0.5	0.5	0
Cohesion	0.5	2	1.5	0	0.5	0.5
Markers	0.5	2	1.5	0.5	0.5	0
Concordance	1	2	1	0	0	0
Spelling	0	1	1	0	0	0
Punctuation	0.75	1	0.25	1	0.75	−0.25
Segmentation	0.75	1	0.25	0.75	0.75	0
TOTAL	9	18.5	9.5	7.25	6.5	−0.75

Taken together, the data presented above for oral and written communication suggest that the experimental triad, in comparison with the control, used a more dialogic style of interaction after their participation in the LT programme. This change was accompanied by an improvement in the quality of their written article.

DISCUSSION

Research on children's learning to write has established how developing novice writers move from rudimentary and serial engagement in some processes of text production (such as planning, composing and reviewing) to a reflexive and iterative engagement with such processes (Flower & Hayes, 1980; Scardamalia & Bereiter, 1986). More expert text production is seen to be characterised by back and forth reflexive movement between aspects of text production, as well as the text and their prior experience, in a dynamic and interdependent fashion (ibid.; Sharples, 1999). However, in the Mexican context (which is the focus of this study) as well as others, children's competences in understanding, producing and synthesising texts have been found to be deficient, reflecting the more basic types of engagement characterized by the authors mentioned above (cf. Guzman & Rojas-Drummond, 2012; INEE, 2006; Mazón, Rojas-Drummond, & Vélez, 2005; Rojas-Drummond et al., 2012). This presents a core challenge of how these children's development of writing can be supported to acquire more expert like practices. This study extends our understanding of this problematic.

A growing body of research suggests that small-group dialogic activities are a beneficial way of supporting children's learning (Alexander, 2008; Mercer, 2000; Mercer & Littleton, 2007; Littleton & Howe, 2010). However, dialogic collaborative interactions are rare in Mexican classrooms (Rojas-Drummond, 2000), resonating findings from classroom research across Latin America, Africa and Asia, which have found that teacher lecturing and eliciting brief responses through closed questions continue to dominate classroom interaction with very little time given to active student engagement in group tasks or whole-class discussion (see e.g., Ackers & Hardman, 2001; Frost & Little, 2014; Hennessy, Hassler & Hofmann, 2015; Sankar & Linden, 2014; Stallings, Knight, & Markham, 2014). Moreover, research also suggests that, even when group discussions actually take place in many classrooms, these are often of little educational value (e.g. Alexander, 2004; Bennett & Cass, 1989). One of the central reasons for this is that children do not necessarily posses the abilities to work collaboratively in productive ways. High quality dialogue that can lead to improvements in learning requires that children learn to participate effectively in collaborative activities (Rojas-Drummond & Mercer, 2003; Rojas-Drummond & Peon, 2004). Given these challenges, we need to ask if collaborative activities actually have the potential of supporting the development of literacy and writing in settings in which the levels of literacy, communicative abilities and collaborative group work are low.

This investigation addresses this puzzle. It looked at whether it is possible to increase the quality of collaborative talk among children in settings where productive forms of communication are found to be rare. Furthermore, the research asked whether an increase in effective collaborative talk would support literacy learning. In particular, the study analysed the outcomes of an intervention designed explicitly to promote oracy and literacy in elementary students, involving supporting dialogic interactions, reading comprehension and text production strategies, called 'Learning Together' (LT) (see Rojas-Drummond et al., 2010). The programme has been developed following a sociocultural perspective which conceptualises literacy as a situated, social and cultural practice (Scribner & Cole, 1981; Street, 2005). At the same time, the present report includes an analysis of the quality of the children's textual productions drawing on a rubric developed based on the work by Cassany (2000), and linking this analysis to models of expert competences in text production such as those of Flower and Hayes (1980) and Scardamalia and Bereiter (1986).

Considering the quality of the texts produced by the children in this study using the rubric mentioned above, results illustrate that experimental and control groups were at similar levels with regard to literacy at the start of the study. Strikingly, they also illustrate that the control group made very little progress over the academic year. These latter results are disappointing, but resonate with the findings discussed earlier that the abilities involved in comprehending and composing texts are not promoted effectively or are not addressed adequately as part of the regular, established classroom practices in some state run Mexican schools (INEE, 2006; 2007). In contrast to results for the control group, the experimental one improved significantly between tests. While the data suggest that both groups had similar levels of knowledge of basics such as spelling, the experimental group, after the intervention, was better able to organise, structure and synthesise their ideas through using more sophisticated linguistic strategies for text production.

The findings of this study suggest that children in the experimental group appropriated discursive abilities related to coherence, grammar and linguistic conventionalities required for working on their ideas and texts to such a degree that they were able to use them to produce higher quality texts in their groups. Significantly, the results further suggest that the experimental children appropriated the literacy abilities promoted by LT so that they could apply them not only when working with their peers, but also in a self-regulated and autonomous fashion.

The theoretical perspective of this chapter assumed that collaborative co-construction and exploration of ideas through joint interactions can support such learning (Hennessy, Mercer, & Warwick, 2011; Mercer & Howe, 2012; Mercer & Littleton, 2007; Rojas-Drummond et al., 2010; Rojas-Drummond et al., 2013; Wells, 1999). Our interest was in particular examining children's talk throughout the whole writing process, at planning, writing and review stages (rather than peer review talk after it), which has been highlighted as potentially important for supporting children's learning about these processes in previous research (Fisher et al., 2010). At the same time, our earlier research had found that, after children were explicitly inducted into using effective ways of communication involving critical and constructive engagement with ideas, and particularly 'Exploratory Talk', they adapted these productive forms of engagement to the type of task being solved, as well as the type of text being produced. Thus, children used 'Exploratory Talk' in activities involving logical problem solving and when writing argumentative texts. However, they used 'Co-constructive Talk' when they were synthesising ideas after reading various texts and when producing informative, expressive and narrative pieces (Rojas-Drummond et al., 2006; Rojas-Drummond et al., 2008; Rojas-Drummond et al., 2010).

So what new evidence does the present study offer about the extent to and ways in which talk can act as a 'vehicle' for developing knowledge and understanding of critical and reflexive engagement with text and ideas in the context of the above kinds of writing activities? To contribute to this question, this study further explored close-up the processes of productive dialogue and collaborative text production to gain insight into the appropriation of these strategies.

The findings suggest that the experimental group's discussion in the post-test involved a much higher overall number of utterances than the control group's, and than both groups at pre-test. The pedagogically important question is, so what was happening in this talk? To answer this question, this study applied a novel set of tools, drawing jointly on the Ethnography of Communication (Hymes, 1972; Saville-Troike, 2003; Rojas-Drummond et al., 2006) and a new collaboratively developed coding scheme to analyse high quality educational dialogue, SEDA (Hennessy, Rojas-Drummond et al., in press). The findings from these analyses illustrate that some of the relevant types of activities for text production are present at pre-test in both groups, involving reading, planning, highlighting and discussing the writing. However, few dialogic engagements among the students were taking place with regard to the processes of text production. Significantly, the micro-analyses illustrate that, after the intervention in the experimental group, children used more dialogic styles of engagement with their ideas and their texts. At the same time, the processes of text production became a lot more sophisticated and focused. So, while it appears that the children in the typical situation were aware that such processes were required for collaboratively producing an expository text, only after the intervention did they learn to apply them in a way that enabled them to plan and interrogate the text. These plans in turn allowed them to engage with, and improve, concrete elements of the text, such as the title, the introduction and the text body in a strategic and reflexive fashion.

The close-up study also gives illustration of how children's engagement took place in the talk during group work. While at pre-test children in both groups were suggesting some ideas for the task and taking action to move the collaborative activity forward (forms of talk also identified in earlier research with similar writing tasks, cf. Rojas-Drummond et al., 2006; Rojas-Drummond et al., 2010), the post-intervention discussion in the experimental group went well beyond this. This group's discussion shows evidence of further critical and reflexive engagement with the ideas proposed by the group members, through interrogating those ideas and making the reasoning behind those ideas explicit, as well as taking those ideas further by clarifying or reformulating them.

We assume that this iterative process of working further on ideas proposed by students to explore and improve them – rather than just express and accept them – is central to enhancing children's literacy. Such a dynamic and iterative engagement with ideas is discussed as central for expert-like text production in the research literature on writing (Flower & Hayes, 1980; Scardamalia & Bereiter, 1986; Sharples, 1999). This engagement with ideas is also at the heart of the approach we have here called dialogic, involving bringing this iterative and dynamic engagement with people's ideas into the shared communicative space. Herein lies a further contribution of such an approach to learning to write. In collaboratively discussing their ideas in the process of producing a shared text, students not only have an opportunity, as has been shown in this study, to improve their literacy, but also improve their oracy abilities. This in turn has value for developing children's social and communicative repertoires not only in but also beyond school (Mercer, 2000; Rojas-Drummond & Mercer, 2003; Rojas-Drummond et al., 2013). These are the kinds of actions children need to take on their (own and others') ideas to make a group work activity dialogic, more than simply everyone sharing their own idea and recording it to provide some kind of output from the group task. This analysis suggests that it is possible for children in a context in which literacy attainment is generally low, to develop, and successfully implement, such abilities.

This strongly suggests that further research on the conditions under which such learning may become possible at scale is needed and worthwhile. While it is not possible in this chapter to tease apart the relative effects of specific aspects of the LT programme and its implementation, this study illustrates the LT programme's potential to provide a realistic and productive framework for such an endeavour. Simply asking teachers to stop doing what they currently, and habitually, do and what pupils know to expect in their sociocultural setting, is not an effective way of changing classroom practice (Hofmann & Mercer, 2015). The LT programme provides a concrete proposal for changing classroom interactive practice which this study suggests can be productive. This chapter also illustrates the usefulness of the methodological tools employed in uncovering some of the patterns by which the difference became possible. Therefore, in addition to the LT programme, the methodological tools used in this study contribute to uncover and illustrate some of the kinds of communicative acts that children need to engage in to make group work productive as well as the strategies that are effective for producing high quality texts.

This study used a combined macro and micro level approach to analysis of educational practices related to enhancing oral and written communication in elementary classrooms. On the micro level, a novel analytical scheme was trialled, SEDA, in conjunction with tools from the Ethnography of Communication, to interrogate the level and kind of dialogic talk the children were engaging in during peer collaboration. These tools were able to tap into the nuances of children's collaborative text production in a very concrete and grounded way. Theoretically, it contributes to our understanding of the relationship between specific forms of talk among children and their development of literacy. However, the findings are not only interesting theoretically, but for teachers aiming to change their interactive practices, and children's oracy and literacy abilities in their classrooms. This study illustrates that the LT programme, as well as the tools applied in the analyses of oral and written communication, can illustrate to practising teachers in settings in which productive collaborative talk is currently rare and literacy outcomes low, the kinds of communicative ideas and strategies that are relevant – and possible – to teach to children to enable them to engage in collaborative discussions around text production in more effective ways that support their development of both oracy and literacy. Methodologically, these new tools offer an exciting opportunity for researchers and practitioners interested in understanding educational dialogue and its benefits, to explore and examine oral and written communication in an in-depth, subtle and systematic fashion.

ACKNOWLEDGEMENTS

The work reported in this chapter was supported by the Dirección General de Asuntos del Personal Académico of the National Autonomous University of Mexico (UNAM) (DGAPA-UNAM) (PAPIIT Project Number: IN303313) for the years 2013–2015. The authors wish to express their gratitude for this generous support. We would also like to thank the Ministry of Education in Mexico, as well as all the staff and students within the participating schools for their commitment to the programme of research. Professor Rojas-Drummond would like to thank the Faculty of Education at the University of Cambridge, UK for hosting her as Visiting Scholar while part of this manuscript was being prepared. Her visiting Scholarship was funded by the National Council of Science and Technology in Mexico (CONACYT Project Number: 160873). In addition, some of the methodological tools used in the study reported derived from a collaborative work carried out for a project entitled 'A Tool for Analysing Dialogic Interactions in Classrooms' (http://tinyurl.com/BAdialogue) funded through the British Academy International Partnership and Mobility Scheme (ref. RG66509), between January 2013–December 2015. We are most grateful to colleagues on the project teams who made significant contributions and helpful input during development and testing of the scheme, including Sara Hennessy, Neil Mercer, Paul Warwick, Christine Howe, Rocío García Carrión, Rupert Higham, Ruth Kershner and Maria José Barrera (UK team); Flora Hernández, Ana Laura Trigo, Mariana Alarcón, Maricela Velez, Rosa María Ríos, Omar Torreblanca and Nube Estrada (Mexico team). We appreciate the support of the Economic and Social Research Council, sponsor of most of the UK team's work in this area over the years.

REFERENCES

Ackers, J., & Hardman, F. (2001). Classroom interaction in Kenyan primary schools. *Compare, 31*(2), 245–261.
Alexander, R. (2001). *Culture and pedagogy: International comparisons in primary education.* Oxford & Boston, MA: Bñackwell.
Alexander, R. (2004). *Towards dialogic teaching: Rethinking classroom talk.* Leeds: Dialogos.

91

Alexander, R. (2008). *Toward dialogic teaching: Rethinking classroom talk.* York: Dialogos.
Bennett, N., & Cass, A. (1989). The effects of group composition on group interactive processes and pupil understanding. *British Educational Research Journal, 15*(1), 19–32.
Cassany, D. (2000). De la gramática a la reflexión lingüística. *Novedades educativas, 119,* 38–52.
Cole, M. (1996). *Cultural psychology: A once and future discipline.* Cambridge, MA: Harvard University Press.
Daniels, H. (2001). *Vygotsky and pedagogy.* New York, NY: Routledge/Falmer.
Dawes, L., Mercer, N., & Wegerif, R. (2000). *Thinking together: A programme of activities for developing thinking skills at KS2.* Birmingham, UK: Questions Publishing.
Edwards, D., & Mercer, N. (1987). *Common knowledge: The development of understanding in the classroom.* London: Methuen.
Fernández, M., Wegerif, R., Mercer, N., & Rojas-Drummond, S. M. (2001). Re-conceptualizing "scaffolding" and the zone proximal development in the context of symmetrical collaborative learning. *Journal of Classroom Interaction, 36*(2), 40–54.
Fisher, R., Myhill, D., Jones, S., & Larkin, S. (2010). *Using talk to support writing.* London: Sage
Frost, M., & Little, A. W (2014). Children's learning practices in Ethiopia: Observations from primary school classes. *Oxford Review of Education, 40*(1), 91–111.
Guzmán, K., & Rojas-Drummond, S. M. (2012). Escritura colaborativa en alumnos de primaria. Un modo social de aprender juntos. *Revista Mexicana de Investigación Educativa, 17*(52), 217–245.
Hennessy, S., Mercer, N., & Warwick, P. (2011). A dialogic inquiry approach to working with teachers in developing classroom dialogue. *Teachers College Record, 113*(9), 1906–1959.
Hennessy, S., Hassler, B., & Hofmann, R. (2015). Pedagogic change by Zambian primary school teachers participating in the OER4Schools professional development programme for one year. *Research Papers in Education.* doi:10.1080/02671522.2015.1073343
Hennessy, S., Rojas-Drummond, S. M., Higham, R., Márquez, A. M., Maine, F., Ríos, R. M., García, R., Torreblanca, O., & Barrera, M. J. (in press). Developing a coding scheme for analysing classroom dialogue across cultural and educational contexts.
Hofmann, R., & Mercer, N. (2015). Teacher interventions in small group work in secondary mathematics and science lessons. *Language and Education,* 1–17.
Howe, C. (2010). Peer dialogue and cognitive development: A two-way relationship? In K. Littleton & C. Howe (Eds.) *Educational dialogues: Understanding and promoting productive interaction* (pp. 32–47). London: Routledge.
Hymes, D. (1972). Models of interaction in language and social life. In J. J. Gumperz & D. Hymes (Eds.), *Directions in sociolinguistics: The ethnography of communication* (pp. 35–71). London: Basil Blackwell.
Instituto Nacional para la Evaluación de la Educación [INEE]. (2006). *Resumen ejecutivo de la prueba EXCALE.* Ciudad de México: INEE [electronic version]. Retrieved from: http://www.inee.edu.mx/
Instituto Nacional para la Evaluación de la Educación [INEE]. (2007). *El aprendizaje en tercero de primaria en México.* Retrieved from: http://www.inee.edu.mx/
Lave, J., & Wenger, E. (1991). *Situated learning. Legitimate peripheral participation.* Cambridge: Cambridge University Press.
Littleton, K., & Howe, C. (2010). *Educational dialogues: Understanding and promoting productive interaction.* London: Routledge.
Maybin, J. (2006). *Children's voices: Talk, knowledge and identity.* Basingstoke: Palgrave.
Mazón, N., Rojas-Drummond, S. M., & Vélez, M. (2005). Efectos de un programa de fortalecimiento de habilidades de comprensión de textos en educandos de primaria. *Revista Mexicana de Psicología, 22*(1), 91–102.
Mercer, N. (2000). *Words and minds: How we use language to think together.* London: Routledge.
Mercer, N. (2008). Talk and the development of reasoning and understanding. *Human Development, 51*(1), 90–100.
Mercer, N., & Howe, C. (2012). Explaining the dialogic processes of teaching and learning: The value and potential of sociocultural theory. *Learning, Culture and Social Interaction, 1,* 12–21.

Mercer, N., & Littleton, K. (2007). *Dialogue and the development of children's thinking: A socio-cultural approach*. London: Routledge.

Organisation for Economic Cooperation and Development [OECD]. (2010). PIS*A 2009 results: What students know and can do – student performance in reading, mathematics and science* (Vol. 1).

PISA. (2003). *Reading literacy*. Retrieved from http://www.pisa.oecd.org

Rogoff, B. (1990). *Apprenticeship in thinking: Cognitive development in social context*. New York, NY: Oxford University Press.

Rojas-Drummond, S. M. (2000). Guided participation, discourse and the construction of knowledge in Mexican classrooms. In H. Cowie & D. van der Aalsvoort (Eds.), *Social interaction in learning and instruction: The meaning of discourse for the construction of knowledge* (pp. 193–213). Exeter: Pergamon Press.

Rojas-Drummond, S. M., & Mercer, N. (2003). Scaffolding the development of effective collaboration and learning. *International Journal of Educational Research, 39*, 99–111.

Rojas-Drummond, S. M., & Peon, M. (2004). Exploratory talk, argumentation and reasoning in Mexican primary school children. *Language and Education, 18*(6), 539–557.

Rojas-Drummond, S. M., Mazón, N., Fernández, J. M., & Wegerif, R. (2006). Explicit reasoning, creativity and co-construction in primary school children's collaborative activities. *Journal of Thinking Skills and Creativity, 1*(2), 84–94.

Rojas-Drummond, S. M., Albarrán, C. D., & Littleton, K. S. (2008). Collaboration, creativity and the co-construction of oral and written texts. *Thinking Skills and Creativity, 3*(1), 77–91.

Rojas-Drummond, S. M., Gómez, L., & Vélez, M. (2008). Dialogue for reasoning: Promoting exploratory talk and problem solving in the primary classroom. In B. van Oers, W. Wardekker, E. Elbers, & R. van der Veer (Eds.), *The transformation of learning. Advances in cultural-historical activity theory* (pp. 319–341). Cambridge: Cambridge University Press.

Rojas-Drummond, S. M., Littleton, K., Hernández, F., & Zúñiga, M. (2010). Dialogical interactions among peers in collaborative writing contexts. In C. Howe & K. Littleton (Eds.), *Educational dialogues: Understanding and promoting productive interaction. Advances in learning and instruction* (pp. 128–148). London: Earlbaum.

Rojas-Drummond, S. M., Littleton, K., Mazón, N., & Vélez, M. (2012). Developing reading comprehension through collaborative learning. *Journal of Research in Reading, 37*(02), 138–158.

Rojas-Drummond, S. M., Torreblanca, O., Pedraza, H., Vélez, M., & Guzmán, K. (2013). 'Dialogic scaffolding': Enhancing learning and understanding in collaborative contexts. *Learning, Culture and Social Interaction, 2*, 11–21.

Sankar, D., & Linden, T. (2014). *How much and what kind of teaching is there in elementary education in India? Evidence from three States*. Washington, DC: World Bank.

Saville-Troike, M. (2003). *The ethnography of communication*. Oxford, United Kingdom: Blackwell Publishing Ltd.

Scardamalia, M., & Bereiter, C. (1986) Research on written composition. In M. Wittrock (Eds.), *Handbook of research on teaching*. London: MacMillan.

Scribner, S., & Cole, M. (1981). *The psychology of literacy*. Cambridge: Harvard University Press.

Sharples, M. (1999). *How we write*. Londres: Routledge.

Stallings, J. A., Knight, S. L., & Markham, D. (2014). *Using the stallings observation system to investigate time on task in four countries*. Washington, DC: World Bank.

Street, B. (2005). Recent applications of new literacy studies in educational contexts. *Research in the Teaching of English, 39*(4), 417–423.

Vass, E., Littleton, K., Miell, D., & Jones, A. (2008). The discourse of collaborative creative writing: Peer collaboration as a context for mutual inspiration. *Thinking Skills and Creativity, 3*(3), 192–202.

Wegerif, R. (2007). *Dialogic, education and technology: Expanding the space of learning*. New York, NY: Springer.

Wegerif, R., & Mercer, N. (1997). A dialogical framework for investigating talk. In R. Wegerif & P. Clevedon (Eds.), *Computers and talk in the primary classroom* (pp. 49–65). Clevedon: Multilingual Matters.

Wegerif, R., Rojas-Drummond, S., & Mercer, N. (1999). Language for the social construction of knowledge: Comparing classroom talk in Mexican pre-schools. *Language and Education, 13*, 133–151.

Wells, G. (1999). *Dialogic inquiry: Towards a sociocultural practice and theory of education.* New York, NY: Cambridge University Press.

Wertsch, J. (1998). *Mind as action.* New York, NY: Oxford University Press.

Sylvia Rojas-Drummond
Faculty of Psychology
National Autonomous University of Mexico (UNAM)

Ana María Márquez
Faculty of Psychology
National Autonomous University of Mexico (UNAM)

Riikka Hofmann
Faculty of Education
University of Cambridge (UC)

Fiona Maine
Faculty of Education
University of Cambridge (UC)

Ana Luisa Rubio
Faculty of Psychology
National Autonomous University of Mexico (UNAM)

José Hernández
Faculty of Psychology
National Autonomous University of Mexico (UNAM)

Kissy Guzmán
Instituto Nacional para la Evaluación de la Educación (INEE)

APPENDIX A:
SCHEME FOR EDUCATIONAL DIALOGUE ANALYSIS (SEDA)

	I Invite elaboration or reasoning		
	Key words	*Definition*	*Description*
I1	Ask for explanation or justification of another's contribution	Ask participant(s) to explain or justify another's or collective ideas, reasoning or the process of arriving at a solution.	Invite participants to take up someone else's or collective ideas, perspectives, reasoning, position, concept, hypothesis, viewpoint, academic content, or the process of arriving at a solution in order to respond critically to them through explanation, justification or argumentation. Asking someone to 'put themselves into another's shoes'. The invitation has to be explicit through phrases such as: 'explain what Jane meant by…'. 'why do you think Ana said that?'. It does not include simply asking others to repeat someone else's statement.
I2	Invite building on/ elaboration/ (dis) agreement/ evaluation of another's contribution or view	Use previous contribution to *elicit further* responses, inviting addition to or elaboration/ clarification/ (dis) agreement/ positioning/ comparison/ evaluation of another's contribution or idea.	This act includes: 1. Inviting participants to take up others' contribution(s) in order to promote the clarification, paraphrasing, extension, elaboration, or deepening of ideas. Includes bringing private contributions or knowledge objects (e.g. outcomes from group work) into the public arena, when further responses/additions are then invited. *Reference to specific prior ideas/ contributions/views/theories must be explicit* (through naming an individual or referring to a specific idea). Excludes ambiguous cases such as "What do you think, Mary?" Consider E1 – 'Invite opinions/beliefs/ideas' for this. 2. Inviting *ideas that are different or similar* to others', or inviting others to identify whether ideas are similar or different. 3. Asking participants to *evaluate or comment on or compare/agree/disagree* with another's argument/position/conclusion by: • Asking participants to take a position in relation to the topic at hand or to agree/ disagree with possible courses of action; • Asking for confirmatory or alternative perspectives. Consider additionally coding C1 – 'Refer back' where positioning is invited in relation to a reference back to an earlier contribution.

(Continued)

I3	Invite possibility thinking based on another's contribution	*Invite speculation/ imagining, hypothesis,* conjecture, or question posing based on another's contribution.	Invite participants to imagine new scenarios and to wonder, speculate, predict or formulate hypotheses about possibilities connected to previous contributions. Typically this might include a conjunction linking to a previous comment: e.g. 'So, what might happen if…' or 'Based on Billy's idea, who has a further question?' The important feature of this code is that, whilst it includes invitations to participants to ask open-ended questions, which are typical of creative and divergent thinking, it explicitly links these to ideas already expressed, rather than inviting new ideas (which would be coded as I5 – 'Invite possibility thinking').
I4	Ask for explanation or justification	Ask other(s) for *justification/* evidence or explanation of reasoning or the process of arriving at a solution.	Ask others to make their reasoning explicit. Includes asking for: explanation, justification, argumentation, analogy, categorisation, making distinctions, use of evidence, providing the meaning of concepts/ideas. Invitations must *explicitly* ask for reasoning, typically (but not sufficiently) with the use of key words such as 'why?', 'how?', 'what caused…?'. Otherwise, consider E1 – 'Invite opinions/ beliefs/ ideas' when ideas/views are invited; or I6 – 'Ask for elaboration or clarification' for invitations to add information or clarify previous ideas.
I5	Invite possibility thinking or prediction	*Invite speculation/ imagining, hypothesis,* conjecture, or question posing.	Invite participants to imagine new scenarios and to: wonder, speculate, predict, make a conjecture, pose a question, or formulate hypotheses about possibilities and theories to explain a phenomenon based on present information or activity. Often involves extrapolation. Invitations must *explicitly* ask for possibilities, not just ideas/views; typically (but not sufficiently) identified through use of conditional tenses or thought experiments as in phrases such as 'what would/could/might happen if…?' Invitations sometimes use future or conditional tense (e.g. thought experiments; especially use of 'would', 'could' or 'might'). Also consider E1 – 'Invite the expression of different opinions/ideas/beliefs', including for open-ended creative thinking; or I4 – 'Ask for explanation or justification' for post-hoc explanations/justifications.

I6	Ask for elaboration or clarification	Probe/ask for clarification *or elaboration or extension or example.*	Ask someone to clarify, paraphrase, extend (say more about), elaborate, deepen or provide an example for their *previous* response/idea/ contribution. It may imply asking someone to add information to the previous idea or changing it qualitatively. Note that a probe is not always an explicit question, an invitation may be implicit. This category does not apply when the participant asks for confirmation.
			Also consider I4 – 'Ask for explanation or justification', which involves making reasoning explicit.
		R Make reasoning explicit	
	Key words	*Definition*	*Description*
R1	Explain or justify another's contribution	Provide or elaborate justification/ evidence or explanation of another's reasoning or the process of arriving at a solution.	Explain or justify someone else's or collective ideas, perspectives, reasoning, position, or the process of arriving at a solution by: providing an argument or a counter-argument, drawing analogies, making distinctions, or breaking down or categorising topics/ideas. It may also include bringing evidence from inside or outside the current context into the dialogue to support an argument, opinion, proposal, prediction or theory.
			As in 'stepping into another's shoes'. The reference to another's contribution has to be explicit. It does not include simply repeating someone else's statement.
R2	Explain or justify own contribution	Provide or elaborate justification/ evidence or explanation of own reasoning or the process of arriving at a solution.	This category encompasses various forms of reasoning, including: providing an argument or counter-argument, explaining, drawing analogies, making distinctions, and breaking down or categorising topics/ideas, as well as accounting for the process of arriving at a solution. It may also include bringing evidence from inside or outside the current context into the dialogue to support an argument, opinion, proposal, prediction or theory.
			Also consider B2 – 'Clarify/ elaborate own contribution' for clarifications without explicit reasoning.

(Continued)

R3	Speculate or predict on the basis of another's contribution	Speculate, hypothesise, conjecture, imagine or express one or more different possibilities on the basis of another's contribution	Speculate, predict, hypothesise, conjecture, imagine or express one or more different possibilities and theories to explain a phenomenon on the basis of another's contribution. Includes thought experiments or more explicit predictions/hypotheses. It also includes the expression of different possibilities based on present information or activity. The reference to another's contribution has to be explicit. Often involves using future or conditional tense (e.g. 'if... then', 'not... unless', 'would', 'could' or 'might').
R4	Speculate or predict	Speculate, hypothesise, conjecture, imagine or express one or more different possibilities or theories.	Speculate, predict, hypothesise, conjecture, imagine or express one or more different possibilities or theories to explain a phenomenon. Includes thought experiments or more explicit predictions/hypotheses. It also includes the expression of different possibilities based on present information or activity. Often involves using future or conditional tense (e.g. 'if... then', 'not... unless', 'would', 'could' or 'might'). It is different from compare/evaluate alternative views in P2, which requires exploring the difference between at least two possibilities or theories. Also consider R1 – 'Explain or justify reasoning or solution' for post-hoc explanations/justifications.

B Build on ideas			
	Key words	*Definition*	*Description*
B1	Build on/ clarify others' contributions	Build on, clarify, revoice, elaborate, make explicit, highlight or transform contributions provided by other(s) or collective idea, opinion or reasoning.	Make a responsive contribution based on another person's previous comment, argument, idea, opinion or information. This is used when building on, clarifying, reformulating, exemplifying, elaborating or transforming someone else's idea/opinion/ suggestion. It goes further than the original contribution did: it may either clarify (to them and/or to others), add something, or change it qualitatively. It includes: <ul><li>Paraphrasing (but not just repeating) another's contribution to emphasise, clarify or make it explicit to others,</li><li>Explicitly recognising the contribution made by another, but not just by praising.</li><li>Completing an idea or comment and chaining ideas between two or more participants; -introducing a different, new idea that is related to a previous contribution.</li><li>Rephrasing technical terms used by a previous speaker.</li><li>Identifying one's own idea(s) as similar or different to another's.</li></ul>
B2	Clarify/ elaborate own contribution	Clarify, elaborate, exemplify or extend own opinion/ idea/ belief or question.	Applies when the same person makes a new comment/response based on their previous comment or elaborates their own previous question (without a justification). It goes further than the original contribution did: it may either clarify (to them and/or to others), add something, or change it qualitatively. Also consider R2 – 'Explain or justify reasoning or solution' for justification. Also consider E2 – 'Make relevant contribution' for extended contributions including elaboration of a new idea.

(Continued)

	E Express or invite ideas		
	Key words	*Definition*	*Description*
E1	Invite opinions/ beliefs/ideas	Invite the expression of opinions/ ideas/beliefs/ knowledge from others.	Ask for opinions/ideas/beliefs, without either: • an explicit reference to previous speakers, comments or ideas in the dialogue; or: • an explicit relation to evidence, theories, disciplinary knowledge, support or further argumentation. Emphasis on promoting participation by the collective, but includes asking just one person. Typically involves asking a question like 'What do you think?' Contrasts with invitations to guess the one 'right' answer. Excludes just calling on someone in order to invite them to speak (which is uncoded unless another function is explicit). Includes inviting open-ended creative thinking, but consider I5 – 'Invite possibility thinking', when inviting speculation, hypothesis, conjecture or question posing. Also consider I4 – 'Ask for explanation or justification', which asks for reasoning, not just ideas/views.
E2	Make other relevant contribution	Offer a pertinent, contribution/ suggestion/ idea/ perspective/ information that progresses the collective activity at hand.	Offer a pertinent, contribution/suggestion/idea/ perspective/information that progresses the collective activity at hand. Includes generating ideas during a brainstorm or bringing ideas from a small group discussion into a larger discussion on the same topic – without making links to others' contributions. To use this code, the contribution has to bring something not yet expressed to the discussion that is related to the general subject, and it must be pertinent to the task at hand. Does not apply when someone repeats or emphasises their own prior contribution, except when doing so to someone not present before. Includes simple feedback such as "I think that's a good point" or "I can see that point", but not simple "yes" or "no" responses. Important: Always use a more specific code (only) where one applies.

	Key words	Definition	Description
		P Positioning and coordinating	
P1	Synthesise ideas	Synthesise or summarise others' or collective ideas	Bring multiple perspectives or ideas into inter-relation and draw out or distil a key idea(s)/conclusion/implication. Must include ideas from more than one person/source (two in total is sufficient), or own ideas in the collective synthesis. May include ideas from immediately preceding discussion or earlier in lesson/lesson sequence; as well as integrating or summarising or recapping. e.g. after class brainstorm or during/at the end of a group discussion. Also consider B1 – 'Build on/explain/clarify other's contributions'.
P2	Compare/ Evaluate alternative views	Compare/ evaluate different opinions/ perspectives/ beliefs.	Compare/evaluate at least two arguments/positions/suggestions (may include own or other's), with explanation or justification. Also consider B1 – 'Build on/explain/clarify other's contributions' for identifying similarity or difference between ideas without judging their value. Also consider R4 – 'Speculate, hypothesise or predict' for speculations, hypotheses and predictions.
P3	Propose resolution	Propose a resolution after discussing a task, issue or problem.	This act includes the result of seeking consensus/agreement, either by suggesting a solution that could be shared by all, or by suggesting that participant should partially agree, or disagree entirely, after discussing a task, issue or problem. Other participants need not agree or share the viewpoint.
P4	Acknowledge shift in position	Participants acknowledge that they have shifted their position in response to the preceding dialogue.	It includes clarifying a misconception or changing opinions/ideas/beliefs. There has to be evidence of the shift/adjustment in position or change of mind in the dialogue. E.g. change in the argument or idea that the participant was exposing earlier. It requires an explicit statement. Also consider P6 – 'State (dis)agreement/position'.

(Continued)

P5	Challenge viewpoint	Challenge viewpoint/ assumption	Challenge/confront others' view/assumption/ argument. The challenge must be evident through verbal (or nonverbal) means, including questioning. This should not be used when a simple 'no' response is given. Includes partial agreement. If it is an explicit statement of disagreement use P6 – 'State agreement or disagreement'.
P6	State (dis) agreement/ position	State that one or more participants (dis)agree with others or acknowledge differences	One or more participants state that they agree or disagree with at least one other. This act includes the result of seeking agreement, either by arriving at a solution or acknowledging participants' differences after discussing a task, issue or problem. For agreement; at least 2 positions must have been expressed previously so that one is chosen over the other. For disagreement or partial agreement, a simple statement is sufficient (since we assume two perspectives have been compared). Includes agreeing a course of action (under above conditions). Positioning in relation to other must be explicit. For a statement of different viewpoint, consider P5 – 'Challenge viewpoint'. If a reason is given, also code with R2 – 'Explain or justify reasoning or solution.'
		RD	*Reflect on dialogue or activity*
	Key words	*Definition*	*Description*
RD1	Talk about talk	Participants talk about talk, reinforce protocols of dialogue, or model effective dialogic techniques.	This includes: • talking about or constructing ground rules for communication. Refers to metacognitive talk about talk rules/protocols, whether rules are established or not. • Modelling productive ways of interacting, e.g. by showing how to 'think aloud'; how to explain; how to argue by providing reasons, justifications and evidence; and how to hypothesise. Includes talk about quality or purpose of talk. Does not include reflection on use of language, e.g. technical terminology; consider RD2 – 'Reflect on learning process/purpose/value'.

| RD2 | Reflect on learning process/ purpose/ value | Comment/ talk about the process of carrying out the collective activity or evaluate own performance. Or reflect on the importance, usefulness, purpose or outcomes of learning or of the task, as part of a collective activity. | This includes:
1. Analysing the processes involved in the development of the task and/or the effectiveness of their (individual or collective) performance during a collective activity. Participants might reflect on how they are learning/have learned (including from others) or whether they are/ were using effective strategies for the task at hand; how well they performed; their level (or lack) of understanding; what they can do to improve their performance; what the next steps are to complete the task; to what extent they have achieved the goals of the activity, etc. Assumes an element of evaluation or reflection. In this act there has to be an explicit statement that refers to the collective activity. Includes affective dialogue: feelings/experiences about working together; E.g. How did I feel when we were doing the task together? What do I feel about my performance? What do I feel about the outcome of the collective activity?
2. Analysing, reflecting on or evaluating the importance of learning and/or outcomes. Includes discussing and reflecting on past-present-future trajectory. E.g. Why do we need to learn x? How/where can we apply what we learned? When will it be useful? Includes talk about the purpose of a shared discussion activity, where there may be no ground rules explicitly operating. Includes reflecting on use of language, e.g. technical terminology. Also consider RD1 – 'Talk about talk'. |
| RD3 | Invite reflection about process/ purpose/ value of learning | Invite others to reflect on the importance, usefulness, processes or outcomes of learning from collective activity. | Encourage others to analyse or evaluate their own learning processes and/or outcomes. There has to be an explicit statement that refers to the collective activity. Includes inviting to reflect on purposes/ goals of learning or the activity or on past-present-future trajectory (e.g. Why do you learn x? How/ where can you apply what you learned?); and encouraging affective dialogue, such as feelings/ experiences about working together (e.g. How did you feel when you were doing the task together? What do you feel about your performance? What do you feel about the outcome of the collective activity?) |

(Continued)

C Connect			
	Key words	*Definition*	*Description*
C1	Refer back	Refer back to prior contributions or observations or knowledge objects or discussions after contributions.	This code should be used when explicitly reviewing, referring to or bringing in a specific contribution (by an individual or group; of one's own or another's) or observation, linking prior knowledge, concepts, beliefs, hypotheses, agreements/conclusions reached, opinions, arguments, ideas, learning content to the current topic or activity. Contributions could come from the current or previous lessons. Includes reference back to prior learning from interaction with texts including multimedia resources where these are linked to present/future activities. Consider E2 – 'Build on others' contributions' when responding rather than explicitly referring back, even if the contribution responded to was earlier than the preceding turn. Consider C2 – Making learning trajectory visible (if reference is to activity or to prior learning from/interaction with texts including multimedia resources, rather than contributions).
C2	Make learning trajectory explicit	Make learning trajectory explicit, providing continuity within and across lessons, including by highlighting relevance to prior or future activity.	This code should be used when reviewing past activities and linking them to present/future activities, as part of making the trajectory explicit. Includes referring forward to an activity or contributions to be requested and encouraging others to record ideas and/or outcomes of dialogue. May include making explicit goals or purpose of learning trajectory. Also consider C1 – 'Refer back' for linking to past contributions. Consider B1 – 'Build on/clarify others' contributions'.

| C3 | Link learning to wider contexts | Make links between what is being learned and a wider context. | Bring knowledge from outside of the classroom or school (i.e. beyond, before or after the current lesson) into the discussion of what is being learned, relating previous experiences within or outside the school, linking given and new information. This relates to the temporal dimension of learning (in different time frames, from very local to very extended in time, and also creation of inter-textual and inter-contextual relations). Includes generalising to other similar instances/contexts. This may include personal experience/memory, analogy or anecdote, especially from younger children and/or when used to justify. Consider C1 – Refer back – if the reference is to previous contributions or lesson activities. |
| C4 | Invite inquiry beyond the lesson | Ask others to pursue their own inquiry before, or after lessons. | Ask others to pursue inquiry prior to teaching a topic or to deepen knowledge afterwards. (This leaves open the possibility for inquiry. It sustains and extends dialogue across time and space). This may include asking others to pursue individual or shared enquiry, withholding information, evaluation and feedback, or ending a lesson in suspense. It may also include inviting individuals or groups to conduct an independent investigation beyond the lesson and bring back results to be collated and/or discussed as a whole class. For enquiry within the lesson consider G2 – 'Propose action or inquiry activity' or I5 – Invite possibility thinking. |

(Continued)

G Guide direction of dialogue or activity			
	Key words	*Definition*	*Description*
G1	Encourage student-student dialogue	Encourage student-student dialogues by giving pairs/groups or class the responsibility for the direction and/or outcomes of the dialogue or the collective activity.	Includes allocating responsibility to students, pairs or groups for the dialogue or the activity – whether or not the teacher is moderating the discussion. Not used when simply setting group work or asking pairs to work together; there needs to be some dialogic element in the task.
G2	Propose action or inquiry activity	Propose possible courses of action or an inquiry activity.	Propose a course of action in the context of a dialogue or collective activity, or propose an inquiry activity. It may also include inviting individuals or groups to conduct an independent investigation and bring back results to be collated and/or discussed as a whole class within the same lesson This is not applicable to simple instructions which are not of a dialogic nature (such as reading out a task or question, which is uncoded). Consider R2 – 'Explain or justify reasoning or solution' if it includes explanation or justification of reasoning. For inquiry beyond the lesson use C4 – 'Invite inquiry beyond the lesson'. Also consider I5 – Invite possibility thinking.

G3	Introduce authoritative perspective	Explicitly introduce authoritative perspective or explanation as part of the flow of dialogic interaction, in response to participants' level of understanding.	Implies invoking voice/perspective of expert from beyond the present dialogue, e.g. to challenge others' thinking or to take on that perspective. This may include authoritative contribution – i.e. making a teaching point – that builds on a learner's contribution or knowledge. Includes introducing or bringing in technical terms. NOTE: Determining if it is adjusted to learner's level is difficult and needs to be established through the particular context of the dialogue. In addition, an authoritative explanation deals with reliability and knowledge of the content. Act may be accompanied by diagnostic strategies such as closed questions or prompting to confirm that students have understood or learned target concepts, but these strategies are not part of the CA.
G4	Provide informative feedback	Provide informative feedback on which others can build.	This refers to formative or diagnostic feedback instead of simple positive, negative or non-committal judgment, or mere repetition of the respondent's answer. This code may be used alongside others that indicate the form of feedback, e.g. B1 – 'Build on/ explain/clarify others' contributions', or it may be accompanied with justification, explanation or elaboration, in which case assign two codes.

(Continued)

G5	Focusing	Focusing the dialogue on key aspects of the activity	This may be used when guiding or focusing the dialogue in a certain desired direction or towards certain key aspects of the activity. Involves feeding in/highlighting salient ideas. This act may involve: 1. feeding in through questioning or suggesting or pointing out salient information about the task or problem. This includes clarifying the task or problem or deepening the discussion. May help to narrow the field of focus or pre-empt undesirable conclusions. This includes bringing participants back to the matter at hand. Excludes repeating an earlier question. 2. extending the field by stimulating thinking in another direction not yet thought about. 3. encouraging others to 'discover' new knowledge (as in scaffolding). Excludes simply reading out or turning to a task or set question (which is uncoded). G5 may be used alongside other codes that indicate the form of focusing, e.g. I6 – 'Ask for elaboration or clarification', I4 – 'Ask for explanation or justification' or R3 – 'Speculate on the basis of another's contribution'.
G6	Allow thinking time	Invite or propose to pause to think, reflect, or respond or talk.	An explicit invitation or proposal to pause, for example to think or reflect or decide. OPTIONALLY: Code when the elicitation is not verbally explicit and there is a pause of at least 3 seconds after an invitation. Code only pauses within the exchange.

SUSANNE JURKOWSKI AND MARTIN HÄNZE

7. FOSTERING KNOWLEDGE CO-CONSTRUCTION THROUGH TRAINING IN TRANSACTIVE COMMUNICATION

Evidence for Training Effects from Analysing Students' Discourse

INTRODUCTION

Transactive communication is defined as referring to and building up on a learning partner's idea. Thereby, the partner's idea is transformed into a more elaborate one. Examples for transactive statements are critiquing the partner's idea, extending the partner's idea or integrating the partner's idea with an idea of one's own. Several studies have shown that students' transactive communication is positively related to their learning outcomes when working in small groups. A previous study by the authors using self-reports on transactive communication has already shown positive effects of a training module for transactive communication on students' knowledge co-construction. In analysing students' discourse, the present study uses a more precise measurement of transactive communication. Eighty university students participated in an experiment with pre-test and post-test measurement. Transactive communication was measured in a group learning situation before the training and in another group learning situation after the training. Students' communication during group learning was audiotaped, transcribed, and coded concerning different forms of transactive statements: Critique, extension, and integration. Furthermore, concerning the topic of the post-test group learning situation, knowledge was pre-tested and post-tested. In addition, at both pre-test and post-test engagement in the learning process and relationship quality were assessed in order to control for non-specific training effects. Between the pre-test and the post-test, the experimental group received the training in transactive communication while the control group completed a filler-task. Analyses revealed that trained students outperformed controls in extensions of their partner's ideas. However, trained and untrained students did not differ in the other forms of transactive statements. Furthermore, the training had a positive effect on students' knowledge acquisition, which was partially mediated by students' improved transactive communication.

A. Surian (Ed.), Open Spaces for Interactions and Learning Diversities, 109–119.

BACKGROUND

Group learning is used in elementary school (Ginsburg-Block, Rohrbeck, & Fantuzzo, 2006; Rohrbeck, Ginsburg-Block, Fantuzzo, & Miller, 2003), secondary school (Slavin, 1995), and higher education (Roseth, Johnson, & Johnson, 2008; Springer, Stanne, & Donovan, 1999). By using group learning teachers intend to promote students' active involvement in the learning process as well as their social and academic learning (Antil, Jenkins, Wayne, & Vadasy, 1998). Overall, these expectations are supported by empirical evidence. For example, a recent review of meta-analyses by Hattie (2009) revealed positive effects of group learning, compared to competitive or individual learning, on learning results. However, the quality of students' discourse is important for group learning to have these positive effects on students' learning results (Mercer & Howe, 2012). Therefore, learners need to be prepared for working together with other students (Webb, 2009, 2010).

For students, group learning provides the opportunity to elaborate about the subject matter collaboratively and, thus, to co-construct knowledge which no singular group member had before working together with the others (van Boxtel & Roelofs, 2001). In knowledge co-construction, students not only elaborate on their own ideas but also on the ideas of their learning partners (Barron, 2000; van Boxtel & Roelofs, 2001; Webb, 2009, 2010). The process of knowledge co-construction is indicated by students' statements; including critiquing the partner's idea, extending the partner's idea or integrating the partner's idea with an idea of one's own (Barron, 2000; Webb, 2009, 2010). This type of communicative activity is also termed transactive communication (Berkowitz, Althof, Turner, & Bloch, 2008; Berkowitz & Gibbs, 1983). Several studies have shown that students' transactive communication is positively linked to their learning outcomes when working in small groups (Berkowitz et al., 2008). Therefore, training learners in transactive communication is expected to increase their knowledge acquisition in group learning. In the present study, a training module for transactive communication was developed and evaluated concerning its impact on both students' transactive communication and their knowledge acquisition when working in small groups.

Research on Transactive Communication

The term transactive communication was first introduced by Berkowitz and Gibbs (1983). According to the authors, transactive communication includes different forms of statements which have in common referring to or building up on the learning partner's idea and, thereby, transforming the partner's idea into a more elaborate one. Examples for transactive statements are the following: Critiquing the partner's idea by pointing to a missing thought or to contradicting thoughts, extending the partner's idea by adding a further thought or integrating the partner's idea with an idea of one's own by combining two or more ideas (Azmitia & Montgomery, 1993; Berkowitz & Gibbs, 1983; Kruger, 1992, 1993).

Berkowitz and Gibbs (1983) found transactive statements during a discussion of moral dilemmas with a partner to be positively related to the moral stage development of young adults. Studies by Kruger (1992, 1993) also revealed that transactive statements during a discussion of moral dilemmas with a partner correlated positively with the moral stage development of eight-year-old children. Following these studies in the domain of moral development, the importance of transactive communication was investigated for other aspects of learning and development. For example, in a study by Azmitia and Montgomery (1993) transactive statements during scientific problem-solving in small groups were positively related to children's subsequent performance in solving such scientific problems. Furthermore, McDonald, Miell, and Morgan (2000) found that transactive statements during a composition of a piece of music in small groups in year seven classes correlated positively with the quality of this composition. Moreover, in a study by Russell (2005) adolescents discussed their performances in a before administered test about genetics. Students' transactive statements during this group discussion were positively related to their performance in a final exam about genetics. For university students as well, their transactive statements during a group work on tasks about educational psychology correlated positively with their subsequent performance concerning this issue (Jurkowski & Hänze, 2010).

Reviewing past research, Berkowitz et al. (2008) conclude that transactive communication has proven to be positively linked to a variety of outcomes when working in small groups. The authors also note that past research focuses on the spontaneous production of transactive statements, while no attempts have been made yet to enhance learners' transactive communication. Past studies' descriptive results yielded a range of 7% (McDonald et al., 2000; Russell, 2005) to 27% (Berkowitz & Gibbs, 1983) of students' statements to be transactive. These results indicate that there is still much potential to increase transactive communication.

The Present Study

We developed a training module for transactive communication. This training module has already been analysed with regard to its effects on students' transactive communication using students' self-reports (Jurkowski & Hänze, 2012). This previous study revealed positive effects of the training on students' transactive communication during a group work as well as on their knowledge acquisition which was tested individually after the group work. Furthermore, the positive training effects on students' knowledge acquisition were partially mediated by their improved transactive communication. In order to investigate the impact of the training more precisely, in this study, we recorded students' discourse during a group work and measured different forms of transactive statements. Thus, this study provides more detailed insights whether students can be prepared for working in small groups through the training module for transactive communication.

In an experimental design, a condition with the training and a condition with a filler task were tested concerning both transactive communication and knowledge acquisition in group learning. In order to measure transactive communication, students' discourse during the group work was audiotaped, transcribed, and coded. Compared to the control condition, we expected that the training would enhance students' transactive communication (hypothesis 1) and would also increase their knowledge acquisition (hypothesis 2). Furthermore, we assumed that the increased knowledge acquisition would be mediated by the enhanced transactive communication (hypothesis 3).

METHODS

Participants

Participants were 80 students (M_{age} = 22.5 years, SD_{age} = 2.9 years) studying at university to become a teacher. Students attended one of three comparable courses in educational psychology in which the present study was conducted. The study covered four consecutive sessions which were fully embedded into the subject of the courses.

Design and Procedure

The training in transactive communication was varied between students. They were randomly assigned to one of two conditions. Under the experimental condition, students received the training, whereas under the control condition, students completed a filler task on educational psychology. Pre and post to this intervention, group learning took place. In both group learning situations, students worked in pairs.

Knowledge was pre-tested in the first session. In the second session, group learning was pre-tested with regard to students' transactive communication. The topic of this group learning situation was scientific observation. The training and the filler task were implemented in the third session. In the fourth session, group learning was post-tested concerning students' transactive communication. The topic of this group learning situation was prosocial behaviour. Furthermore, following the group learning at the post-test, knowledge was post-tested. Pre-test and post-test of knowledge referred to the topic of the post-test group learning situation, that is prosocial behaviour. Additionally, serving as control variables, for both group learning situations, students' engagement in the learning process as well as the relationship quality between the learning partners was assessed.

Both group learning situations followed three steps: The topic was divided into two portions and each student prepared one portion by reading a text and completing a task on this text (first step, 15 minutes). Following this individual work, the learning partners reported each other on their particular portion of the topic (second step, 10 minutes). Afterwards, student pairs worked together on tasks that required them to link and to integrate both portions of the topic (third step, 30 minutes). During this group work (third step), students' discourse was audiotaped.

Training in Transactive Communication

The training module consisted of six components, needing one session of 100 minutes. The sixth component was not included in the session since it was a homework students were assigned to. In order to enhance students' knowledge about transactive communication and to promote their performance of transactive communication, we used well established training techniques: Modeled and verbal instruction, practice, and feedback. The components were as follows:

1. First, students watched a video of two models strongly referring to and building up on each other's ideas. Afterwards, students watched a video of two models almost never communicating transactively.
2. Students gained information about transactive communication through a lecture and a text. More precisely, the trainer explained the benefits of transactive communication for students' learning and illustrated different forms of transactive statements, including examples.
3. Participants identified different forms of transactive statements in a written dialogue.
4. Students attended three short sessions of group work. The trainer encouraged students to perform different forms of transactive statements. After each session, students received feedback from their peers concerning their transactive communication.
5. Students' training experiences and implications for further practice were discussed.
6. For homework, students were given a learning journal and they filled in when and how they used transactive communication in other group work during the following week.

Measurements

Pre-test and post-test of knowledge. Knowledge was pre-tested by one open-ended question; the post-test of knowledge included two open-ended questions. The two post-test questions required students to link and to integrate the two portions on prosocial behaviour. Thus, students' answers to these questions can be assumed to be the individual outcome of student pairs' knowledge co-construction. Students' answers to the three questions were compared to a sample solution provided by an expert and credits were given depending on the accuracy of a student's answer according to the sample solution. Over the three questions, absolute inter-rater agreement ranged from ICC = .97 to ICC = .98.

The bivariate correlation between the performance in the two post-test questions was significant, $r = .48$, $p < .01$. Hence, the total of these questions served as the post-test of knowledge. For the post-test of knowledge, students could attain up to 21 credits ($M = 6.71$, $SD = 2.55$). For the pre-test of knowledge, a maximum of six credits was given ($M = 2.41$, $SD = 1.08$).

Coding of students' discourse. The communication between learning partners during group work (third step) was audiotaped, transcribed, and coded at both points of measurement.

In past research, various coding systems have been used. Basically, two approaches can be distinguished to measure transactive communication. Following the first approach, transactive communication is analysed in detail by coding different forms of transactive statements (cf. Azmitia & Montgomery, 1993). According to the second approach, transactive communication is coded whenever a student's statement refers to or builds up on the partner's preceding idea, independent of the form of transactive statement (cf. Schuitema, van Boxtel, Veugelers, & ten Dam, 2011).

In the present study, both approaches were used. The first approach provided detailed information about the training effects on transactive communication. Thus, it could be analysed whether the different forms of transactive statements could be trained to the same extent. Transactive communication is assumed to be positively linked to learning outcomes independent of the form of transactive statement. Hence, the second approach served to investigate the impact of the training on students' knowledge acquisition mediated by their transactive communication.

The following three forms of transactive statements were coded: (1) critiquing the partner's idea by pointing to a missing thought or to contradicting thoughts, (2) extending the partner's idea by adding a further thought, (3) and integrating the partner's idea with an idea of one's own by combining two or more ideas. In addition, the total of these three forms of transactive statements served to measure transactive communication on a general level. Absolute inter-rater agreement was $ICC = .92$ for critique, $ICC = .97$ for extension, and $ICC = .95$ for integration.

In the following, we give an example of students' discourse and the coding of transactive statements. Students were planning a donation campaign for cancer suffering children (third step).

Student A: People should know whom they are donating money to. So, we could show some pictures of the children in hospital.

Student B: Then, people would also feel more empathy for the children [extension]. But we should consider that they could also get into a bad mood because of the photos, and then they would not donate that much money. Happy children would be better [critique].

Student A: But we could tell them that they can really do something for the children and show both pictures of children in hospital and pictures when these children have recovered [integration].

Control variables. Using the transcripts of students' communication, the engagement in the learning process was measured with two variables: Number of spoken words and number of externalizations during group work (third step). Following Weinberger and Fischer (2006), externalizations were coded whenever a student contributed a content related idea without referring to or building up on the idea of the learning partner. Absolute inter-rater agreement for externalization was ICC = .99.

Following the *Group Environment Questionnaire* (Carron, Widmeyer, & Brawley, 1985), eight items were formulated in order to measure the relationship quality. Sample items included: "How much did you like your learning partner", "How much could you rely on your learning partner". Cronbach's alpha coefficient was .94 at the pre-test and .93 at the post-test.

RESULTS

Results are based on 79 students with a complete set of data. In order to analyse the training effects on control variables, transactive communication, and knowledge acquisition, analyses of covariance were conducted. These analyses included the factor training (training/no training) as the independent variable, the post-test measure as the dependent variable, and the corresponding pre-test measure as the covariate. Furthermore, a path analysis was conducted to examine the impact of the training on students' knowledge acquisition mediated by their transactive communication. In the path analysis, transactive communication and knowledge were residuals resulting from regression analyses of the post-test measure on the corresponding pre-test measure. In all analyses of covariance, group membership was nested within conditions; in path analysis group membership was set on level two.

At the post-test, trained and untrained students neither varied in the number of spoken words, $F(1,38) < 1, p > .40, \eta^2 = .01$, nor in the number of externalizations, $F(1,38) < 1, p > .40, \eta^2 = .01$. Furthermore, there was no difference in the relationship quality, $F(1,38) < 1, p > .40, \eta^2 = .00$.

As supposed, trained students displayed more post-test transactive communication than those in the control group, $F(1,38) = 24.68, p < .01, \eta^2 = .39$. In detail, at the post-test trained students showed more extensions than untrained students, $F(1,38) = 17.90, p < .01, \eta^2 = .32$. However, no differences were found with regard to critique, $F(1,38) = 2.37, p > .05, \eta^2 = .06$, nor were there any differences in integration, $F(1,38) = 1.77, p > .05, \eta^2 = .05$. As expected, trained students outperformed untrained students in their post-test knowledge, $F(1,38) = 39.66, p < .01, \eta^2 = .51$. Descriptive statistics are presented in Table 1.

Table 1. Estimated marginal means and standard deviations at the post-test in the experimental group and the control group

	Training		No training	
	M	SD	M	SD
Transactive communication	9.17	3.71	5.46	4.36
Critique	1.49	1.93	0.94	1.20
Extension	7.21	2.84	4.30	3.68
Integration	0.47	0.83	0.23	0.59
Knowledge	7.81	2.63	5.26	1.65

Path analysis (see Figure 1) revealed a direct path from the training to students' post-test transactive communication as well as to their post-test knowledge. As expected, the indirect path from the training to the post-test knowledge, mediated by students' post-test transactive communication, was significant, $\beta = .21$, $p < .05$.

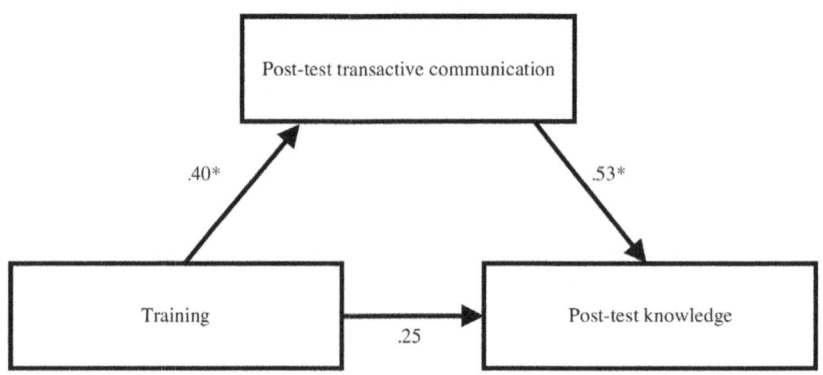

Figure 1. Training, transactive communication, and knowledge at the post-test. Training is coded as follows: 0 = no training, 1 = training. Standardized path coefficients are presented. * p < .05, ** p < .01.

DISCUSSION

The results show that the training in transactive communication had a large effect both on students' transactive communication and their knowledge acquisition. Thus, the training could foster students' knowledge co-construction to a considerable degree. These results indicate that students can be prepared for working in small groups through this training module. Past research has focused on the spontaneous production of transactive statements (Berkowitz et al., 2008). Therefore, the present training can be considered to be the first training module which was developed for transactive communication. The results also provide experimental evidence for the importance of transactive communication for working in small groups.

In detail, the training had a positive effect on extensions. Hence, trained students were more likely than untrained students to add further thoughts to their partner's ideas and, thereby, to transform their partner's ideas into more elaborate ones. However, other forms of transactive statements could not be enhanced by the present training. Berkowitz and Gibbs (1983) assume that different forms of transactive statements vary in their difficulty. This may result in some forms of transactive statements to be more easily produced by learners and, therefore, more easily enhanced through training than other forms of transactive statements. In the control group, students rarely criticized their partner's idea or integrated their partner's idea with an idea of their own. Therefore, critique and integration are probably more difficult to be produced than extension. However, it could also be that the tasks we used for group work predominantly required students to extend their partner's ideas while criticizing or integrating where not stimulated by these tasks. Yet, our findings are in line with the results of Azmitia and Montgomery (1993) as well as McDonald et al. (2000) who also report low absolute frequencies of integration, compared to extension. Consequently, a further development of the present training should include special exercises for the practice of critique and integration.

The positive training effects on students' knowledge acquisition were partially mediated by their improved transactive communication. Still, a direct effect of the training on students' knowledge acquisition remained. This direct effect cannot be explained by non-specific training effects on students' engagement in the learning process, nor can it be explained by students' improved relationship quality. One possible explanation is that the training had a positive effect not only on transactive statements produced in verbal communication but also on students' thoughts. In particular, if students did not get the chance to take their turn because their partner continued speaking they might have produced transactive statements without speaking aloud. In order to investigate this phenomenon, future studies could additionally use self-reports which distinguish between transactive statements produced in verbal communication and transactive statements produced in thoughts.

In sum, the training in transactive communication could foster students' knowledge co-construction to a considerable degree. The results suggest that a further development of this training module could support group learning even to a greater extent.

REFERENCES

Antil, L. R., Jenkins, J. R., Wayne, S. K., & Vadasy, P. F. (1998). Cooperative learning: Prevalence, conceptualizations, and the relation between research and practice. *American Educational Research Journal, 35*, 419–454.

Azmitia, M. & Montgomery, R. (1993). Friendship, transactive dialogues, and the development of scientific reasoning. *Social Development, 2*, 202–221. Retrieved from http://dx.doi.org/10.1111/j.1467-9507.1993.tb00014.x

Barron, B. (2000). Achieving coordination in collaborative problem-solving groups. *The Journal of the Learning Sciences, 9*, 403–436. Retrieved from http://dx.doi.org/10.1207/s15327809jls0904_2

Berkowitz, M. W., & Gibbs, J. C. (1983). Measuring the developmental features of moral discussion. *Merrill-Palmer Quarterly, 29*, 399–410.

Berkowitz, M. W., Althof, W., Turner, V. D., & Bloch, D. (2008). Discourse, developments, and education. In F. Oser & W. Veugelers (Eds.), *Getting involved: Global citizenship development and sources of moral values* (pp. 189–201). Amsterdam, The Netherlands: Sense Publishers.

Carron, A. V., Widmeyer, W. N., & Brawley, L. R. (1985). The development of an instrument to assess cohesion in sport teams: The group environment questionnaire. *Journal of Sport Psychology, 7*, 244–266.

Ginsburg-Block, M. D., Rohrbeck, C. A., & Fantuzzo, J. W. (2006). A meta-analytic review of social, self-concept, and behavioral outcomes of peer-assisted learning. *Journal of Educational Psychology, 98*, 732–749. Retrieved from http://dx.doi.org/10.1037/0022-0663.98.4.732

Hattie, J. (2009). *Visible learning. A synthesis of over 800 meta-analyses relating to achievement.* Abingdon: Routledge. Retrieved from http://dx.doi.org/10.4324/9780203887332

Jurkowski, S., & Hänze, M. (2010). Soziale Kompetenzen, transaktives Interaktionsverhalten und Lernerfolg: experimenteller Vergleich zweier unterschiedlich gestalteter Gruppenunterrichtsbedingungen und Evaluation eines transaktivitäts-bezogenen Kooperationsskriptes [Social skills, transactive communication, and academic achievement – comparison of different collaborative arrangements and evaluation of scripting transactive communication]. *Zeitschrift für Pädagogische Psychologie, 24*, 241–257. Retrieved from http://dx.doi.org/10.1024/1010-0652/a000020

Jurkowski, S., & Hänze, M. (2012). F& Hänze, M. (2012). 10-0652/a000020ogie, 24and academic achievement – comparison of different collaborative arrangements and evaluation of scripti [Fostering transactive interaction: Effects of training in transactive interaction on learning results in cooperative learning]. *Zeitschrift für Entwicklungspsychologie und Pädagogische Psychologie, 44*, 209–220. Retrieved from http://dx.doi.org/10.1026/0049-8637/a000074

Kruger, A. C. (1992). The effect of peer and adult-child transactive discussions on moral reasoning. *Merrill-Palmer Quarterly, 38*, 191–211.

Kruger, A. C. (1993). Peer collaboration: Conflict, cooperation or both?. *Social Development, 2*, 165–182. Retrieved from http://dx.doi.org/10.1111/j.1467-9507.1993.tb00012.x

MacDonald, R., Miell, D., & Morgan, L. (2000). Social processes and creative collaboration in children. *European Journal of Psychology of Education, 15*, 405–415. Retrieved from http://dx.doi.org/10.1007/bf03172984

Mercer, N., & Howe, C. (2012). Explaining the dialogic processes of teaching and learning: The value and potential of sociocultural theory. *Learning, Culture, and Social Interaction, 1*, 12–21. Retrieved from http://dx.doi.org/10.1016/j.lcsi.2012.03.001

O'Donnell, A. M. (2006). The role of peers and group learning. In P. A. Alexander & P. H. Winne (Eds.), *Handbook of educational psychology* (pp. 781nal p. Mahwah, NY: Lawrence Erlbaum. Retrieved from http://dx.doi.org/10.4324/9780203874790

Rohrbeck, C. A., Ginsburg-Block, M. D., Fantuzzo, J. W., & Miller, T. R. (2003). Peer-assisted learning interventions with elementary school students: A meta-analytic review. *Journal of Educational Psychology, 95*, 240–257. Retrieved from http://dx.doi.org/10.1037/0022-0663.95.2.240

Roseth, C. J., Johnson, D. W., & Johnson, R. T. (2008). Promoting early adolescents' achievement and peer relationships: The effects of cooperative, competitive, and individualistic goal structures. *Psychological Bulletin, 134*, 223–246. Retrieved from http://dx.doi.org/10.1037/0033-2909.134.2.223

Russell, H. A. (2005). *Transactive discourse during assessment conversations on science learning.* Retrieved May 15, 2014, from http://scholarworks.gsu.edu/epse_diss/

Schuitema, J., van Boxtel, C., Veugelers, W., & ten Dam, G. (2011). The quality of student dialogue in citizenship education. *European Journal of Psychology of Education, 26*, 85–107. Retrieved from http://dx.doi.org/10.1007/s10212-010-0038-1

Springer, L., Stanne, M. E., & Donovan, S. S. (1999). Effects of small-group learning on undergraduates in science, mathematics, engineering, and technology: A meta-analysis. *Review of Educational Research, 69*, 21–51. Retrieved from http://dx.doi.org/10.3102/00346543069001021

van Boxtel, C., & Roelofs, E. (2001). Investigating the quality of students discourse: What constitutes a productive student discourse. *Journal of Classroom Interaction, 36,* 55–62.

Webb, N. M. (2009). The teacher's role in promoting collaborative dialogue in the classroom. *British Journal of Educational Psychology, 79,* 1–28. Retrieved from http://dx.doi.org/10.1348/000709908x380772

Webb, N. M. (2010). Peer learning in the classroom. In P. Peterson, E. Baker, & B. McGaw (Eds.), *International encyclopedia of education* (Vol. 6, pp. 636–642). Oxford: Elsevier. Retrieved from http://dx.doi.org/10.1016/B978-0-08-044894-7.00616-3

Weinberger, A., & Fischer, F. (2006). A framework to analyze argumentative knowledge construction in computer-supported collaborative learning. *Computers & Education, 46,* 71–95. Retrieved from http://dx.doi.org/10.1016/j.compedu.2005.04.003

Susanne Jurkowski
Institute of Educational Psychology
University of Kassel

Martin Hänze
Institute of Educational Psychology
University of Kassel

ANIKÓ ZSOLNAI AND LÁSZLÓ KASIK

8. COPING STRATEGIES AND SOCIAL PROBLEM SOLVING IN ADOLESCENCE

INTRODUCTION

Social competence has traditionally been defined as the complex system of social abilities, habits, skills and knowledge (e.g. Rose-Krasnor, 1997; Semrud-Clikeman, 2007). Social competence has the function to organise social behaviour, and to trigger the operation of the individual elements of the system (Nagy, 2007). International surveys agree that social competence is a very important factor for both individuals' inner balance and a satisfactory social co-existence. Within social competence the functioning of social problem solving and coping strategies are very relevant. However, the investigation of this social components is not very common in Hungary, thus we do not have adequate data about this area. Their developmental effect must be investigated because these results are very important for planning a social competence promotion programme in schools.

THEORETICAL BACKGROUND

According to the well-established psychological view, social competence is a complex system of various social, emotional, cognitive (both inherited and learnt) abilities and motives (Rose-Krasnor, 1997). Within social competence social-problem solving and coping strategies are very important factors (Fülöp, 2009).

According to D'Zurilla et al. (2002, 14.), the *social problem solving* (SPS) is "the self-directed cognitive-behavioural process by which a person attempts to identify or discover effective or adaptive ways of coping problematic situations encountered in the course of everyday living". Based on the Maydeu-Olivares and D'Zurilla's research (1996), SPS has five different factors: positive problem orientation, negative problem orientation, rational problem solving, impulsivity/carelessness, and avoidance. Longitudinal studies with adults suggest that negative orientation predicts future depression, anxiety and stress (Ciarrochi & Scott, 2006). According to Ciarrochi et al. (2009), some adolescents also experience an increasingly negative orientation, and the negative orientation is in connection with worsening affect. Adolescents with higher levels of positive orientation had higher levels of positive emotional and empathy. Higher levels of positive orientation were

A. Surian (Ed.), Open Spaces for Interactions and Learning Diversities, 121–126.

also related to better family quality of life (fewer parent-adolescent social problems and conflicts). The parents-adolescent relationship has an important and positive effect on relationship with peers and on social problem solution in school. D'Zurilla and Nezu (1990) suggested that having rationality improve the social behaviour of both children and adults. Rationality reduces impulsivity, as measures of impulsivity remained lower at one year follow up (e.g. Shure, 1999). However, some results (e.g. Cooper, 2011) indicated that having rationality alone does not improve behaviour in adolescence; for example, the early adolescents (11-year-olds) reported strong rationality and high aggressive behaviour (Kasik, 2014, p. 144).

Coping strategies are essential components of social behaviour. Several coping strategies can be used in different frustrating situations, and both aggressive and prosocial behaviours have their role in coping. By applying coping strategies the individual makes cognitive and behavioural efforts to solve the particular situation (Margitics & Pauwlik, 2006; Englert, Bertrams, & Dickhauser, 2011). The frequency and efficiency of the use of different coping techniques have been identified mainly in teenagers and adults but according to recent research results coping models contain several elements which can be found at an earlier age, even in nursery-school children.

According to Lazarus and Launier (1978) as well as Lazarus and Folkman (1984), individuals use two basic types of coping technique: the problem-focused and the emotion-focused strategies. In the case of the problem-focused technique the individual makes an attempt to solve, avoid or modify the problem by focusing on the problem or the situation in order to be able to avoid it in a similar situation. During the coping process the individual can apply several coping strategies, which may aim at the problematic situation and also on the individual or individuals themselves, and their application is in close relation with the development of several cognitive areas, for example the development of problem-solving skills. In the case of the emotion-focused strategy the main purpose is to resolve and soothe emotional reactions evoked by certain situations, and to surmount overwhelming negative emotions, moreover, we also use this strategy when the situation cannot be changed (Lazarus, 1990). The application of this strategy also depends on the level of development of cognitive areas, however the relation is smaller-scale than in the other strategy, and the emotion-focused strategy is in a closer relation with how the nervous system works.

AIMS AND HYPOTHESES

The aim of our research was to explore the functioning of coping strategies and social problem solving ability at the ages of 8, 12, 15 and 18, to reveal associations between these social forms and some background factors, such as age, gender, school success (grade average) and family background (e.g. mothers' and fathers' educational level, family type), and to investigate the relationship between raters' judgements.

We hypothesised that significant differences would be found between the younger (8, 12) and the older (15, 18) cohorts; to find out about how raters' responses (children's, teachers', and mothers') relate to each other. Based on our earlier findings (Zsolnai, Lesznyák, & Kasik, 2011; Zsolnai, Kasik, & Braunitzer, 2014) we hypothesised that the social problem solving and coping strategies are influenced the most by family type; and the correlation between the school success (grade average) and coping strategies and social problem solving shows increasing tendency.

PARTICIPANTS AND INSTRUMENTS

The participants were 888 students (8: 222; 12: 210; 15: 221; 18: 235 – whole simple: male 46%; female 54%) and their teachers (N = 34 – one per group) and mothers (N = 888). The native language of all participants was Hungarian. Two questionnaires were adapted (CSQ, Coping Strategies Questionnaire for children and teacher – Tremblay et al., 1992; SPSI, Social Problem Solving Inventory for children, mothers, teachers – D'Zurilla, Nezu, & Maydeu-Olivares, 2002). These instruments proved to be highly reliable (Cronbach α are between .83 and .92).

The Tremblay questionnaire assesses social and emotional skills involved in the operation of coping strategies by items that represent problematic social situations either for the children themselves or their mates. The items are grouped into four categories: disruptive (13 items), anxious (5 items), inattentive (4 items) and prosocial (10 items). In our study, the reactions of the children were coded into seven, literature-based categories (e.g. Fabes & Eisenberg, 1992). These categories were solely behavioural and we did not code cognitive coping responses. The behavioural coping categories used were as follows: Asking for help (adult); Asking for help (peer); Overt aggression; Verbal aggression; Avoidance; Impulsivity; Negotiation. Each response category received a proportion score ranging from 0 to 1.

The SPSI assesses the five factors of SPS: PPO = Positive Problem Orientation; NPO = Negative Problem Orientation; RPS = Rational Problem Solving; ICS = Impulsivity/Carelessness Style; AS = Avoidance Style. All factors include 5 items (resulting in a total of 25 items). PPO covers elements of constructive problem solving, such as self-efficacy and positive outcome expectancy. NPO covers a set of dysfunctional cognitive-emotional schemas like low self-efficacy and negative outcome expectancy. RPS can be defined as a constructive problem solving style that is characterized by rational, deliberate, and systematic application of effective problem-solving skills. ICS is a set of dysfunctional problem solving attempts like impulsivity and carelessness. AS is a dysfunctional dimension characterized by passivity and attempts to shift the responsibility of problem solving to others. The SPSI subscales consist of 5-point (from 0 to 4) Likert-type items where: 0 = Not at all true of me; 1 = Slightly true of me; 2 = Moderately true of me; 3 = Very true of me; 4 = Extremely true of me.

RESULTS

Functioning of Social Problem Solving (SPS) and Coping Strategies (CS)

The relationship between children's and mothers' responses is the strongest in most cases, and the largest divergence is observed between teachers' and parents' responses. Based on the total values (means of the raters' judgements), three *SPS* factors (negative problem orientation, rational problem solving and avoidance) show increasing tendency with age, contrary to positive problem orientation and impulsivity ($p < .05$). Gender differences can be found especially among children between 15 and 18 (for example the 15- and 18-year-old boys show more rationality than girls, and girls show more avoidance than boys).

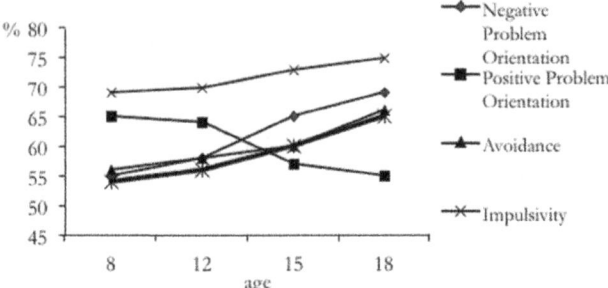

Figure 1. Social problem solving (based on the total values)

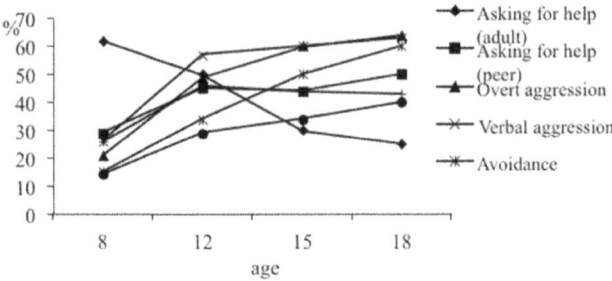

Figure 2. Coping strategies

The relationship between the values of CS of children and adults is similar in the age groups. Overt aggression, impulsivity and avoidance were used by the two older (15, 18) groups in a significantly higher proportion than by the two younger (8, 12) groups. Asking for help (peer), verbal aggression, impulsivity and negotiation were used by the older (12, 15, 18) children in a significantly higher proportion than by the youngest (8) children. In contrary, asking for help (adult) was used by the younger (8, 12) children in a significantly higher proportion than by the older (15, 18) children. In the oldest age group (18), boys were rated significantly more aggressive than girls.

Relationship SPS Factors, CS, Family Background and School Success

The values between positive problem orientation and rationality, impulsivity and negative problem orientation are positive (Pearson r are between .23 and .44) in all age groups and in the case of all raters. The correlation between rationality and avoidance, impulsivity and rationality are negative (Pearson r are between −.27 and −.37) in all age groups and in the case of all raters.

The correlations between overt and verbal aggression, avoidance and negotiation are positive (Phi r are between .22 and 73) in all age groups and in the case of all raters. Based on the total values, the SPS factors and CS are influenced the most by family type, and less by mothers' educational level in all age groups. In the youngest group, school success (grade average) already shows high positive correlation with SPS factors and CS, and these values increase with age. In the older (15, 18) groups, the highest values can be found between rational problem solving and mathematics and biology, between impulsivity and history and literature.

CONCLUSION

According to our results, (1) negative problem orientation, rational problem solving and avoidance show increasing tendency with age; (2) overt aggression, impulsivity and avoidance as coping strategies were used by older children in a significantly higher proportion than by younger children; (3) family characteristics (family type, mothers' educational level) play a major role in the development of social problem solving and coping strategies, school success shows positive correlation with social problem solving and coping strategies, and these values increase with age. These results strengthen unequivocally international research experience in the same domain (Englert et al., 2011; Fiske, 2004; Pruitt, 1998).

It is essential for researchers and educators to have appropriate and sufficient knowledge on the development of coping strategies and social problem solving, as this can inform the development of adequate learning environments for children. It is still a research issue to decide at what ages can coping strategies and social problem solving be developed most effectively.

ACKNOWLEDGEMENT

The research reported here would not have been possible without the funding of TÁMOP 3.1.9/08/01-2009-0001.

REFERENCES

Ciarrochi, J., & Scott, G. (2006). The link between emotional competence and well-being: A longitudinal study. *British Journal of Guidance and Counselling, 34*, 231–244.
Ciarrochi, J., Leeson, P., & Heaven, P. C. L. (2009). A longitudinal study into the interplay between problem orientation and adolescent well-being. *Journal of Counseling Psychology, 56*, 441–449.

Cooper, J. O. (2011). Aggression and rational problem-solving skills of early adolescence. *UMI Dissertation Publishing.*

D'Zurilla, T. J., & Nezu, A. M. (1990). Development and preliminary evaluation of the social problem-solving inventory. *Psychological Assessment: A Journal of Consulting and Clinical Psychology, 2,* 156–163.

D'Zurilla, T. J., Nezu, A., & Maydeu-Olivares, A. (2002). *Social Problem-Solving Inventory – Revised (SPSI–R): Technical manual.* North Tonawanda, NY: Multi-Health Systems.

Englert, C., Bertrams, A., & Dickhauser, O. (2011). Dispositional self-control capacity and trait anxiety as relates to coping style. *Psychology, 2*(6), 598–604.

Fiske, S. T. (2004). *Social beings. Care motives in social psychology.* West Sussex: John Wiley & Sons.

Fülöp, M. (2009). Socialization for cooperative and competitive citizen: A classroom observation study. *Social Science Tribune. From a national identity to a European one. 55*(19), 59–87.

Kasik, L. (2014). Development of Social Problem Solving–A longitudinal study (2009–2011) in a Hungarian context. *European Journal of Developmental Psychology, 12*(2), 142–158.

Lazarus, R. S. (1990). Stress, coping and illness. In H. S. Friedman (Ed.), *Personality and disease* (pp. 84–86). New York, NY: Wiley.

Lazarus, R. S., & Folkman, S. (1984). *Stress, appraisal, and coping.* New York, NY: Springer.

Lazarus, R. S., & Launier, R. (1978). Stress related transactions between person and environment. In L. Pervin & M. Lewis (Eds.), *Internal and external determinants of behaviour* (pp. 126–149). New York, NY: Plenum Press.

Margitics, F., & Pauwlik, Zs. (2006). *Megküzdési stratégiák preferenciájának* összefüggése *az* észlelt *szülői nevelői hatásokkal* [The relationship between the preference of coping strategies and perceptions of parenting]. *Magyar Pedagógia, 106*(1), 43–62.

Maydeu-Olivares, A., & D'Zurilla, T. J. (1996). A factor-analytic study of the Social Problem-Solving Inventory: An integration of the theory and data. *Cognitive Therapy and Research, 20*(6), 115–133.

Nagy, J. (2007). *Kompetencia alapú kritériumorientált pedagógia* [Criterion referenced pedagogy]. Szeged: Mozaik Kiadó.

Pruitt, D. G. (1998). Social conflict. In T. D. Gilbert, S. T. Fiske, & G. Lindzey (Eds.), *Handbook of social psychology* (pp. 470–503). New York, NY: McGraw-Hill.

Rose-Krasnor, L. (1997). The nature of social competence: A theoretical review. *Social Development, 6,* 111–135.

Semrud-Clikeman, M. (2007). *Social competence in children.* New York, NY: Springer.

Shure, M. B. (1999). *I can problem solve. An interpersonal cognitive problem-solving program.* Washington, DC: National Institute of Mental Health.

Tremblay, R. E., Masse, B., Perron, D., & Leblanc, M. (1992). Early disruptive behavior, poor school achievement, delinquent behavior and delinquent personality: Longitudinal analyses. *Journal of Consulting and Clinical Psychology, 60,* 64–72.

Zsolnai, A., Kasik L., & Braunitzer, G. (2014). Coping strategies at the ages 8, 10 and 12. *Educational Psychology, 35*(1), 73–92. doi:10.1080/01443410.2014.916397

Zsolnai, A., Lesznyák, M., & Kasik, L. (2011). Preschool children's aggressive and prosocial behavior in stressful situations. *Early Child Development and Care, 181*(11), 1503–1522.

Anikó Zsolnai
Institute of Education
University of Szeged

László Kasik
Institute of Education
University of Szeged

PART 3

ADDRESSING CULTURAL DIVERSITY

KSENIJA KRSTIĆ, LJILJANA B. LAZAREVIĆ AND
IVANA STEPANOVIĆ ILIĆ

9. DROPOUT AS A RESULT OF EDUCATION WITH NO SPACE FOR DIVERSITY

INTRODUCTION

Traditionally, educational system in Serbia, with prevalence of ex-cathedra teaching methods, focuses on the reproductive level of knowledge, as the results of international assessment studies (TIMSS, PISA) shown (OECD, 2013; Pavlović, Babić, & Baucal, 2013; Martin et al., 2012). Beside that, educational practices in Serbian primary and secondary schools are mostly responsive just to the needs of children from majority of the population (students from educated middle class families). In teaching and learning settings like that, there is no space for diverse instructional and learning needs of children who are not already adapted to such kind of education.

Dropping out of school is a serious educational and social problem. Several extensive studies dealing with factors of dropout indicated that a combination of different factors, like individual, family, school, and systematic, rather than a single factor, causes dropout (Lyche, 2010; Dowrick & Crespo, 2005). Dropout can be observed as a final consequence of a longer process of disengagement, which begins with frequent absenteeism, decrease of school grades, and decrease in social interactions with teachers and peers.

Most dropouts have serious educational deficiencies that limit their economic and social well-being throughout their lives (Rumberger, 1987). Early school leaving may lead to a weaker position in society and in the labour market (European Commission, 2009). Young people who drop out of school have a difficulties securing and maintaining stable employment and, on average, earn less than those who graduates from high school (Bradshaw et al., 2008). Students who drop out of school have 2 to 5 times more chance to live socially excluded, below a poverty line and to depend on the social assistance system (Christle, Jolivette, & Nelson, 2007; Nevala et al., 2011). Additionally, dropping out of school has severe consequences for society as well, since the society experiences a loss of productive workers, a loss of earnings and tax revenues they would have generated. Also society has a higher costs for every early school leaver because of increased incarceration, health care and social services (Bridgeland et al., 2006). Economical analyses from Finland and

A. Surian (Ed.), Open Spaces for Interactions and Learning Diversities, 129–136.

Holland have shown that every early school leaver costs the society between 1.1 and 1.8 million euros (NESSE, 2010). Cutting the number of young people who leave education early is one of the five key targets of the *Europe 2020 strategy to boost growth and create jobs* (Europe, 2020, 2010). Therefore, many countries are striving to define the system and school measures that could prevent children from dropping out at different levels of schooling.

This chapter aims to show why some children dropout from schools in Serbia before they earned a higher secondary education diploma or ISCED 3c diploma (ISCED, 1997). Serbia has a major problem with high dropout rate. In 2013, in Serbia there were 25.3% of young people between 18 and 24 years who were not in education, employment or training system (MICS, 2014). Dropout rates are even higher for children from marginalised groups. According to data from MICS 2014 study (MICS, 2014), dropout rate is more than 78% for children from Roma community.

This work is a part of the larger study, where goal was to study and analyse factors causing dropout from Serbian educational system. Study focuses on the analysis of educational system and school context from the perspective of students who left school. The main aim was to analyse case studies of early school leavers in order to get better understanding of factors influencing dropout, to describe the risks and barriers in educational system which increase a chances for dropout, and to indicate the causes and mechanisms causing dropout.

Method

The entire study was realised in 8 primary and 13 secondary schools with highest dropout rates in 17 municipalities in Serbia. During the field work interviews and/ or focus groups were done with school principles, school psychologists, teachers, pedagogical assistants, representatives of parents and students, representatives from Regional school administrations, Centres for social work, Youth offices, and police makers from Ministry of Education, National Educational Council, National Institute of Evaluation of Quality of Education.

The results shown in this chapter are based on the analyses of 12 case studies of children who dropout from school in Serbia. They were chosen based on the recommendation from schools, as examples of dropouts from schools in the sample. Specifically, 8 boys and 4 girls, 12 to 18 years old (mean age 15.1) participated in case studies. Among them, five students dropped out from primary school, two didn't enrol any secondary school after they finished primary, and five students dropped out from secondary school. Those children are from poor, low-income families, often dysfunctional (due to alcoholism, imprisonment, and domestic violence) or incomplete (one of the parents is death or working abroad). In addition, case studies included also interviews with four parents, two mothers and two fathers. Data obtained from other informers from schools (like teachers, psychologists, students) served as a context in which data obtained from dropout students and their parents in case studies were analised.

This part of the study has applied a phenomenological approach, focusing on the students' own experience in order to understand how and what meanings they construct around their everyday events and experiences (Bodgan & Biklen 2003). Researchers have underlined the need to describe the students' own representations of their educational experience in order to understand the processes underlying early school leaving (Eivers, Ryan, & Brinkley, 2000). In this study original answers and ecological context in which they were gathered are kept. Keeping that in mind, every single case might be treated as representative of whole class of cases, but not as just one analysed case.

Both qualitative and quantitative data gathering techniques were used. Children from case studies participated in semi-structured in-depth interview, focusing on following topics: socio-demographic, family medical history, data about school achievement and absence, behavioural problems, family structure and quality of family relations, relations with friends and school employees, reasons for dropout, family and peer reactions on student's decision to leave the school, student's and family educational aspirations, family duties and hobbies. As part of interview, they completed questionnaires assessing motivation for learning, attitudes toward school and education, teachers' educational habits and practices within the school, and free-time activities.

After the statistical analysis of questionnaires and qualitative content analysis of the interviews, several factors highly related to dropout were singled out.

RESULTS

Students who drop out of school are usually from minority, vulnerable groups and from poor, socially disadvantage families and early school leaving just reproducing "a circle of poverty".

Although the immediate causes for school leaving are usually individual ones, like low academic achievement, grade repetition, lack of motivation for learning, law educational aspirations, they lead to dropout only when there is no adequate school support. Qualitative analysis indicates that common factor in each 12 cases is *inadequate school practice*.

The analysis points out the following school factors that influence the risk of dropping out:

- low quality of teacher-student interaction,
- lack of adequate learning support (e.g., remedial classes),
- lack of individualised teaching,
- failure in recognising student's developmental or emotional problems.

Low Quality of Teacher-Student Interaction

On the one hand, most of our dropout students, as well as interviewed parents, do not express dissatisfaction with cooperation with school staff. All children from case studies can single out at least one person in the school (psychologist, classroom teacher…) with whom they had a good relationship. Parents stated that school staff did talk with them about their child absenteeism and school leaving but that didn't lead to positive outcomes. This school failure in preventing their child from dropping out had established or intensified parental beliefs that the child is "heavy" or that a child "is a problem" and that there is no way to change that. However, parents couldn't specify what exactly school representatives did besides talking with them.

On the other hand, all students from case studies did experience some kind of discrimination or neglect from teachers in the school. They were faced with low expectations from teachers, unequal criteria for marks, sometimes even insults and ridicule. We've got several examples of disparagement of students from teachers: "*You cannot learn for B*"; or after the expressed desire of Roma student to enrol in (medical) secondary school: "*Why are you so unrealistic?*"

Students describe most of their teachers as strict, showing no understanding or interest in students. Paradoxically, their only understanding of students' problems or difficulties was shown as tolerance for students' absenteeism or ignorance. Almost all of children from our sample stated that if they had any problem in school they wouldn't ask a teacher for help.

Lack of Adequate Learning Support

Lack of adequate learning support in classroom is one of the key school factors for risk of dropout. It is a risk factor especially for students with learning problems or lack of learning motivation. It usually goes in combination with low quality of teacher-student interaction—sometimes teachers do not support students' learning but they also belittle students and discourage them, and deepen their personal insecurity and lack of interest for schooling. Our data show that teachers often blame the child and the family for dropout and do not recognise their own responsibility for school leaving. Students from our sample indicated that most teachers do not give them any explanation for marks they've got nor they point out on the students' mistakes or what else they should learn from previous lessons.

Remedial classes are singled out as one of basic forms of learning support. Both primary and secondary schools in Serbia are obliged to organise remedial classes and they formally exist in all schools from our sample. But, in the practice that does not work. Interviewed dropout students answered that although they had learning difficulties they didn't attended remedial classes, and they didn't got adequate support or help in learning. Sometimes school does not organise remedial classes, but even if those classes exist students often do not attend them and teachers do not try to motivate them to participate. Based on our data, lack of remedial classes or students' absence should be treated as a significant risk factor for dropout.

Lack of Individualised Teaching

Quality of teaching referring to teachers activities aimed at individualised teaching, adjustment of teaching process and teaching demands to developmental and educational needs of their students is one of the key factors for prevention of school failure and school dropout as a result of failure. The very existence and the quality of individualised teaching is a major precondition for equal learning opportunities for all students, e.g., for equal chances for learning and development.

Most teachers in primary and secondary schools in Serbia still teach in traditional way. By using ex-cathedra teaching methods and insisting on reproductive knowledge acquisition (OECD, 2013; Pavlović, Babić, & Baucal, 2013; Martin et al., 2012) they do not support learning and skills development which can be transferred in everyday life and future work context. They often do not introduce any innovations in teaching and do not adjust their methods to students' particular needs. Hence, there is no room for diversified instructional methods and individualisation of teaching process. Students from our sample mention just few teachers who make an effort to support all students to achieve learning goals during lessons and to adapt their teaching approach to educational needs of different student.

Individual educational plan is one of the educational instruments, introduced through the Law on Foundations of the Education System (adopted in 2009), which aim is to support the education and learning of children with educational or developmental difficulties through personalised methods of work (Parliament of the Republic of Serbia, 2009; Kovács et al., 2014). Although in all primary and secondary schools teaching staff have some experiences with individualised educational plan for students with educational or developmental difficulties, often that is not a really individualised teaching but rather decrease of learning expectations and marking criteria. In some cases, teachers are showing their "understanding" for students' difficulties by decreasing criteria and by "pulling" student to a higher grade without achieving learning goals that are needed for success in the higher grade. Consequently, as shown in our study, student dropout of school in final years of the primary education because he/she couldn't cope with curriculum demands due to the lack of basic writing and reading skills.

Failure to Recognise Student Developmental or Emotional Problems

Students from our case studies have pointed out that their teachers have shown "understanding" for their problems, but that understanding was usually tolerance for student's absenteeism and low expectations regarding their achievement.

Beside financial and material support (in clothing, school books, etc), other forms of support, help or encouragement for students' development and education are missing. Teachers often lack specific knowledge and skills for such kind of work with children in schools. One of the main reasons for that can be found in the lack of pre-service training. Namely, they are trained as specialist for certain field (physics, biology, history, etc.), without sufficient knowledge and practice regarding different teaching methods and supporting students' learning. As an example, we can provide a case of a student who repeated the same grade for five times, and at the end, dropped out of school because of exam anxiety which was not recognised and adequately treated.

CONCLUSIONS

Each of our twelve case studies provide insight into specific pattern of risk factors related to school practices that might cause children to leave school. As our data show, reasons for dropout from educational system are multiple and often followed by many different social, school and/or family and individual factors. None one of these factors is sufficient risk factor for dropout separately. Rather, interaction of these factors, without adequate measures of prevention and intervention, heightens the risk that student will drop out of school.

Although dropout is not just an educational problem, it happens in educational system and in schools. Almost all aspects of school functioning could be the factors increasing a chance of dropping out of educational system, but if they are used in adequate manner, they could also be an important (significant) resources of dropout prevention measures.

We can conclude that systemic support for students from minority, vulnerable groups should include an adequate recognition and overview of whole student situation and living context, taking into account all personal, family and socio-cultural factors (like socio-cultural deprivation, lack of learning support at home, cultural patterns regarding schooling, etc.), with a provision of timely and focused social-emotional support with individualised teaching and learning methods.

If student alone or with a support from other family members cannot cope with learning and doing homework, it will lead to weaker school performance, lower school marks, grade repetition, sense of failure and decrease in self-esteem. Taken together, it leads to school dropout.

Providing individualised teaching, with diversified instructional methodology and adjustable teaching process, encourages all students during classes, and promote cooperation between students. Consequently, it would make schools more inclusive and more successful in providing equal learning opportunities for student coming from different social contexts.

REFERENCES

Bogdan, R. C., & Biklen, S. K. (2003). *Qualitative research for education: An introduction to theories and methods* (4th ed.). New York, NY: Pearson Education group.

Bradshaw, C., O'Brennan, L., & McNeely, C. (2008). Core competencies and the prevention of school failure and early school leaving. In N. G. Guerra & C. P. Bradshaw (Eds.), *Core competencies to prevent problem behaviours and promote positive youth development. New Directions for Child and Adolescent Development, 122*, 19–32.

Bridgeland, J., Dilulio, J., & Morison, K. (2006). *The silent epidemic: Perspectives of high school dropouts*. Washington, DC: Civic Enterprises, LLC.

Christle, C. A., Jolivette, K., & Nelson, C. M. (2007). School characteristics related to high school dropout rates. *Remedial and Special Education, 28*(6), 325–339.

Dowrick, P. W., & Crespo, N. (2005). School failure. In T. P. Gullotta & G. R. Adams (Eds.), *Handbook of adolescent behavioural problems: Evidence-based approaches to prevention and treatment* (pp. 589–610). New York, NY: Springer Science and Business Media.

Eivers, E., Ryan, E., & Brinkley, A. (2000). *Characteristics of early school leavers: Results of the research strand of the 8-to-15 year old early school leavers initiative*. Dublin: Educational Research Centre, St. Patrick's College.

European Commission. (2009). Progress towards the Lisbon objectives in education and training. Indicators and benchmarks 2009. Commission staff working document. SEC (2009) 1616 final. Retrieved November 23, 2009, from http://aei.pitt.edu/42902/

European Commission. (2010). *EUROPE 2020. A strategy for smart, sustainable and inclusive growth*. Brussels: European Commission. Retrieved from http://ec.europa.eu/eu2020/pdf/COMPLET%20EN%20BARROSO%20%20%20007%20-%20Europe%202020%20-%20EN%20version.pdf

Government of the Republic of Serbia (2014). Second National Report on Social Inclusion and Poverty Reduction in the Republic of Serbia. Government of the Republic of Serbia.

ISCED. (1997). International Standard Classification of Education: I S C E D 1997. UNESCO: Author. Retrieved from http://www.unesco.org/education/information/nfsunesco/doc/isced_1997.htm

Kovács Cerović, T., Babić, D. P., Jovanović, O., Jovanović, V., Jokić, T., Rajović, V., & Baucal, I. (2014). *Monitoring framework for inclusive education in Serbia*. Belgrade: Social Inclusion and Poverty Reduction Unit and UNICEF.

Lyche, C. (2010). Taking on the completion challenge: A literature review on policies to prevent dropout and early school leaving *(OECD Education Working Papers, No. 53)*. Paris: OECD Publishing.

Martin, M. O., Mullis, I. V. S., Foy, P., & Stanco, G. M. (2012). *TIMSS 2011 international results in science*. ChestnutHill, MA: TIMSS & PIRLS International Study Center, BostonCollege.

MICS. (2014). Serbia Multiple indicator Cluster Survey, 2014; UNICEF.

NESSE. (2010). Retrieved from https://www.spd.dcu.ie/site/edc/documents/nesse2010early-school-leaving-report.pdf

Nevala, A., Hawley, J., Stokes, D., Slater, K., Souto Otero, M., Santos, R., Duchemin, C., & Manoudi, A. (2011). *Reducing early school leaving in the EU*. Brussels: European Parliament.

OECD. (2013). *PISA 2012 results: What students know and can do – tudents kperformance in mathematics, reading and science* (Vol. 1). Paris: OECD Publications.

Parliament of the Republic of Serbia (2009). Zakon o osnovama sistema obrazovanja i vaspitanja [Law on Foundations of the Education System]. Službeni glasnik Republike Srbije, no. 72.

Pavlović Babić, D., & Baucal, A. (2013). *Podralndar bić, Dications.ISA 2012 u Srbiji: Prvi rezultati* [Support Me, Inspire Me: PISA 2012 in Serbia: First Results]. Belgrade: Centar za primenjenu psihologiju.

Rumberg, R. (1987). High school dropouts: A review of issues and evidence. *Review of Educational Research, 57*(2), 101–121.

RZS (2012). *Istraživanje višestrukih pokazatelja u Republici Srbiji 2010: Finalni izveštaj* [Multiple indicators cluster survey in Republic of Serbia 2010: final report]. Beograd, Republika Srbija: Republički zavod za statistiku. Retrieved from http://www.unicef.rs/files/Publikacije/mics4_srb_nov.%2022.%202012.pdf

Ksenija Krstić
Department of Psychology
University of Belgrade
Ljiljana B. Lazarević
Institute of Psychology
University of Belgrade

Ivana Stepanovic Ilić
Institute of Psychology
University of Belgrade

TEUTA MEHMETI AND ANNE-NELLY PERRET-CLERMONT

10. SEEKING SUCCESS OF MIGRANT STUDENTS THROUGH DESIGNED TASKS

A Case Study with Albanian Students in Switzerland

INTRODUCTION

Revisiting School (Un)Success of Migrant Children

Some groups of minority students are well known for being at risk of school failure. Different trends of research in sociology, psychology and education have explored the processes that affect their school performances and careers. A bias of causal attribution, known in social psychology as "blaming the victim" (Ryan, 1971), is likely to infiltrate these lines of research when researchers take for granted that being unsuccessful is "normal" for these groups and then start to look for causes that can explain this "obvious fact". The causal attribution is then made to individual (competencies, motivations, attitudes towards school and learning, involvement, cognitive and social skills, etc.) or group traits (family culture, differences between school and home, type of socialisation, values, etc.), as if characteristics of those who are failing were responsible for the failure, leaving out alternative explanations such as educational design, social prejudices, teachers' behaviour and other processes pertaining to the situation and its other actors.

Some studies have taken an opposite standpoint and have started to investigate the success of minority students, opening ways to better understand complex phenomena that cannot be reduced to quasi mechanical causal interactions between supposedly independent factors (Cesari Lusso, 2001; César, 2013; César & Kumpulainen, 2009; Hudicourt-Barnes, 2003; Mehmeti, 2013; Rosebery, Ogonowski, DiSchino, & Warren, 2013; Warren, Ballenger, Ogonowski, & Rosebery, 2001). These results have encouraged us to inquire further in two directions: (1) to better understand what are the pedagogical designs that favour success of the participants, (2) to reconsider more attentively the cognitive processes that are afforded or required by these pedagogical designs and (3) to better understand the communication dynamics between students and teachers. Indeed, there can also be a hidden attribution bias: students are failing on a cognitive task but the researcher looks for non-cognitive explanations for this failure (motivation, cultural differences, etc.). We would like here to remain centred on the cognitive and communication demands and their management by both students and teacher.

A. Surian (Ed.), Open Spaces for Interactions and Learning Diversities, 137–150.

We will focus on a particular group of migrant children known particularly for their failure in school, i.e., Albanian-speaking children in Switzerland.

The Case of Albanian-Speaking Students in Switzerland

In the Swiss context, Albanian-speaking children are said to face difficulties in their social integration. Many negative social representations are conveyed by the media and through political discourse (e.g., Burri-Sharani, Efionayi-Mader, Hammer, Pecoraro, Soland, Tsaka, & Wyssmüller, 2010; Dahinden, 2009; Leuenberger & Maillard, 1999; Piguet, 2005), but also at school. Educational reports show that Albanian-speaking children are particularly inclined to school failure. Some studies (CDIP, 2003; Coradi Vellacott & Wolter, 2005; Kronig, Haeberlin, & Eckhart, 2000; Müller, 2001) suggest that the structure and functioning of the school system might be obstacles for these children's school success. Others point to teachers' negative representations due to a supposedly sociocultural distance between them and the children (Coradi Vellacott & Wolter, 2005). In this perspective, Klein, Nicolet and Grossen (2000) report how a Kosovar student's performances in mathematics were assessed as low by a Swiss teacher even though the researchers did not observe particular difficulties for this child. And Hauswirth and Roshier (1999) give the example of a Kosovar student who was considered a brilliant student in her country of origin but could hardly meet the school requirements and teachers' expectations in spite of the fact that she was demonstrating great involvement.

The general image depicts Albanian-speaking children in Switzerland as poor performers at school, apparently not able to display some important socio-cognitive skills. Our aim here is to go the distance with this general discourse and with the search for external factors to explain students' failure in order to observe what really happens in concrete cases around precise tasks: what are the cognitive and communicational processes behind students' performances in school?

RESEARCH QUESTIONS AND METHODOLOGY

This study will explore how these children, who are so often expected to fail at school, take part in a pedagogical activity that has been designed to foster argumentation and reasoning skills. The following questions will be addressed: (1) How do the children deal with the task: do they get involved and take active part in it? (2) Do they display important skills such as argumentation and complex reasoning? (3) How do teachers and students communicate?

A Pedagogical Activity Designed to Offer Interactive and Thinking Space

The activity was designed by the first author with the goal of promoting active involvement of all students and argumentation. It invites students to discuss a current issue of world importance. Students are considered as the main protagonists of the activity whereas the teacher is expected to intervene only when children need any help or when she needs to recall the instructions. Interactions among children are therefore preferred. As a guide for the activity, the teacher is supposed to provoke and foster argumentative discussions by requiring from the students that they share, confront and discuss their answers and to encourage the children to feel comfortable participating and to develop their own thinking. Following its design, this activity avoids the pressure of normative assessments that are well-known to inhibit children's competencies (Butera, Buchs, & Darnon, 2011).

A protocol describing the planned activity is given to the teachers. It contains four steps:

1. The teacher introduces the researcher: a friend who studies psychology and education and is interested in what children do during classroom activities. She will then explain that this lesson is different from usual lessons: children have to be active and play an important role conducting the discussion; and the teacher will be confined to a more passive role, helping with questions of vocabulary or other such matters.

2. The teacher then tells the students that she expects them to work first in dyads. She organises these dyads, and informs them that she will give two photographs (see Figure 1)[1] to each dyad. She then writes three questions on the blackboard:
   1. *What do you see in these pictures? Describe.*
   2. *Where could these two pictures have been taken?*
      2.1. *What are the characteristics of this country?*
   3. *What creates pollution?*

Figure 1. Photographs distributed by the teacher

She then tells the children that they have to discuss these questions in their dyad. When they have reached an agreement, they will have to write their answers on the blackboard. The dyads discuss the questions.

3. The teacher then asks the dyads to choose which member of the dyad will write the answers on the blackboard and then s/he does so. Once this is finished, the

teacher explains to them that they are now going to discuss one another's answers and that, for this, she will appoint one dyad to discuss the answers of another dyad. Dyads who discuss other dyads' answers are expected to ask questions if something is not clear, to show disagreement if they do not agree and to explain why.

4. The teacher draws attention to some of the answers written on the blackboard, and to some of the issues raised by the children, and opens the discussion to the whole class.

Participants and Collection of the Data

Two regular Swiss school teachers (the second one with Albanian as mother tongue) have volunteered to test this pedagogical design. Three classes were involved: a class of 8- to 9-year-old children (among which are a few Albanian speakers) during the regular school time; and two classes (one of 5- to 8-year-old students and one of 8- to 13-year-old students) of Albanian language and culture, organised by the local Albanian community and held by the second teacher in an official school building as an extra hour. Both teachers had received their training in Switzerland.

Our analysis is based on written notes taken during these lessons (we didn't want to use the video camera as it is very intrusive). Thanks to shorthand, some of the dialogues have been noted word for word.

In the three classrooms, the designed activity was a success and even more so than what we had expected: the teachers happily accepted the protocol and implemented it as it was; the students got readily involved and all of them (including the Albanian students of the regular classroom) displayed motivation to the point of neglecting the recess time in order to pursue the activity; they interacted a lot among themselves, respecting each other's points of view and spontaneously asking their peers to explain their standpoints.

In this chapter, we will "zoom" in on interactive moments in the class with the older Albanian children. We will first provide the reader with a view of these children's attitudes during the activity, of the answers they gave, and of their argumentative discussions. We will then consider in detail a specific moment of interaction between the teacher and three students that attracted our attention because it seemed particularly rich. The analysis will consist of a very fine grained analysis of their communication and argumentation, using the analytical model proposed by van Eemeren, Grootendorst, and Snoeck Henkemans (2002).

A CASE STUDY

An Overview of Students' Involvement in the Task

We have observed that when the students received the two photographs, they spontaneously started to discuss in dyads, and this even before the teacher had a chance to give the planned instructions. Obviously they were interested and felt concerned. All the dyads discussed the questions and came to conclusions.

When the students wrote their answers on the blackboard, we could see that answers to question 1 (*What do you see on these pictures? Describe*) were generally detailed descriptions of the pictures (*tailpipe, garbage, black smoke, gas, etc.*). When trying to answer question 2 (*Where could these two photographs have been taken? What are the characteristics of this place*), students mostly mentioned cities from either Kosovo or Albania. For question 3 (*What creates pollution?*), most of them mentioned poverty and citizens' lack of sensitivity to the issue of pollution.

We have also noticed that some students – even when not designated by the teacher as being in charge of discussing another dyad's answers – raised their hands and asked questions to their mates, such as: "why does carbonic gas create pollution?" Children then offered different answers such as: ozone layer, disappearance of water, global warming, etc., and then discussed the comparison between carbonic and natural gas.

During the discussions, we have observed that, even if a dyad simply agreed with the statements of another dyad, students would nevertheless tend to explicitly discuss others' answers and defend their own, backing them up with arguments. This finding, thanks to a very simple design of the pedagogical activity, was a nice surprise as it is often reported that argumentation can be difficult to foster in formal school situations.

These observations tend to show that the students really got involved in the activity, were active and started argumentative discussions.

An Interaction in Which Students Demonstrate That They Are Actively Using Argumentative Skills

An important aim of the designed task was to promote students' expression and offer them the opportunity to enter into argumentation. We are now going to "zoom" in on a specific moment in order to observe closely how this happens. This closer look will confirm the general impression of active and argumentative students, but we will see that the phenomenon is more complex: even when she tries, the teacher does not really support – at least in this case – the argumentative processes that she wants to promote.

For our analysis, we will partially refer to the analytical model of argumentation proposed by van Eemeren, Grootendorst, and Snoeck Henkemans (2002) because it can help us to identify the students' standpoints, to observe if they confront their partners with their standpoints, and to see if they defend their standpoints with arguments. It also helps to trace the children's reasoning and see whether they are able to follow it till the end or eventually forget it if interrupted by their peers or teacher. Using this model to analyse the data also invites taking into account "unexpressed premises" (van Eemeren & Grootendorst, 1992; Gerritsen, 2001; Greco Morasso, Miserez-Caperos, & Perret-Clermont, 2015). They are implicit elements in the interlocutors' statements that can be reconstructed in regard to the context. We will also consider whether their standpoints are fixed or evolved during the social interactions.

Introduction of the Extract

The following extract is located in the third step of the activity (when all the students have written their answers on the blackboard and the teacher designates a dyad X to discuss the dyad of a group Y). Most students answered question 2 (*Where could these two pictures have been taken?*) by mentioning a city from Albania or Kosovo. But the dyad formed by Burim[2] and Arlind has written on the blackboard: "We don't know". When the teacher asks a dyad to comment on Burim and Arlind's answer, a discussion starts with Burim explaining his dyad's answers (turn 1), followed by the teacher asking a question (turn 2). Later (turn 6), two other students intervene, Valon and Shpresa, who were not necessarily in charge of discussing Burim and Arlind's answers.

Burim's Argumentation

Let's now reconstruct Burim's argumentation from turns 1 to 5. Unexpressed premises are written in parentheses.

Standpoint	
1.	We don't know (where the two images could have been taken) (turn 1)
Arguments	
1.1.1	Pollution is a current problem everywhere (on earth) (turn 1)
(1.1.1'a)	(Cities of Albania or Kosovo, among others, but not only, are on earth)
(1.1.1'b)	(Pollution is not exclusively in places where there are garbage and tailpipe)
(1.1.1'b'.1)	(Garbage and tailpipe are not the only sources of pollution)
(1.1.1'b'.1'.2)	(Pollution is a problem present in Switzerland too (among other places) (turn 3))
1.1.1.1b.1.2.1a	[in Switzerland] there are lot of companies and industries (turn 5)
1.1.1.1b.1.2.1b	they produce a lot, this also pollutes (turn 5)

The reconstruction of Burim's argumentation makes clear that he starts by declaring a standpoint: "we don't know (where the two pictures could have been taken)" and that this is a standpoint that he immediately backs up with the argument that "pollution is a current problem everywhere". In turn 2, the teacher challenges Burim's argument when she asks: "And does it mean that in Switzerland too?". Burim answers in turn 3 with "yes", meaning that pollution is a problem present in

Table 1. Participants: Three students (Burim, Valon, Shpresa) and the teacher.
Dialogues are in French because the teacher allowed the students to use the
French language if they wanted to as they had declared that they
lacked the proper vocabulary in Albanian to discuss pollution.

1	Burim	J'ai écrit «on ne sait pas» [à la question 2] mais pour dire que je ne suis pas d'accord avec les autres parce que [la pollution] c'est un problème qui est présent partout	I wrote "we don't know" [to question 2] but to say that I don't agree with the others because it [pollution] is a current problem everywhere
2	Teacher	Et ça veut dire qu'en Suisse aussi?	And does it mean that in Switzerland too?
3	Burim	Oui	Yes
4	Teacher	Ah oui, et où par exemple?	Oh yes, and where for example?
5	Burim	Ben j'ai déjà vu mais aussi parce qu'il y a plein de grandes entreprises et industries qui produisent des choses, ça aussi ça pollue	Well, I have already seen it but also because there are lot of companies and industries which produce things, this also pollutes
6	Valon	Oui mais quand même en Suisse y'a beaucoup moins parce que par exemple y'a pas ces déchets comme ca partout	But still in Switzerland there is much less because for example there is not so much garbage everywhere like that
7	Teacher	Et comment ça se fait?	And how does it come about?
8	Shpresa	Ben parce que la Suisse c'est pas un pays pauvre	Well because Switzerland is not a poor country
9	Teacher	Et donc?	So what?
10	Valon	On peut payer pour enlever les déchets	We can pay to remove garbage
11	Teacher	Où paye-t-on pour ça? comment ça se passe ?	Where do we pay for it? How does that work?
12	Burim	Les impôts	Taxes

Switzerland, too (see 1.1.1'b.1'2) and finally gives coordinative arguments (see for instance 1.1.1.1b.1.2.1a and 1.1.1.1b.1.2.1b) to sustain this. We can thus observe that Burim is able to answer and defend his standpoint and to deploy a rather complex argumentation.

This is relevant to point out in terms of the level of complexity in Burim's argumentation. A closer look at how we have deciphered his unexpressed premises allows us, moreover, to point out that Burim seems to reflect both on the place where the images could have been taken and on the sources of pollution (what creates pollution). This can indicate that he integrates question 3 (*what creates pollution*) in his reasoning and seeks a coherent sense of the questions asked.

As said, Burim's interventions are situated during the third step of the activity, when all the answers have been written on the blackboard and therefore exposed to the whole class. Thus, different standpoints have been exposed and discussed. Burim is most probably taking into account the other answers on the blackboard when he says that "[he doesn't] agree with the others". A possible interpretation of Burim's claim in turn 1 could be: "I wrote we don't know (standpoint) in order to say that I don't agree with the others (others think that pollution is specific to the cities of Albania or Kosovo), because it [pollution] is a problem current everywhere (and it is not only present – contrarily to what the photographs suggest – in the places where there are abandoned garbage and smoking tailpipes because these are not the only sources of pollution). If this reconstruction is correct, then it indicates that Burim is attentive to what has been said by his mates and that he does not want to directly attack someone else's answer – a sign of social competence. It could also indicate that Burim refuses to take the two photographs given by the teacher as representative of the phenomenon of pollution and moreover of the pollution in a specific place. On the contrary, his classmates seem to accept such premises. Burim's arguments show that he is considering both the place and the sources of pollution.

We can see that Burim keeps a line of reasoning in turns 1 to 5. It is also interesting to see that the teacher's challenge of Burim's standpoint (turn 2) does not make him abandon his standpoint. On the contrary, he maintains it.

Burim's expression of a standpoint that he supports with different arguments and that he maintains from turns 1 to 5, also when it is challenged by the teacher, invites us to think that the frame of the activity allows him to do so and that he feels secure enough in the activity to propose a standpoint and arguments unshared by his classmates.

Burim's argument, "pollution is a problem present in Switzerland too", seems to back up the standpoint "we don't know where the pictures could have been taken". The teacher, by her question in turn 2 ("and does it mean that in Switzerland too?"), seems to suggest a different standpoint than the one proposed by Burim. The new standpoint would be: pollution is not a problem present in Switzerland. Burim, however, rejects this standpoint, and it could be that this rejection indicates that he is still keeping to his own previous standpoint.

Valon's Argumentation

In this extract, we can observe another student who seeks actively to develop his standpoint: In turn 6, Valon counters Burim's argumentation on the industries in Switzerland that produce a lot and hence pollute; "But still in Switzerland there is much less because for example there is not so much garbage everywhere like that". As other students did, Valon previously mentioned a city in Kosovo as a place where these pictures could have been taken. Taking this into account, a possible reconstruction of Valon's argumentation would be the following (unexpressed premises in parenthesis):

Standpoint

1.   The two images could have been taken in a city of Kosovo

Arguments

(1.1)   (The two images represent a tailpipe and a container filled with garbage)

(1.1.1') (There are smoking tailpipes and containers filled withgarbage in Kosovo)

1.2   The two images were probably not taken in Switzerland

1.2.1a   there is much less pollution in Switzerland [than in a city of Kosovo]

1.2.1b   for example [in Switzerland] there is not so much garbage everywhere like that (turn 6)

Valon is actively reasoning. He has a standpoint that he defends with arguments. While Burim proposed arguments that consider both the question of the place where the pictures could have been taken and the sources of pollution, Valon seems to be centred only on recognizing the place where the photographs could have been made. He seems to take for granted that the pictures are representative of a specific place, and he focuses on question 2 (*Where these two pictures could have been taken?*). Valon's intervention is particularly interesting because it could mean two things: he could be trying to state his standpoint and to confront Burim with it. It could also be that Valon wants to ensure that he and Burim are talking about the same object: indeed, Valon was probably very attentive to Burim's claim and could have noticed that he had mentioned other elements (industries) than those in the pictures. Anyhow, one thing is clear: Valon is involved in the activity, is trying to put his own thinking at play and is able to take the others' perspectives into account.

This second example again shows the student's involvement in the activity and both his cognitive and social competencies.

The Role of the Teacher

In this extract, what role does the teacher play in the interaction and how does it affect the students?

The teacher intervenes in many turns: In turn 2, she makes a suggestion ("Does it mean that in Switzerland too there is pollution?"); in turn 4, she invites Burim to give a precise example ("where for example?"*).* Then, in turns 6,7 and 9, she asks questions again about the students' claims. Her interventions seem to have different impacts. From turns 2 to 5, she invites Burim to deploy his thinking, but orients him on what she wants him to talk about. This does not directly stop Burim's course of reasoning. However, in turns 5 and 6, when a discussion begins between Burim and Valon, her intervention stops the discussion between the two students by giving authority to Valon's statement, in turn 7. Valon's statement becomes the new standpoint to be discussed (*there is not much pollution in Switzerland or pollution is not really present in Switzerland*). The students are then oriented towards this new standpoint. Burim, who initially had a different standpoint, seems to play the game of entering into the discussion of this new standpoint and, in turn 12, contributes with a suggestion compatible with the statements made by his classmates.

In the designed activity, the teacher was expected to help the students to critically discuss each other's answers. In this extract her interventions do not seem to fit this aim. Indeed, in some turns she seems to interpret students' statements and takes a particular position on them (i.e., judges them). For example, in turn 6, Valon's intervention could be interpreted as a conversational skill: he wants to make sure that he and Burim are talking about the same object. But the teacher uses Valon's intervention to make her point. The teacher does not offer support for both students to mutually discuss their different views. Similarly, it is difficult to know whether Valon wanted to back up his standpoint with arguments such as the opposition between rich and poor countries, but the teacher, in turn 9, gives authority to Shpresa's argument ("Because Switzerland is not a poor country", turn 8) and hence guides him towards such a line of reasoning.

DISCUSSION

The aim of this case study was to offer children who are reputed to fail at school a pedagogical activity in which they would likely deploy their cognitive and social skills and in particular their argumentative competencies. We were happy to see that in conditions where they are explicitly invited to be active and develop their own thinking and confront their peers with it, these students showed great involvement, were active, and deployed argumentations that the analysis reveals as more complex than they could have seemed at first hand. They defend their standpoints and give arguments. The in-depth analysis of a particular interaction reveals that this happens in spite of the fact that the teacher intervened all the time, not always respecting the child's line of thinking, and as a consequence, did not leave much open space for the children to discuss among themselves their own different standpoints. The teacher had initially announced her intention to foster a discussion that would take place among the students, but she suddenly became the main interlocutor for each child.

Altogether these results can help shed light on the complexity of formal conversations in schools when children are supposed to develop their own reasoning and teachers have a hard time refraining from constantly intervening (for further examples of this type, see Giglio, 2015; Perret-Clermont & Giglio, in press). A closer look at children's answers in classroom dialogues can help to better understand the complexity of the task required from them: understanding the questions, the aim of the activity, the intent of the teacher in her interventions, reasoning, bringing arguments, but also their awareness of being in interactions with others who do not necessarily share the same standpoints, especially the teacher. While school performances tend to be assessed according to the "final response" expected by the teacher, this study suggests that children's capacities are likely to be underestimated in this perspective because it does not grant them the possibility to use their different premises, to bring in new issues, and to receive attuned feedback from the teacher on what they are trying to say.

Beyond the case of Albanian-speaking children in these schools, we understand these observations as an invitation for further research to explore school success (or non-success) in migrant children. In this pedagogical activity, children have been invited to discuss a scientific and civic issue, namely pollution, and could draw on their personal knowledge and experience. They have been very explicitly allowed to express their own standpoints and even required to do so. Results suggest that they took this object of discussion very seriously. They were actively seeking to deal with the questions set by the teacher. They did reflect on the phenomenon of pollution. Not only were the children active in the discussion, but they also deployed rather complex argumentation (a result that is in line with the evidence of Greco Morasso, Miserez-Caperos, & Perret-Clermont, 2015; Perret-Clermont, Arcidiacono, Breux, Greco, & Miserez-Caperos, 2015) and this in spite of the fact that the teacher did not manage to see and hence to acknowledge the complexity of their argumentation.

We also feel encouraged to better understand how children's reasoning and argumentation are dialogical and not independent either from issues such as identity, previous experience, scope of the conversation, position management, etc. (Muller Mirza & Perret-Clermont, 2009; Sinclaire-Harding, Miserez, Arcidiacono, & Perret-Clermont, 2013).

Studies on the challenges of multicultural education (e.g., de Haan & Elbers, 2004; de Haan, Keizer, & Elbers, 2010; Gorgorio & Planas, 2005) have already raised many issues on why migrant children face important obstacles at school and have opened paths to avoid them. Our study suggests that children could also encounter difficulties not because of a potential cultural distance or discontinuity (de Haan & Elbers, 2004; Gorgorio & Planas, 2005) with the teacher (in the present case study they are all Albanian-speaking and here to advance their knowledge of their own language and culture) but because the teacher just seems to behave like many other teachers (e.g., observations of teachers in different countries by Giglio, 2015): confronted with a student's unexpected answer, she just (involuntarily) dismisses it by sticking to her own standpoint and intentions without making these explicit.

In educational contexts, there seems to be a tendency to attribute to the children (and to *their* supposed lack of competencies) their failure in school tasks. And this is so especially if they come from lower socioeconomic backgrounds. It is much less often the case that failure is attributed to the pedagogical design or to the teacher's pragmatic moves. In this case study, children did have the skills required by the assigned task, notably argumentative skills; however, the teacher was not able to capitalize on them because (certainly inadvertently) she rejected or stopped the children's actualisation of their argumentative reasoning. A better understanding by researchers and teachers of the conversational dynamics involved could probably help to advance quality and equity.

ACKNOWLEDGMENTS

We would like to thank Margarida César, Sara Greco, and the anonymous reviewers for their stimulating contributions to this discussion (even if we take complete responsibility for what is written here); Alessio Surian for his encouragement; and Athena Sargent for her precious help with the English language.

We are grateful to the Swiss National Science Foundation for its support (contract n°100019-156690/1 Perret-Clermont/Greco/Iannaccone/Rocci) to our studies on the implicit in children's argumentation.

NOTES

¹   The two images were found by the researcher on the internet:
   Image 1: https://kasaselimi.files.wordpress.com/2010/03/mbetruina.jpg
   Image 2: thinkstockphotos/stockbyte: http://cache4.asset-cache.net/xr/56530327.jpg?v=1&c=
   IWSAsset&k=3&d=8A33AE939F2E01FF5442AB8FC2AF2ED849B62DCF13617E5E26F109DF6
   8AEEBDABCC685C059D63657
²   All the names are pseudonyms.

REFERENCES

Burri-Sharani, B., Efionayi-Mader, D., Hammer, S., Pecoraro, M., Soland, B., Tsaka, A., & Wyssmüller, C. (2010). *La population kosovare en Suisse*. Berne: Office fédéral des migrations (ODM).

Butera, F., Buchs, C., & Darnon, C. (Eds). (2011). *L'évaluation, une menace ?* Paris: PUF.

CDIP. (Ed.). (2003). *Le parcours scolaire et de formation des élèves immigrés à "faibles" performances scolaires. CONVEGNO 2002: Rapport final*. Berne: Conférence suisse des directeurs cantonaux de l'instruction publique (CDIP).

César, M. (2013). Collaborative work, dialogical self and inter-/intra-empowerment mechanisms: (Re) constructing life trajectories of participation. In M. B. Ligorio & M. César (Eds.), *Interplays between dialogical learning and dialogical self* (pp. 151–192). Charlotte, NC: Information Age Publishing (IAP).

César, M., & Kumpulainen, K. (Eds.). (2009). *Social interactions in multicultural settings*. Rotterdam, The Netherlands: Sense Publishers.

Cesari Lusso, V. (2001). *Quand le défi est appelé intégration*. Bern: Peter Lang.

Coradi Vellacott, M., & Wolter, S. (2005). *Chancengerichkeit im schweizerischen Bildungswesen*. Aarau: Schweizerische Koordinationsstelle für Bildungsforschung.

Dahinden, J. (2009) "Are you who you know?" – A network perspective on ethnicity, gender and transnationalism. Albanian-speaking migrants in Switzerland and returnees in Kosovo. In C. Westin, J. Bastos, & J. Dahinden (Eds.), *Identity processes and dynamics in multi-ethnic Europe* (pp. 4–20). Amsterdam: Amsterdam University Press.

de Haan, M., & Elbers, E. (2004). Minority status and culture: Local constructions of diversity in a classroom in the Netherlands. *Intercultural Education, 15*(4), 451–453.

de Haan, M., Keizer, R., & Elbers, E. (2010). Ethnicity and student identity in schools: An analysis of official and unofficial talk in multiethnic classrooms. *European Journal of Psychology of Education, 25*(2), 176–191.

Eemeren, F. H. van, & Grootendorst, R. (1992). *Argumentation, communication, and fallacies: A pragma-dialectical perspective*. Hillsdale, NJ: Lawrence Erlbaum Associates.

Eemeren, F. H. van, Grootendorst, R., & Snoeck Henkemans, A. F. (2002). *Argumentation: Analysis, evaluation, presentation*. Mahwah, NJ: Lawrence Erlbaum Associates.

Gerritsen, S. (2001). Unexpressed premises. In F. H. van Eemeren (Ed.), *Crucial concepts in argumentation theory* (pp. 50–80). Amsterdam, The Netherlands: Sic Sat.

Giglio, M. (2015). *Creative collaboration in teaching*. New York, NY: Palgrave Macmillan.

Gorgorio, N., & Planas, N. (2005). Cultural distance and identities-in-construction within the multicultural mathematics classroom. *ZDM, 37*(2), 64–71.

Greco, S., Mehmeti, T., & Perret-Clermont, A. N. (submitted). Discussion in the classroom: An analysis from the perspective of argumentation.

Greco, S., Mehmeti, T., & Perret-Clermont, A. N. (in press). Getting involved in an argumentation in class as a pragmatic move: Social conditions and affordances. In D. Mohammed & M. Lewinski (Eds.), *Proceedings of the 1st European Conference on Argumentation: Argumentation and reasoned action*.

Greco Morasso, S., Miserez-Caperos, C., & Perret-Clermont, A.-N. (2015). L'argumentation à visée cognitive chez les enfants. Une étude exploratoire sur les dynamiques argumentatives et psychosociales. In N. Muller Mirza & C. Buty (Eds.), *Argumentation dans les contextes de l'éducation* (pp. 39–82). Bern: Peter Lang.

Hauswirth, M., & Roshier, C. (1999). Entre fuite et retour: quel asile scolaire? *InterDIALOGOS, 99*(1), 18–23.

Hudicourt-Barnes, J. (2003). The use of argumentation in Haitian Creole science classrooms. *Harvard Educational Review, 73*(1), 73–93.

Klein, P., Nicolet, M., & Grossen, M. (2000). *Regard des élèves sur leur parcours migratoire*. Lausanne: Université. Rapport dans le cadre du Projet National de Recherche 39.

Kronig, W., Haeberlin, U. & Eckhart, M. (2000). *Immigrantenkinder und schulische Selektion. Pädagogische Visionen, theoretische Erklärungen und empirische Untersuchungen zur Wirkung integrierender und separierender Schulformen in den Grundschuljahren*. Bern, Stuttgart, Wien: Haupt-Verlag.

Leuenberger, U., & Maillard, A. (1999). *Les damnés du troisième cercle: les Albanais de la Kosove en Suisse, 1965–1999*. Genève: Les éditions Metropolis.

Mehmeti, T. (2013). Réussite scolaire de jeunes femmes kosovares: quels processus psycho-sociaux. *Dossiers de psychologie et éducation (Université de Neuchâtel), 70*, 5–125.

Müller, R. (2001). Die Situation der ausländischen Jugendlichen auf der Sekundarstufe II in der Schweizer schule: Integration oder Benachteiligung? *Schweizerische Gesellschaft für Bildungsforschung, 23*(2), 265–298.

Muller Mirza, N., & Perret-Clermont, A.-N. (Eds.). (2009). *Argumentation and education: Theoretical foundations and practices*. Dordrecht, Heidelberg, London, New York, NY: Springer.

Perret-Clermont, A. N., & Giglio, M. (in press). Créer un objet nouveau en classe. Un dispositif d'innovation pédagogique et d'observation. In M. Giglio & F. Arcidiacono (Eds.), *Les interactions sociales en classe: réflexions et perspectives*. Berne : Peter Lang.

Perret-Clermont, A. N., Arcidiacono, F., Breux, S., Greco, S., & Miserez Caperos, C. (2015). Knowledge-oriented argumentation in children. In F. H. van Eemeren & B. Garssen (Eds.), *Scrutinizing argumentation in practice* (pp. 135–149). Amsterdam, The Netherlands: Benjamins.

Piguet, E. (2005). *L'immigration en Suisse depuis 1948. Une analyse des flux migratoires*. Zürich: Seismo.

Rosebery, A. S., Ogonowski, M., DiSchino, M., & Warren, B. (2013). "The Coat Traps All Your Body Heat": Heterogeneity as fundamental to learning. *Journal of the Learning Sciences, 19*(3), 322–357.

Ryan, W. (1971). *Blaming the victim*. New York, NY: Pantheon Books.

Sinclaire-Harding, L., Miserez, C., Arcidiacono, F., & Perret-Clermont, A.-N. (2013). Argumentation in the Piagetian clinical interview: A step further in dialogism. In M. B. Ligorio & M. César (Eds.), *The interplays between dialogical learning and dialogical self* (pp. 53–82). Charlotte, NC: Information Age Publisher.

Warren, B., Ballenger, C., Ogonowski, M., & Rosebery, A. S. (2001). Rethinking diversity in learning science: The logic of everyday sense-making. *Journal of research in science teaching, 38*(5), 529–552.

Teuta Mehmeti
Institute of Psychology and Education
University of Neuchâtel

T. MEHMETI & A.-N. PERRET-CLERMONT

Anne-Nelly Perret-Clermont
Institute of Psychology and Education
University of Neuchâtel

FREDRIK RUSK, MICHAELA PÖRN AND FRITJOF SAHLSTRÖM

11. WHOSE QUESTION? WHOSE KNOWLEDGE?

Morality in the Negotiation and Management of L2
Knowledge in a Communicative L2 Programme

INTRODUCTION

Diverse applications of communicative or content-based second language (L2) education are used worldwide in several different contexts, and have yielded good results (e.g. McMillan & Turnbull, 2010; Turnbull & Dailey-O'Cain, 2010). An important issue for research on content-based and communicative language classrooms using L2 as the language of instruction is how participants, in collaboration with each other, solve and handle problems of understanding, and primacy to both own and others L2 knowledge in this specific context when the teacher is supposed to only use the L2. In these situations, the participants rely on limited L2 knowledge when maintaining intersubjectivity[1] (e.g. Hellermann, 2009; Lilja, 2010; Lilja, 2014; Majlesi & Broth, 2012).

Mutual understanding is at the heart of human social interaction (e.g. Schegloff, 2007). To restore lost intersubjectivity participants rely on repair, which is a common set of practices in social interaction, including L2 educational settings (e.g. Hellermann, 2009; Markee, 2000; Seedhouse, 2004). Much conversation analytical (CA) research on L2 educational settings and participants' repair practices in these settings focus on situations involving code-switching, that is first language (L1) use (see, e.g., Cromdal, 2000; Firth & Wagner, 1997; Kurhila, 2001; Üstünel & Seedhouse, 2005). However, trouble(s) in intersubjectivity related to L2 knowledge also occur in situations where participants rely on the L2 to repair the intersubjectivity. These situations differ from situations in which participants rely on code-switching, since the participants have to rely on limited target language knowledge when doing the repair. This brings additional risks for further difficulties in repairing the mutual understanding. These situations, which are the focus of this chapter, are still relatively unexplored in research on L2 learning.

The aim of this chapter is to analyse, using conversation analysis (CA), participants' management of L2 knowledge in interaction when solving the problems of understanding the L2, and how participants negotiate rights and primacy to own and others L2 knowledge. The setting is an introductory Finnish L2 programme for seven-year-old Swedish-speaking children (Pörn & Norrman, 2011; Pörn & Törni, 2010). The programme was a form of introductory Finnish as L2 programme that

A. Surian (Ed.), Open Spaces for Interactions and Learning Diversities, 151–166.

was strongly influenced by communicative and content-based language education (Baker, 2011). The situations analysed are characterised by a L2 learner who has problems understanding the current activity, which involves understanding the L2, and asks for the teacher's help. The analytical focus is on how participants, in these situations, manage their own and each other's L2 knowledge, including primacy to said knowledge. This includes negotiations of access and rights to knowledge.

CONVERSATION ANALYSIS AND L2 LEARNING

CA employs a participant's perspective, according to which the organizations of talk-in-interaction are not automatic running processes; they are on-going sense-making practices of participants' social interaction. How the participants understand the situations then and there is in the centre of the analysis, which in turn is based on systematically established empirical findings situated in naturally occurring settings (Schegloff, 1996, 2007). The main part of the analysis includes aspects that participants make relevant and categories, actions, and activities that participants co-construct in their interaction then and there. Every contribution (e.g. turn, utterance) to the interaction is situated in the context, shaped by the context, and renews the context (Seedhouse, 2004). A precedent turn/action makes a next turn/action relevant (e.g. greeting – greeting, question – answer) and the series of turns can be tracked for what participants may be doing through them, which responses may be relevant or possible, and where the sequence is going – that is, what outcomes the participants pursue (Schegloff, 2007).

There is a growing body of L2 research applying CA to study the social interaction in diverse L2 educational settings (e.g. Brouwer & Wagner, 2004; Firth & Wagner, 1997, 2007; Hall, Hellermann, & Pekarek Doehler, 2011; Hellermann, 2009; Kääntä, 2010; Lilja, 2010; Markee, 1995; Mondada & Doehler, 2004; Mori, 2007; Seedhouse, 2004). These studies argue that CA's participant-oriented analysis of social interaction can help to better understand how language learning in interaction is done and accomplished. Within this body of research, there is a small group that approaches learning as a social action that participants actively do in interaction (e.g. Lee, 2010; Lilja, 2014; Pallotti & Wagner, 2011; Rusk & Pörn, 2013; Sahlström, 2011; Wagner, 2010). This research explores new ways of understanding how learning can be understood as a social action: as something participants demonstrably and explicitly do in the contingency of social interaction. 'Doing learning' is analysed from a participant's perspective and through considering the learning object as something that participants actively orient to and co-construct in social interaction (Lee, 2010; Sahlström, 2011). In other words, learning and the learning object are approached from a participant's perspective: they are not externally or theoretically defined as readymade analytical categories. Whether learning is done (as an action), and whether participants orient to the social practices as learning, is an empirical question. In her analysis of conversations between L1 and L2 speakers, Lilja (2014) shows that L2 user and L2 learner are two separate entities. Her analysis reveals how participants make the two different roles locally relevant depending on the contingency of the interaction. It is relevant for the analyst to keep the concepts separate. The social action of learning is co-constructed in the social interaction by the participants.

This body of research considers epistemics in interaction, knowing, and the dynamic relationships in participants' knowledge as crucial in the practices used to do learning as a social action (e.g. Rusk & Pörn, 2013; Sahlström, 2011). Furthermore, the body of L2 research that employs CA's analysis of epistemics in interaction is continuously growing (e.g. Jakonen, 2014a, 2014b; Jakonen & Morton, 2015; Koole, 2010; Käänätä, 2014; Piirainen-Marsh & Tainio, 2014; Sert, 2013; Sert & Jacknick, 2015). Knowledge asymmetries and claims of knowledge are constantly actualized in the interaction between a teacher and a student. Participants' expressed knowing in relation to different domains of knowledge can be used as a resource for, and by, teachers and students when determining whether someone has understood what is taught and what someone has learned or needs to learn. The roles of teacher and student are not (necessarily) predefined, but instead the participants make them relevant and talk them into being in the contingency of social interaction (Lilja, 2014). This involves a negotiation of who knows what and to which extent, as well as who has primacy to which knowledge (e.g. Melander & Sahlström, 2010).

EPISTEMICS IN INTERACTION

Mutual action and understanding depend on participants' abilities to acknowledge what co-participants know or do not know regarding a specific epistemic domain and adjust actions accordingly (cf. Enfield & Levinson, 2006; Garfinkel, 1967). In the organization of dynamic epistemic relationships in social interaction, participants orient to each other's relative knowledge of a domain of knowledge (epistemic status) and express their knowing (epistemic stance) in the unfolding interaction (Heritage, 2012a, 2012b, 2012c). *Epistemic status* involves a participant's epistemic access to a domain of knowledge; what is known, how it is known, and the rights and obligations to know it (Drew, 1991; Heritage & Lindström, 1998; Pomerantz, 1980; Stivers, Mondada, & Steensig, 2011). Epistemic access is distributed among participants in interaction so that they occupy more knowledgeable (K+) or less knowledgeable (K–) positions in relation to the domain and to each other. The epistemic status is an established and settled matter for many domains of knowledge. Participants are usually treated as having more knowledge than others of domains close to them (e.g. relatives, friends etc.) and about domains that are in their expertise (Heritage, 2012a, 2012c). However, a participant's epistemic status vis-à-vis epistemic domains can be altered and/or challenged in the moment-by-moment interaction (Heritage, 2012a; Mondada, 2011).

In the negotiation of epistemic status, participants express their *epistemic stance* on a moment-by-moment basis (Heritage, 2012a, 2012c). A participant can express a 'knowing' and/or an 'unknowing' stance in relation to different epistemic domains (Heritage, 2012a). Participants usually preserve a consistency, or *epistemic congruence*, between status and stance (Heritage, 2013). Epistemic congruence refers to participants' mutual understanding of each others' knowledge states; it stretches over several turns or even entire sequences (Heritage, 2012b). Expressed epistemic stances can also be incongruent for a variety of motives and contingencies, and participants who wish to seem more or less knowledgeable than they are may dissemble their epistemic status (Drew, 2012; Heinemann, Steensig, & Lindström, 2011; Heritage, 2013; Raymond & Heritage, 2006). Epistemic incongruence in the form of exam questions may be considered as face-threatening or challenging in ordinary conversation outside of classrooms, since they, in part, invade on the co-participant's epistemic territory (e.g. Heritage, 2011; Raymond & Heritage, 2006; Sidnell, 2005). However, exam questions appear to play an important part in the dynamic epistemic relationships that are at play in classrooms (Gardner, 2012).

This present study analyses the management of L2 knowledge, including rights and obligations to L2 knowledge, in communicative L2 education. The aim of this chapter is to examine, using CA and the epistemics framework, how participants handle and solve situations in which a child at a Finnish L2 programme has problems understanding the current activity, which involves understanding the L2, and asks the teacher for help. The focus is on situations in which the L2 learner expresses an unknowing epistemic stance regarding the L2 and current activity and bids for help from the K+ participant.

RESEARCH CONTEXT AND DATA CONSTRUCTION

The empirical material consists of video recordings of a Finnish as L2 programme organised during two school semesters in 2008–2010. The programme was organised four days per week for 45 minutes. It was optional and administered outside of the school. The purpose of the L2 programme was to function as an introduction to Finnish as L2 education in accordance with the Finnish national curriculum (cf. Opetushallitus, 2004). The content of the programme was based on different concrete themes that were familiar to the participating children (e.g. their home environment and hobbies). The overall aim of the programme was communicative, that is, to help the children understand Finnish in simple everyday situations (Pörn & Törni, 2010; Pörn & Norrman, 2011). By using L2 as the language of instruction, the children got a chance to learn to understand spoken Finnish, but had no obligation to respond in Finnish (Baker, 2011). In other words, the children were allowed to use Swedish in their interaction with both the teacher and their peers, but the teacher uses the L2.

The analysis focuses on video recordings from the first year (2008–2009) of the language programme, during which the children were recorded for four separate weeks from November 2008 to April 2009. The recordings were conducted with one video camera and no external microphone. The data construction focused on the entire group of seven children. The aim was to capture the teacher's social interaction with the children. The interaction has been transcribed using CA conventions

(Hepburn & Bolden, 2012).[2] The initial data selection focused on situations in which the children explicitly bid for help. Situations in which the problem of understanding was the L2 were transcribed in greater detail. In the data of approximately 12 hours, there were 27 instances in which the children expressed an unknowing stance regarding the L2 and requested the teacher for help.

ANALYSIS

The analysis includes three excerpts. The first excerpt is an example of how the participants in this context usually orient towards each other's primacy to knowledge, and epistemic status and stance, when a child asks for help. The second excerpt exemplifies a situation in which the teacher asks an exam question, that is, adopts an incongruent unknowing stance. The third, and last, excerpt exemplifies a situation in which there appear to be misunderstandings with regard to participants' expectations of others' and own knowledge, partly, because of how primacy and obligations to L2 knowledge is negotiated.

Participants' Management of Epistemic Congruence

The following excerpt (1) represents the most often occurring forms of handling and solving situations involving the children's expressed unknowing stances regarding the L2. Excerpt (1) exemplifies a typical instructional situation in the Finnish as L2 programme, where the participants preserve a consistency between their epistemic status and stance. The teacher has laid pictures of familiar animals on the floor and instructs and explains what the group is supposed to do next. In the next activity, the children are supposed to wander around the room while the teacher plays the piano; when the music stops, the teacher says the name of an animal in the L2, and the children are then supposed to stand on a picture of the named animal as fast as possible. There is a lot happening in this excerpt, but the focus of this analysis is on how the participants manage own and others L2 knowledge in the talk-in-interaction.

The teacher begins the sequence by projecting an instructional sequence as she asks the children to be quiet and listen (line 1). In doing so, the teacher points at her ear. She often uses semiotic resources to make her message as clear as possible for the children to understand her use of the L2 (Finnish). Throughout this instructional sequence, she uses gestures to illustrate what she is saying. The teacher is oriented to as the K+ participant and the children convey possible knowing stances, answers, of what they are supposed to do next throughout the sequence (lines 11, 13, 18, 22 and 33). In between each of the incorrect possible knowing stances, the teacher restarts the instructions and demonstrates what she is saying by stepping on and pointing at the pictures (lines 15 and 23). Thus, the children's possible answers are rejected, and the participants in this situation are oriented towards changing the children's status from K– to K+ with regard to understanding the next activity (Drew, 2012; Heritage, 2012c). The children are engaging in a shared understanding

```
  01 Te: aaa (1.0) kuunnelkaa (.) ⌈kuunnelkaa kaikki ⌉(1.0)
         uuu        listen        │listen     everyone│
  02                              ⌊((points at her ear))⌋
  03     mä soitan (.) ⌈musiikkia? (1.0)            ⌉ja ⌈te kävelette             ⌉
         I play        │music?                      │and│you walk                  │
  04                   ⌊((plays piano in the air))  ⌋   ⌊((points at the children))⌋
  05     (1.0) ⌈kävelette täällä                ⌉
               │you walk  here                   │
  06           ⌊((stands up and walks around)) ⌋
  07     ja (1.0) sitten kun (.) musiikki ⌈loppuu,                     ⌉
         and      then   when     the music│stops                       │
  08                                       ⌊((holds up hand/shows 'stop'))⌋
-> 09 R:  och,
          and,
  10 Te: niin (1.0) mä sanon ⌈jo- (.)        ⌉⌈mä sanon⌉⌈jonkun eläimen.         ⌉
         then       I say    │so-            ││I say    ││some   animal.           │
-> 11 Mi:                    │ska  vi stiga  ││på den   ││                         │
                            ⌊should we step ⌋⌊on it    ⌋│                         │
  12                                                   ⌊((points att papers on floor))⌋
-> 13 R: >ja vet (.) alltså när musiken ha stanna då   ska   man hitta ett pa:
         >I know    like   when the music has stopped then should one find  a   pair
  14     fo:rt<
         fa:st<
  15 Te: aaa. (.) mä sanon jonkun- sanon (.) jonkin ⌈eläimen.           ⌉
                  I say    some-   I say     some    │animal.             │
  16                                                 ⌊((pekar på pappren)) ⌋
  17     ⌈esimerkiks              ⌉hevonen niin silloin (.)
         │for example             │horse   so   then
-> 18 R: │man tar opp en (    )   │
         ⌊you pick one up (    ) ⌋
  19 Te: ⌈tarttee löytää hevonen⌉ (1.0) ⌈tai hevonen              ⌉
         │you need to find a horse│      │or  a horse              │
  20     ⌊((steps on a paper))   ⌋      ⌊((steps on another paper))⌋
  21     (4.0)
-> 22 R: ska    jag först ställa mig    på båda två (av denhä hevonen)
         should I    first stand myself on both two (of that  horse)
  23 Te: a. schh (1.0) ⌈mä soitan (.) eeks nii, (1.0) pianoa lalalalalala⌉
         a. shhh       │I play        right,           piano  lalalalalala│
  24                   ⌊(( p l a y s  p i a n o  i n  t h e  a i r ))    ⌋
  25 Te: musiikki loppuu (.) musiikki loppui (1.0) sitten (1.0)⌈minä         ⌉sanon
         the music stops     the music stops       then        │I            │say
  26                                                            ⌊((points at herself))⌋
  27 Ma: ⌈mina sanon⌉
         │I    say   │
  28 Te: │ö:        │
         ⌊u:        ⌋
  29 Te: jää (.) minä (.) sanon (.)⌈kissa (.)        ⌉ niin⌈kaikkien             ⌉
         yes     I        say       │cat              │ then │everyone              │
  30                               ⌊((points at paper))⌋     ⌊((points at children))⌋
  31     pitää (.)⌈<löytää>        ⌉(.) kissa. ((points at paper))
         have to   │<find>          │    cat.
  32              ⌊((spanar i luften))⌋
-> 33 Mi: ⌈aj ska   vi- (.) säger du en g- en grej⌉⌈så ska   man fort stiga på den⌉=
          │oh should we-    you say  one t- one thing││so should one fast  step  on it│
  34      ⌊(( p o i n t s  &  g a z e s  a t  T e ))⌋⌊(( points & gazes at papers ))⌋
  35 Te: =jää ⌈(1.0)        ⌉niin just⌈(1.0) hyvä            ⌉
         yes  │              │exactly   │      good             │
  36          ⌊((points at Mi))⌋         ⌊((stands up & goes to piano))⌋
  37 Mi:  ⌈jaa
          ⌊yeah
```

Excerpt 1. Djurpapper (Animal papers)

as they express their knowing. They make it available for the other children to assess and help them in understanding what the next activity may be. In line 33, Mikael provides a possible understanding, a weak knowing stance, which is confirmed in

156

the next turn and accepted as correct by the teacher (lines 35–36). The teacher's confirmation of Mikael's correct answer in the third turn reaffirms her position as K+ (cf. Drew, 1981; Sinclair & Coulthard, 1975). Mikael's turn in line 33 is prefaced with a change-of-state token (Heritage, 1984; Lindström, 2008), which indicates that he now knows something he previously did not know; however, this knowing is still contingent on the teacher's confirmation, as she is the K+ participant, and oriented to as such. After this correct understanding, the teacher projects the entire group of children as K+, since Mikael gave them the answer in their L1, when she stands up and walks to the piano to begin the actual activity.

The children are displaying how they understand the instructions for the upcoming activity. They provide possible answers, knowing stances, in their L1 (Swedish), and the instructor uses the L2 (Finnish) as it is the target language. As a child displays his/her understanding of the instructions, they also share it with the group. As one child understands the activity, the entire group understands it as they then are given the instructions in Swedish since the child who understood the instructions asks for confirmation of his/her understanding. The sequence is a typical instructional sequence, from the analysed data, where the participants are oriented towards an understanding of the instructions and what the next activity is going to be. The teacher's K+ status regarding both L2 and content is institutionally sanctioned (Sidnell, 2012) and part of the practice in the L2 programme, and participants orient towards it as such. In other words, the teacher has primacy to L2 knowledge and content.

Excerpt (1) is an example of how the teacher and children reach a shared understanding of their activities then and there through the use of the L2 and semiotic resources, as well as a shared understanding regarding the L2 and the current and subsequent activities. Participants commonly withhold congruence between the epistemic stance they express and their epistemic status. The participants project and orient to a K– status, for the children, and project and orient to the teacher's status as K+. Epistemic congruence appears to be part of doing instruction and learning in these situations. The children's understanding and knowledge of the L2 and the activities are made available to both the children and the teacher as they express their stances in the social interaction. Through this management of knowledge, the participants do not claim knowledge of anything that they may not have epistemic access to.

Epistemic Incongruence to Explicate Accountability of Knowing

The next situation, excerpt (2), exemplifies situations in which the teacher dissembles her institutionally sanctioned K+ status and repeats the child's initial question, regarding problems understanding the L2, in the form of an incongruent *counter* (cf. Markee, 1995, 2004; Schegloff, 2007). This way of responding to a child's explicitly displayed problem of understanding the L2 differs from launching an instructional sequence (as exemplified in excerpt [1]).

Excerpt (2) is an example of how participants negotiate primacy to knowledge, as well as who knows what regarding the learning object that is oriented to. Mikael expresses an unknowing stance regarding L2 knowledge, which the teacher orients to as known to him, or at least as something that he should know. The children are doing assignments on a paper and in one of the assignments they are supposed to draw a red triangle. The assignments are written in the L2 (Finnish) on the paper.

```
      01 Mi: ⌈va      e kolmio:.    ⌉
             |what  is triangle:.   |
      02 Er: |klar                  |
             |done                  |
      03     (0.9)                  |
      04 Er: nu  e  ja⌈klar         |
             now I  am |done        |
  ->  05 T:            |<kolmio  mikä on kolmio>
                       |<triangle what  is triangle>
      06 Er: nu  e  ja|klar         |
             now I  am |done        |
      07 Mi:          |de e triangel|
                      |it is triangle⌋
      08 T:  jåå.
             yes.
```

Excerpt 2. Kolmio (Triangle)

Mikael asks the teacher what 'kolmio' (triangle) is (line 1). The teacher repeats the trouble-source in the second turn ('kolmio', triangle) and repeats Mikael's initial question in the form of an incongruent counter (line 5). In the third turn (line 7), Mikael confidently says 'de e triangel' (it is triangle). The teacher confirms his answer in the fourth turn (line 8). This situation is an example of how participants negotiate who has the right to know, and ask, what regarding L2 knowledge. By countering the child's question, the teacher projects the child as possibly knowing, that he has asked a question to which he knows the answer. In other words, the teacher is orienting towards the child's epistemic status as being K+ regarding the learning object that is oriented to. Mikael displays his knowledge by giving the correct answer without hesitation in the third turn. The teacher appears to orient to the assignment as one that is testing knowledge that Mikael already should have. The exchange of turns in (2) was rather common in the data analysed. The teacher often countered questions regarding L2 knowledge that the children, in her opinion, should have and that they have done learning on before.

Markee (1995, 2004) found that teachers in small group work situations in English as Second Language (ESL) classrooms had a tendency to use similar questions as those in excerpt (2). According to Markee (1995, 2004), this action appears to be typical for L2 classrooms; he also criticizes the incongruent counter as not being 'communicative' and demonstrates how participants appear to socially construct situations that may prevent actions that could promote L2 understanding and learning (Markee, 2004). In other words, the use of an incongruent counter is a delicate matter, since the knowing or unknowing of a particular participant is made explicit in the interaction. In our data, the teacher appears to be sensitive to when the children have a chance of knowing the answer themselves. Excerpt (2) exemplifies this use of an incongruent counter. Through this action, the teacher makes it explicit that the L2 learner has asked a question to which s/he knows the answer him-/herself. The K− participants are projected as knowing, and responsible for the learning and the task. The incongruent interrogative appears to be a preferred next action in this line of turns, and the K+ participant in this context appears to have limited epistemic access to know what the L2 learner does or does not know. One reason for the incongruent counters, which do invade on the epistemic territories of the K− participants (e.g. Heritage, 2011; Raymond & Heritage, 2006; Sidnell, 2005), to be oriented to as unproblematic is that the teacher (K+ participant) is invited to help. They are asked to help and the incongruent counters appear to be oriented to as part of scaffolding and support (e.g. Lantolf, 1994; Lerner, 1995; Wood, Bruner, & Ross, 1976).

Misunderstandings in the Management of Epistemic Congruence in Interaction

The next situation, excerpt (3), is an example of a misunderstanding that occurs when a child does not understand what the teacher is saying and/or doing with her talk. Two minutes before line 1, the teacher has said to the group that they can take their drawings home and finish them there. The children are drawing pictures and Elin asks the teacher if they are supposed to colour their drawing (line 1). The teacher looks at her wristwatch and says that there is not enough time, since it is time for a snack (lines 3–4).

Erik sits in the vicinity of the teacher and Elin. He overhears their exchange of turns and orients to it as he tells the teacher that he cannot colour his picture, since a monster that makes everything black and white has just walked by (lines 5–6). The teacher translates Erik's turn and acknowledges what he has just said (lines 7–8). In the next turn (line 8), the teacher repeats (what she said earlier) that they can take their drawings home today. The initial word, 'mut' (but), in the turn indicates that she orients to it as a repeat of information that should be known to the group. While doing this, she points at Erik's drawing (line 9). Erik says with a soft and insecure voice that he is not going to colour it (line 11). The teacher acknowledges it and says that he does not have to, but he can take it home (line 13). She repeats the word 'kotiin' (home) at the end of her turn, thereby emphasising it. After a long pause, Erik expresses a strong unknowing stance regarding the teacher's entire turn: 'vadå' (what, line 15). The teacher replies by using an incongruent interrogative and asking Erik to display his knowledge of what the Finnish word 'kotiin' (home) means (line 16). She designs the turn as bilingual and says in Swedish 'va e' (what is) and uses the Finnish word 'koti' (home). The teacher orients to this knowledge as something Erik should know. Erik does not have time to think for longer than 0.9 seconds before a peer, Sussi, walks by and translates the problem-word 'hemma' (home) (line 18). The teacher acknowledges and confirms Sussi's answer and repeats 'saatte

```
01 El:  ska    man färglägga
        should one colourize
02      (1.3)
03 T:  ⌈kello   on niin paljon et (nyt) on    välipala
       │the time is too  late    so (now) it is snack
04     ⌊((looks at her wristwatch))
05 Er: ja får int färglägga (.) föratt- de(d)är monstre gick   förbi:
       I can not colourize     because- tha(t)   monster walked pa:st
06     så då- då blir    allting ⌈(.) då  blir   allt⌉ing vit-⌈vitt svart
       so the-then becomes everything│  then becomes every│thing whit-│white black
07 T:                              │kaikki   on        │        │musta   valkosta
                                   ⌊everything is       ⌋        ⌊black an white
08 T:  jåå. mut tänään (.) saatte ⌈viedä kotiin.  ⌉
       yes. but today      you can│take   home.   │
09                                ⌊((points on paper))⌋
10     (0.7)
-> 11 Er: °int ska ja   färglägg(a)°
          °I'm not gonna colouriz(e)°
12     (0.9)
13 T:  ei tartte       mut saatte viedä kotiin (.) kotiin.
       you don't have to but you can take  home       home.
14     (1.1)
-> 15 Er: vadå?
          what?
16 T:  va  e koti
       what is home
17     (0.9)
-> 18 S: >hemmA.<
         >hOme.<
19 T:  mm-m (.) jå (.) saatte viedä kotiin (.) °(hem)°
       mm-m.    yes     you can take  home       °(home)°
20     (1.1)
21 T:  sit voi    jatkaa kotona jos haluu=
       then you can continue at home if  you wanna=
-> 22 Er: =ska   ja ta  hem den eller
          =should I take home it  or
23 T:  jåå
       yes
24     (1.7)
-> 25 Er: °okej°
          °okay°
```

Excerpt 3. Kotiin (Home)

viedä kotiin' (you can take home) to Erik (line 19). After a long pause, without confirmation or acknowledgement of understanding from Erik's part, the teacher rephrases her previous instructions (line 21). Erik latches on to the teacher's turn and asks for confirmation of his understanding of the turn (line 22). He ends his turn with 'eller' (or), which leaves room for the teacher to accept or reject the understanding. The teacher confirms it (line 23) and Erik closes the sequence by confirming that he has now understood (line 25).

The sequence begins with a misunderstanding on Erik's part, which appears to partially be a consequence of the use of L2 as the language of instruction. He orients towards the issue regarding the colouring of the drawing that Elin asked about in Swedish (hers and Erik's L1). In her response, the teacher launches another instruction in Finnish (the children's L2). Erik orients to the content that was previously oriented to, which Elin asked about, regarding the colouring. Erik's turn in line 11 should be understood in terms of this understanding of the context. The teacher orients to it and says that he does not have to and repeats the instruction. Erik then expresses a strong unknowing stance and the teacher appears to orient towards Erik as knowing regarding the word 'koti' (cf. excerpt [2]). She asks Erik what one word in the instruction means, the keyword, and projects him as knowing. In-and-through this action, the teacher displays that knowing the word is Erik's responsibility. A peer that walks by then gives the possible solution. The peer orients to the children's right to use each other's knowledge as a resource in this educational context. The misunderstanding on Erik's part could possibly have extended and expanded even further if the peer had not helped (e.g. Rusk & Pörn, 2013). This situation was easily resolved through a translation from Finnish to Swedish, since Erik did not appear to understand the L2 used by the teacher (line 15). However, the teacher is not in a position to translate and that is why peers are a resource for additional knowledge in understanding the instructions given in the L2 (cf. excerpt [1]). Especially in situations where the teacher projects the child as knowing and obligated to know.

DISCUSSION

The focus of this article was to better understand the management of participants' L2 knowledge in a communicative L2 programme—that is, to better understand how participants negotiate rights and responsibilities regarding knowledge of the learning objects that are oriented to when engaging in doing L2 learning. The study presented here can not draw very generalized conclusions, because of a limited set of examples offered in the analysis, and because of only studying one communicative L2 context. However, the findings are based on the larger body of analysed material, but they are exemplified through the three excerpts.

The first excerpt (1) exemplifies how most situations, when the children express an unknowing epistemic stance regarding the L2, are characterised by the participants preserving a consistency between their epistemic status and the stance(s) they express. It also exemplifies how the children and the teacher are engaged in, and oriented to, the mutual action of changing the children's knowledge of the L2 from K– to K+ in the specific context and for the specific purpose of knowing what to do in a game or how to complete an assignment.

The second excerpt (2) exemplifies situations when the determination of whether a displayed problem of understanding the L2 is 'truly' seeking for information. The L2 learners in the situations analysed in this article do not appear to have the epistemic authority to determine when or how they know. The teacher appears to have epistemic access and the right to reject (to some extent) the expressed knowing of the children, thereby invading their epistemic territories (e.g. Heritage, 2011; Raymond & Heritage, 2006; Sidnell, 2005). In most cases, this appears to be true, as the child (K– participant) knows the answer without much help from the teacher (K+ participant). This would indicate that the K+ participant uses the incongruent counter when they have done learning on the learning object before. Another aspect that the incongruent counter brings into play is that the K+ participant appears to orient to the current task as the K– participant's responsibility. This orientation explicitly makes them facilitators for the K– participant's learning. The K+ participant is not in a position to 'learn', in the same sense as the K– participant, since the K+ participant already knows. It is the K– participant's task to learn, the K+ participant orients to supporting when learning, and incongruent counters appear to be part of this action (e.g. Lantolf, 1994; Lerner, 1995; Wood, Bruner, & Ross, 1976). The incongruent counter does not appear to be 'communicative' (Markee, 1995) or 'truly' seeking for information; however, with a perspective on learning as an action that participants do, it appears that the incongruent interrogative is specifically designed and used with regard to doing learning.

The third excerpt (3) exemplifies when the K– participant is truly unknowing regarding the requested knowledge (see also Rusk & Pörn, 2013). There appears to be 'complex and difficult epistemic circumstances' in which 'incommensurate epistemic resources are in conflict' (Heritage, 2012a: 5; Sidnell, 2012: 55). In the case of the data analysed for this chapter, it is related to L2 knowledge and who knows what of the L2. There appears to be grounds for misunderstandings regarding how participants orient to and understand each other's knowing of L2, which in turn may lead to breakdowns in intersubjectivity. Moreover, K+ participants need to be sensitive to the clues and claims of knowledge that K– participants express to reach a mutual understanding with regard to what the learning object is, and how they will be doing learning related to that learning object. The use of the L2 in doing this appears to bring in a need for an increased epistemic sensitivity. The management of L2 knowledge in the context under scrutiny seems to be smooth when the task and/or content is partially familiar to the children, and when they are situated in the context then and there. However, L2 learners bring in a special set of knowing and not knowing to which all participants need to be sensitive to maintain intersubjectivity (cf. Schegloff, 2000). Therefore, may the teacher's use of the L2 when resolving the children's problems of understanding the L2 bring into the situations added epistemic domains that the participants need to be aware of. It appears that the intricate linguistic context and epistemic circumstances regarding who knows what regarding the L2 and the content require participants (both K+ and K–) to be vigilant regarding the management of epistemic congruence, epistemic access and rights to knowledge related to the epistemic domains of the L2 and the current activity.

NOTES

[1] The term intersubjectivity is multifaceted and research has been conducted on what it is in several different fields (e.g. sociology and philosophy). In this article we rely on CA-studies and the CA understanding of the term intersubjectivity (e.g. Schegloff, 1992). In talk-in-interaction, as understood from CA perspective, participants display understandings of each others' conduct and actions in the interaction and thus do they build the grounding for intersubjectivity. Intersubjectivity is maintained

moment-by-moment and turn-by-turn on a micro level by the participants in the social interaction, which enables them to have a shared understanding of their mutual social actions and activities that they perform in concert with each other.

[2] The translation of the transcripts is not idiomatic. Instead, they are an attempt to replicate the wordings, prosody, and way of speaking used by the participants in the situations transcribed, but still give the reader a good understanding of what is said. (See e.g. Bucholtz 2000; Temple and Young 2004).

(.)	a micropause less than 0.2 seconds
(0.5)	a silence indicated in tenths of seconds
[text]	overlapping talk or co-occurring embodied actions
<u>text</u>	stress or emphasis
TEXT	louder speech than normal
°text°	markedly quiet speech
:	prolongation/stretching of the prior sound
>text<	faster speech than normal
<text>	slower speech than normal
text-	cut-off or self-interrupted speech
((text))	non-verbal/embodied activity/transcriber's description of events
(text)	likely hearing of speech
(Si) / X	the identity of speaker is not clear
( )	inaudible
=	speech/body language activity latches on previous turn
@text@	animated voice
#text#	creaky voice
?	rising intonation
.	falling intonation
,	continuing intonation
hh (hh)	audible exhale
.hh (.hh)	audible inhale
text	English translation of Finnish
text	English translation of Swedish

REFERENCES

Baker, C. (2011). *Foundations of bilingual education and bilingualism*. Bristol: Multilingual Matters.

Brouwer, C. E., & Wagner, J. (2004). Developmental issues in second language conversation. *Journal of Applied Linguistics, 1*(1), 29–47.

Bucholtz, M. (2000). The politics of transcription. *Journal of Pragmatics, 32*(10), 1439–1465.

Drew, P. (1981). Adults' corrections of children's mistakes: A response to Wells and Montgomery. In P. French & M. MacLure (Eds.), *Adult-child conversation: Studies in structure and process* (pp. 244–267). London: Croom Helm.

Drew, P. (1991). Asymmetries of knowledge in conversational interactions. In I. Markova & K. Foppa (Eds.), *Asymmetries in dialogue* (pp. 21–48). Hemel Hempstead: Harvester/Wheatsheaf.

Drew, P. (2012). What drives sequences? *Research on Language & Social Interaction, 45*(1), 61–68.

Enfield, N. J., & Levinson, S. C. (Eds.). (2006). *Roots of human sociality: Culture, cognition and interaction*. New York, NY: Berg.

Firth, A., & Wagner, J. (1997). On discourse, communication, and (some) fundamental concepts in SLA research. *The Modern Language Journal, 81*, 285–300.

Firth, A., & Wagner, J. (2007). Second/foreign language learning as a social accomplishment: Elaborations on a reconceptualized SLA. *The Modern Language Journal, 91*(Focus Issue), 800–819.

Gardner, R. (2012). Conversation analysis in the classroom. In J. Sidnell & T. Stivers (Eds.), *The handbook of conversation analysis* (pp. 593–611). Chichester, West Sussex: Wiley-Blackwell.

Garfinkel, H. (1967). *Studies in ethnomethodology*. Englewood Cliffs, NJ: Prentice-Hall.

Hall, J. K., Hellermann, J., & Pekarek Doehler, S. (Eds.). (2011). *L2 interactional competence and development*. Bristol: Multilingual Matters.

Heinemann, T., Steensig, J., & Lindström, A. (2011). Addressing epistemic incongruence in question-answer sequences through the use of epistemic adverbs. In T. Stivers, L. Mondada, & J. Steensig (Eds.), *The morality of knowledge in conversation* (pp. 107–130). Cambridge: Cambridge University Press.

Hellermann, J. (2009). Looking for evidence of language learning in practices for repair: A case study of self-initiated self-repair by an adult learner of English. *Scandinavian Journal of Educational Research, 53*(2), 113–132.

Hepburn, A., & Bolden, G. B. (2012). The conversation analytic approach to transcription. In J. Sidnell & T. Stivers (Eds.), *The handbook of conversation analysis* (pp. 57–76). Chichester, West Sussex: Wiley-Blackwell.

Heritage, J. (2011). Territories of knowledge, territories of experience: Empathic moments in interaction. In T. Stivers, L. Mondada, & J. Steensig (Eds.), *The morality of knowledge in conversation* (pp. 159–183). Cambridge: Cambridge University Press.

Heritage, J. (2012a). Epistemics in action: Action formation and territories of knowledge. *Research on Language & Social Interaction, 45*(1), 1–29.

Heritage, J. (2012b). Epistemics in conversation. In J. Sidnell & T. Stivers (Eds.), *The handbook of conversation analysis* (pp. 370–394). Chichester, West Sussex: Wiley-Blackwell.

Heritage, J. (2012c). The epistemic engine: Sequence organization and territories of knowledge. *Research on Language & Social Interaction, 45*(1), 30–52.

Heritage, J. (2013). Action formation and its epistemic (and other) backgrounds. *Discourse Studies, 15*(5), 551–578.

Heritage, J., & Lindström, A. (1998). Motherhood, medicine and morality: Scenes from a medical encounter. *Research on Language & Social Interaction, 31*(3–4), 397–438.

Heritage, J., & Raymond, G. (2005). The terms of agreement: Indexing epistemic authority and subordination in talk-in-interaction. *Social Psychology Quarterly, 68*(1), 15–38.

Jakonen, T. (2014a). *Knowing matters: How students address lack of knowledge in bilingual classroom interaction* (unpublished doctoral dissertation). University of Jyväskylä, Finland.

Jakonen, T. (2014b). Building bridges. How secondary school pupils bring their informal learning experiences into a Content and Language Integrated (CLIL) classroom. *Apples, T. (2014b). Building bridges. How seco*(1), 7–28.

Jakonen, T., & Morton, T. (2015). Epistemic search sequences in peer interaction in a content-based language classroom. *Applied Linguistics, 36*(1), 73–94.

Kääntä, L. (2010). *Teacher turn-allocation and repair practices in classroom interaction: A multisemiotic perspective* (unpublished doctoral dissertation). University of Jyväskylä, Finland.

Kääntä, L. (2014). From noticing to initiating correction: Students' epistemic displays in instructional interaction. *Journal of Pragmatics, 66*, 86–105.

Koole, T. (2010). Displays of epistemic access: Student responses to teacher explanations. *Research on Language & Social Interaction, 43*(2), 183–209.

Lantolf, J. P. (1994). Sociocultural theory and second language learning: Introduction to the special issue. *The Modern Language Journal, 78*(4), 418–420.

Lee, Y.-A. (2010). Learning in the contingency of talk-in-interaction. *Text & Talk, 30*(4), 403–422.

Lerner, G. H. (1995). Turn design and the organization of participation in instructional activities. *Discourse Processes, 19*(1), 111–131.

Lilja, N. (2010). *Ongelmista oppimiseen* (unpublished doctoral dissertation). University of Jyväskylä, Finland.

Lilja, N. (2014). Partial repetitions as other-initiations of repair in second language talk: Re-establishing understanding and doing learning. *Journal of Pragmatics, 71*, 98–116.

Lindström, J. (2008). *Tur och ordning. Introduktion till svensk samtalsgrammatik*. Stockholm: Norstedts Akademiska Förlag.

Majlesi, A. R., & Broth, M. (2012). Emergent learnables in second language classroom interaction. *Learning, Culture and Social Interaction, 1*(3–4), 193–207.

Markee, N. (1995). Teachers' answers to students' questions: Problematizing the issue of making meaning. *Issues in Applied Linguistics, 6*(2), 63–92.

Markee, N. (2004). Zones of interactional transition in ESL classes. *The Modern Language Journal, 88*(4), 583–596.

McMillan, B., & Turnbull, M. (2010). Teachers' use of the first language in French immersion: Revisiting a core principle. In M. Turnbull & J. Dailey-O'Cain (Eds.), *First language use in second and foreign language learning*. Bristol: Multilingual Matters.

Melander, H., & Sahlström, F. (2010). *Lelander, H., & Sahls*. Stockholm: Liber.

Mondada, L. (2011). The management of knowledge discrepancies and of epistemic changes in institutional interactions. In T. Stivers, L. Mondada, & J. Steensig (Eds.), *The morality of knowledge in conversation* (pp. 27–57). Cambridge: Cambridge University Press.

Mondada, L., & Pekarek Doehler, S. (2004). Second language acquisition as situated practice: Task accomplishment in the French second language classroom. *The Modern Language Journal, 88*(4), 501–518.

Mori, J. (2007). Border crossings? Exploring the intersection of second language acquisition, conversation analysis, and foreign language pedagogy. *The Modern Language Journal, 91*(Focus Issue), 849–862.

Opetushallitus. (2004). *Grunderna ftus. (2004). nal, 91gs? Exploring the intersection of.* Helsinki: Opetushallitus.

Pallotti, G., & Wagner, J. (2011). L2 learning as social practice: Conversation-analytic perspectives. In G. Pallotti & J. Wagner (Eds.), *L2 learning as social practice: Conversation-analytic perspectives* (pp. 1–16). Honolulu, HI: University of Hawai'i.

Piirainen-Marsh, A., & Tainio, L. (2014). Asymmetries of knowledge and epistemic change in social gaming interaction. *The Modern Language Journal, 98*(4), 1022–1038.

Pomerantz, A. (1980). Telling my side: 'Limited access' as a 'fishing' device. *Sociological Inquiry, 50* (3–4), 186–198.

Pörn, M., & Norrman, H. (2011). *Sano se suomeksiman, H. (2011). s.* Vasa: Pedagogiska fakulteten vid Åbo Akademi i Vasa.

Pörn, M., & Törni, J. (2010). *KUKAKO*. Vasa: Pedagogiska fakulteten vid Åbo Akademi.

Raymond, G., & Heritage, J. (2006). The epistemics of social relations: Owning grandchildren. *Language in Society, 35*(5), 677–705.

Rusk, F., & Pörn, M. (2013). Epistemisk positionering som en del av andra- språkslärande i social interaktion. In M. Eronen & M. Rodi-Risberg (Eds.), *Perspektivet som utmaning, Point of view as challenge. VAKKI-symposiumi XXXIII 7.lloint of* (pp. 315–326). Vaasa: VAKKI Publications 2.

Sahlström, F. (2011). Learning as social action. In J. K. Hall, J. Hellermann, & S. Pekarek Doehler (Eds.), *L2 Interactional competence and development* (pp. 43–62). Bristol: Multilingual Matters.

Schegloff, E. (2000). When 'others' initiate repair. *Applied Linguistics, 21*, 205–243.

Schegloff, E. A. (1992). Repair after next turn: The last structurally provided defense of intersubjectivity in conversation. *American journal of sociology*, 1295–1345.

Schegloff, E. A. (1996). Confirming allusions: Toward an empirical account of action. *The American Journal of Sociology, 102*, 161–216.

Schegloff, E. A. (2007). *Sequence organization in interaction: A primer in conversation analysis I.* Cambridge: Cambridge University Press.

Seedhouse, P. (2004). *The interactional architecture of the language classroom*. Malden, MA: Blackwell Pub.

Sert, O. (2013). 'Epistemic status check' as an interactional phenomenon in instructed learning settings. *Journal of Pragmatics, 45*(1), 13–28.

Sert, O., & Jacknick, C. M. (2015). Student smiles and the negotiation of epistemics in L2 classrooms. *Journal of Pragmatics, 77*, 97–112.

Sidnell, J. (2005). *Talk and practical epistemology*. Amsterdam: John Benjamins.

Sidnell, J. (2012). Declaratives, questioning, defeasibility. *Research on Language & Social Interaction, 45*(1), 53–60.

Sinclair, J., & Coulthard, M. (1975). *Towards an analysis of discourse*. Oxford: Oxford University Press.

Stivers, T., Mondada, L., & Steensig, J. (Eds.). (2011). *The morality of knowledge in conversation.* Cambridge: Cambridge University Press.

Temple, B., & Young, A. (2004). Qualitative research and translation dilemmas. *Qualitative Research, 4*(2), 161–178.

Turnbull, M., & Dailey-O'Cain, J. (Eds.). (2010). *First language use in second and foreign language learning.* Bristol: Multilingual Matters.

Üstünel, E., & Seedhouse, P. (2005). Why that, in that language, right now? Code-switching and pedagogical focus. *International Journal of Applied Linguistics, 15*(3), 302–325.

Wagner, J. (2010). Learning and doing learning in interaction: What do participants do in everyday out-of-school second language talk? In Y. Kite & K. Ikeda (Eds.), *Language learning and socialization through conversations* (pp. 51–59). Osaka: Kansai University, Centre for Human Activity Theory.

Wood, D. J., Bruner, J. S., & Ross, G. (1976). The role of tutoring in problem solving. *Journal of Child Psychiatry and Psychology, 17*(2), 89–100.

Fredrik Rusk
Faculty of Education and Welfare Studies
Åbo Akademi University in Vaasa

Michaela Pörn
Faculty of Education and Welfare Studies
Åbo Akademi University in Vaasa

Fritjof Sahlström
Institute of Behavioural Sciences
University of Helsinki

JELENA RADIŠIĆ AND ALEKSANDER BAUCAL

12. "WHAT ABOUT WHEN THE MAJORITY IS EXCLUDED?"

A Critical Eye on Language and Math Classrooms in Serbia

INTRODUCTION

Academic discourse on diversity and inclusiveness in Serbia has, over recent years, become rather strong. Yet, apparently, very little professional practice in the actual classroom has changed. Statutes, such as The Strategy of Development of Education in Serbia until 2020,[1] laws in force, like the Law on Foundations of Education and its consecutive amendments[2] and rulebooks for the teachers (e.g. Rulebook on additional educational, health and social support of children and students)[3] have contributed from a legislative perspective towards the concept of student-centred teaching and learning to become embedded in the system. Particular emphasis has been placed on the system's inclusiveness and the extent to which it is catering for different student needs. In this way it is emphasised that students from different socio-economic backgrounds (e.g. Roma, special needs education, gifted children) should be, more than ever before, paramount in the teachers' focus.

Analysis of the effectiveness of the Serbian education system shows that much improvement is still needed in making practices truly inclusive despite the changes that have been introduced.[4] Several studies show poor effectiveness of the professional development system with regard to teachers' improvement of instruction skills along with the lack of motivating mechanisms for them to perform (SABER teacher country report: Serbia, 2012); while teachers' own perceptions speak in favour of them lacking sufficient knowledge for working with children with special needs (Spasenović & Matović, 2015). As a whole, the education system is evaluated to be insufficiently inclusive with a persistent need for strengthening inclusive practices in Serbian schools at both primary and secondary levels (Government of Republic of Serbia, 2014, Project Report, 2015).[5] Thus, despite the clear policy intention as to how the system should be developed, a substantial gap between policy and practice remains very much visible.

For several decades it has been argued that teachers' practices are particularly important for the outcomes of students' learning (e.g. Hattie, 2009; Vieluf,

A. Surian (Ed.), Open Spaces for Interactions and Learning Diversities, 167–176.

Kaplan, Klieme, & Bayer, 2012; Ing, Webb, Franke et al., 2015), while teachers are seen as the key 'engineers' of the learning environment (Brophy, 2013). What teachers do provides direct scaffolding when students explore and develop their own strengths, skills and competencies (e.g. Stigler & Hiebert, 1999; Hmelo-Silver, 2006; Bell & Pape, 2012). The ways in which teachers orchestrate their lessons varies and much of this variation is dependent upon their own beliefs as to how the teaching and learning process takes place (Pajares, 1992; Bryan & Atwater, 2002; Gregoire Hill & Fives, 2015). A number of researchers have offered different ways to describe teachers' beliefs (e.g. Korthagen, 2004), their development (e.g. Pajares, 1992; Levin, 2015) and how these may be associated with teachers' practices (e.g. Bryan & Atwater, 2002; Baumert et al., 2010; Buehl & Beck, 2015).

As part of effective classroom practices, student centred discussions are seen as a key element in constituting effective teaching in both mathematics and language and arts, since students' participation in conversations about their mathematical activity (i.e. reasoning, interpreting, and meaning-making) or particular literature piece is considered vital for them developing a broad subject matter understanding and a sense of authorship of the knowledge gained (Cobb, Boufi, McClain, & Whitenack, 1997; Nathan & Knuth, 2003; Jones, 2007; Clarke, 2014). However classrooms may not be filled with students thinking alike or different and diverse students may be learning side by side within a classroom. In order for all of them to be included in the activities, as the lesson unfolds in a meaningful way, teachers need to adapt their own instructional styles so as to cater for the needs of all of their students. (Ainscow et al., 2006; Hick & Thomas, 2008)

Having in mind the overall reports on the need to further improve the inclusive practices of the Serbian education system, in this chapter the authors examine how teachers cater for different students' needs even when faced with the mainstream students, which may be considered as a far less challenging population than the students with special needs and children from vulnerable groups. The central question of the chapter is: to what extent teachers from Serbian schools attune their practices to different interests and educational needs of students they work with? Therefore in this chapter we will examine the typical practices in language and mathematics in Serbian classrooms and the extent to which these teachers are sensitive to children's diverse needs when they work with mainstream student groups in an inclusive classroom.

METHODOLOGY

Data are drawn from a study investigating the interplay between teachers' beliefs on the teaching and learning process and their actual classroom practices. The study involves a sample of 96 upper secondary teachers from grammar and vocational schools who teach mathematics (48 teachers) and Serbian language and literature (48 teachers).[6] All the teachers (77% female)[7] work in upper secondary schools in Belgrade, the capital of Serbia, and 13 of the 96 teachers were sampled in the qualitative part of the study (10 women and 3 men) based on criteria described later in the text.

Research design. An explanatory mixed methods design was used in the study. The data were collected through a questionnaire followed by a video study and 'post-lesson video stimulated interview' with each of the teachers involved in the video study.

The quantitative part, a questionnaire, was designed using three scales: the Teacher beliefs scale; Teachers' Sense of Efficacy Scale – Short Form (Tschannen-Moran & Woolfolk Hoy, 2001), adapted for purposes of this research; and List of Teachers' Practice. The aim was to map teachers' beliefs about teaching and learning and to register their classroom practices. Items in the first and second scale were formulated as closed-type questions based on the Likert-type with 4-point rating scales ranging from 1 (don't agree at all) to 4 (totally agree), while the third scale was conceived as a Likert-type with 5-point rating scales ranging from 1 (never/almost never) to 5 (at almost every class).[8] Factor analysis of the first scale singled out several dimensions around which teachers' beliefs regarding teaching and learning could be organized. These dimensions are "modern" (example item – "In order for the students to learn something they should be able to have a discussion about it in the classroom") and "traditional" teacher (example item – The main task of teachers is to transfer knowledge to the students); reliability in the range of $\alpha = 0.783$ to $\alpha = 0.888$. Factor analysis of the Sense of Efficacy Scale – short form (Tschannen-Moran & Woolfolk Hoy, 2001) singled out two dimensions around which teachers' perceptions of their own efficacy could be described using Teachers' Sense of Efficacy Scale – short form (Tschannen-Moran & Woolfolk Hoy, 2001). Both dimensions provided satisfying reliability ($\alpha = 0.836$, and $\alpha = 0.747$) focusing on the self-efficacy in students' motivation and the other on self-efficacy in the domain of classroom management. At the List of Teaching Practices, consisting of a list of twenty-five different classroom practices that teachers may conduct in their work, the factor analysis revealed that three sets of practices could be extracted; participatory practice ($\alpha = 0.812$), practices focused on structuring the class ($\alpha = 0.748$) and practices focused on classroom atmosphere ($\alpha = 0.743$). Following the factor analysis, hierarchical cluster analysis (Ward method) was employed in order to identify the different groups of teachers based on their beliefs about teaching and learning and their dominant practices used while working with the students.

Qualitative data collection (video study and 'post-lesson video stimulated interviews') was organised based on the results of the quantitative part of the study. Using discriminant function typical teachers from each of the identified teacher groups were selected. A total of 13 teachers in the surveyed sample were thus selected for this phase of the research.[9] All teachers were regular teachers for the groups of students that were filmed. With each of the teachers, two classes were videotaped (26 in total). Recording was done using two cameras inside the classroom. All videotaping of the lessons was done following the regular teaching programme.[10] In this way researchers were able to capture typical practices of teachers and regular classroom activities students were partaking.

After the videotaping was conducted a conversation with each teacher took place in the context of a joint view of selected sequences from the class. In this way the authors were able to enter into a dialogue with the teachers on specific practices used during the videotaped lesson and the insights from the dialogues with the teachers were used to frame the subsequent analysis. The lesson sequences were balanced with respect to the teachers' subject matter. Interviews with teachers lasted an hour on average. All video sessions were transcribed using a conversational analysis approach (Jefferson, 2004) while the patterns of interaction were analysed following the I-R-F[11] structure developed by (Sinclair & Coulthard, 1975). Video analysis was also performed against the types of activities over time, the type of interaction between teachers and students, types of content implementation during the lessons and the general atmosphere over the course of the observed lessons.

RESULTS

Four different groups of teachers have been identified. The first group of teachers, labelled as "laissez-faire", perceive themselves as not being very successful in coping with disciplinary issues in the classroom. They report on scarce use of structuring practices or those "stressing class atmosphere". The group labelled "traditional stressing on atmosphere" (further in the text "T/A teacher") reveals the opposite profile. Their highest group scores have been on structuring and atmosphere stressing practices. With respect to other profiles, they believe themselves to be the most competent ones within the domain of disciplinary issues. The "traditional group" of teachers scores the lowest in participatory practices and practices focusing on atmosphere and significantly lower than the other groups in the dimension related to a modern set of beliefs on teaching and again higher than other groups in the traditional set. For this group, teaching is seen as a process during which a teacher transmits knowledge to the students. Finally, teachers labelled as the "modern group" score the highest on participatory and atmosphere stressing practices as well as on the set of modern beliefs on teaching and learning. Teaching is understood as the process during which knowledge is jointly co-constructed and shared between the teacher and the students.

Subsequent analyses show no significant connections between types of teachers and the type of school the teachers were working in ($\chi^2 = 3.864$, df = 3, p > 0.01). Significant connections have been shown between types of teachers and their subject matter ($\chi^2 = 40.951$, df = 3, p < 0.01). Both Mathematics and Language teachers have been represented in each of the four profiles, but with significantly different rates of occurrence. The language teachers are more distributed in the "laissez-faire" (35%) and "modern" labelled groups (51%) while Mathematics teachers mostly occupy "traditional" and "T/A" clusters. About 82% of Mathematics teachers could be found in the two traditionally labelled groups (teachers were equally distributed between the two), whereas only 4% are found within the group labelled to exhibit a modern teaching style.

Lesson observation against the types of teaching/learning activities over the lesson time and the ways content is implemented during the lessons pointed to differences between teachers belonging to four teacher groups. Different types of teachers differ in respect of who delivers the knowledge, to what extent students participate in the activities in the classroom, how many of them participate in the classroom talk, whether it is allowed to have more than one solution to the problem posed and the extent students may share own personal views and discuss them with others. The more traditional teacher beliefs on the teaching and the learning process are (traditional and T/A types especially) the teacher is more in charge of delivering knowledge to the students. These teachers remain as the dominant actor who introduce ideas during the lessons, pose problems to the students, and answer the questions they raised themselves. The starting point of the discussion is not associated with students' experience.

An example from a mathematics lesson held by a teacher belonging to the traditional group will be examined[12]. For this group, it is typical for teacher to have dominance over the solving process while interacting with just a few students (out of 30 which is average in Serbian upper secondary classrooms). In this case the teacher is the one who puts the problem out, but also solves it from the beginning to the very end. Students' participation comes down to coping numbers from the blackboard.

Episode 1. Traditional type teacher, lesson topic – Distance between point and line (grade two).

1. teacher: a:ll right (.) mi:nus three halves plus x plus n $((-3/2 + xn))$ (.) and since it go:es↑ through this very poi:nt (.) n will be how much? (.) this is zero since x is zero >and y mi:nus one half means n will be just mi:nus one half < (3.0) eh (.) tha:t perpe:ndicular is at the same time a perpendicular on b: (.) right? (.) and cu:ts b: at some point come on let it be b:$((B))$ (.) ca:n we fi:nd this point?

2. student: °we:can°

3. teacher: it is an intersection between m and b:$((M,B))$ (4.0) y is mi:nus three halves x mi:nus one half $((-3/2 \ x -1/2))$ (1.0) and b: is (.) two thirds x plus seven thirds $((2/3x + 7/3))$ (.) you can e:quali:ze the side on the right as the one on the left is also equal (3.0) multiply everything with si:x (.)

The teacher speaks out-loud while solving the problem as if the communication between her and the students is two way, yet when she asks a question "n will be how much?" or "can we find this point?" she is the one answering them. Even with the second question, the "*we*" positioning may indicate a shared activity, yet that will not be the case. Despite the fact that the epistemology of language and mathematics do differ, the characteristics such as described above are shared among traditionally oriented teachers irrespective them teaching mathematics or Serbian language.

When encountered with the practices of teachers belonging to the "modern" group, the delivery of knowledge, the extent of students' participation, how many of them do participate in the classroom talk and whether it is allowed to have more than one solution to the problem posed, portrays a different picture (again irrespectively of the subject taught by the teacher). In terms of the use of physical space, the teacher is amongst the students most of the time. The language spoken is the one that the students use, students' ideas are the starting point for solving the problem or starting a discussion, checking for students' understanding is frequent and, finally, the pace of activities is oriented towards the pace of the students. Regardless as to whether a mathematics or a language lesson is observed the majority of students have opportunities to present their opinions and the problems can be solved in a manner different from the one proposed by the teacher (as illustrated in math lesson example 2).

Students were given several new problems to work on (example 2). They work on them individually or in pairs at own pace. After 7–8 minutes of seat work (during this time the teacher fulfils administrative duties) students are given the opportunity to "bid for the floor". Each math problem is solved by a different student.

Episode 2. Modern type teacher, lesson topic – Solving linear equations (grade three).

1. Dejana: so the dog jumps (3.0) jump is two mete:rs a:nd ((*corrects what she just wrote on the board, teacher follows up on what Dejana is writing down, some students solve the task for themselves, others look at the board*))

2. teacher: HERE so if you don't understand (.) who doesn't understand (.) lo:o:k ((*walks in one part of classroom following what is written on the board*))(.) dejana [expla:i:ns]

3. Dejana: [( )] one minute (1.0) then we will so hm dog makes two jumps (.) then he crosses four mete:rs

4. teacher: ri:ght

5. Dejana: and the fox three jumps (.) then it is three mete:rs

6. teacher: ri:ght

7. Dejana: so it mea:ns that for one minute (.) hm the dog approaches fox ((*Dejana writes down everything she is saying at loud*)) four mete:rs minus three mete:rs that is one meter (.) so he will meet her then(.) since this is thi:rty mete:rs ((*points her hand on a drawing of a road she previously draw*)) this whole path

As students take turns in front of the board, the other students remain working on problems that they have not yet solved or check solutions they have with the ones written on the board. What is crucial is that students are both solving the problems and providing explanations as to why something is done in a given manner. The teacher gives comments only after the task is completed by the student(s). Authorship of ideas is handed in to the students. The same set of practices is seen in language lessons of teachers belonging to this group. The researchers' interpretations were backed up by teachers' accounts of their own practice during the video stimulated interviews.

CONCLUSIONS

In this chapter we have explored the typical practices of mathematics and language teachers, examining, in particular, the extent to which teachers are attuned to students' educational and learning needs even at the level of giving them enough time to solve a problem or granting them authorship for ideas produced in class. Despite the fact that current Serbian legislation strongly promotes student centred teaching, our results point to the conclusion that teacher centred methodologies still prevail in Serbian classrooms.

A higher number of teachers supporting the more traditional concept is evident amongst mathematics teachers (82%). When observed at the level of characteristics for the entire group, these remain the same irrespective of the subjects taught by the teachers. Individualized student participation is limited. Rather, these teachers cater for the needs of those students who are interested in gaining relevant knowledge of the "academic" community as this is relevant for the life choices they have made (i.e. their future enrolment at university). After all, these findings are in line with teachers' own beliefs that they are the ones passing on knowledge to students. In the cases when the learning process is seen as a mutual endeavour, taking place in a joint space created by the students and their teachers, authorship of knowledge is distributed in an entirely different manner.

One can question why this is a dominant practice? Are these teachers authoritative figures or is this a dominant culture? We argue that it is a "dominant culture" of specific academic communities who are in charge of initial teacher education. Over the course of decades teachers have been educated to be specialists of subject matter they will teach. Other elements of being a teacher have been seen to be of a lesser or more limited importance.

This leads us to the second question as to whether one can change the practices of learning if one has not yet changed the minds of the community of the teachers? The authors dare to say "No".

There will be teachers who will be bold in doing things differently, like those teachers belonging to the modern cluster, as this is in line with their own beliefs on how teaching should unfold. However, for systemic changes to take place and to be able truly to talk of inclusive practices, the change needs to happen in professional teacher communities as a whole. Since these serve as support systems motivating teachers to perform and to introduce a whole new set of practices, only when the shift occurs within, will the preconditions exist for the actual systemic change to be created.

ACKNOWLEDGEMENT

This work was partially supported by the Ministry of Education and Science of Serbia grants number 179034 and 179018.

NOTES

[1] Government of Republic of Serbia, Official Gazette, 107/2012.
[2] Government of Republic of Serbia, Official Gazette, 72/2009, 52/2011 and 55/2013.
[3] Government of Republic of Serbia, Official Gazette, 72/09.
[4] As the majority of teachers in Serbia, teachers in our study belong to those generations of teachers who were educated for the scientific career in a specific domain, while didactis or methods of teaching were rarely part of the sylabus taught.
[5] The Project "Development of Comprehensive Monitoring Framework for Inclusive Education in Serbia: Pilot Study and Assessment of Inclusiveness of Primary Education" has been jointly conducted by UNICEF; Social Inclusion and Poverty Reduction Unit, Government of Republic of Serbia; Fund for Open Society Serbia and the Institute for Psychology, Faculty of Psychology, University of Belgrade.
[6] Serbian language and literature is a L1 language.
[7] Such a gender representation is typical in the Serbian education system.
[8] All scales were previously tested in a pilot study involving 88 teachers.
[9] Initially 12 teachers were scheduled for filming, three in each cluster. Due to changes in the schedule it seemed one of the teacher was unreachable for the filming, because of which a substitute was found in the sample. When it occurred that the teacher originally planned for the filming was indeed available she was also filmed which lead to the total of 4 teacher being filmed in the 'traditional' group.
[10] In all of the lessons that were filmed the teachers followed regular activities and lesson plans and informed the researchers on which topic was to be filmed during the video study.
[11] "I" stands for the initiation (e.g. through a question from the teacher); "R" stands for response (from the student); and ("F" stands for feedback).
[12] Two episodes from the mathematics lesson are shown in the chapter to facilitate clarity of the given arguments. The episodes were chosen in a way to depict similar processes observed in the Language lessons.

REFERENCES

Ainscow, M., Booth, T., & Dyson, A. (2006). *Improving schools, developing inclusion*. London: Routledge.

Baumert, J., Kunter, M., Blum, W., Brunner, M., Dubberke, T., Jordan, A., Klusman, U., Krauss, S., Neubrand, M., & Tsai, Y-M. (2010). Teachers' mathematical knowledge, cognitive activation in the classroom, and student progress. *American Educational Research Journal, 47*, 133–180.

Bell, C. V., & Pape, S. J. (2012). Scaffolding students' opportunities to learn mathematics through social interactions. *Mathematics Education Research Journal, 24*(4), 423–445.

Brophy, J. (2013). *Motivating students to learn* (3rd ed.). London: Routledge.

Bryan, L. A., & Atwater, M. M. (2002). Teacher beliefs and cultural models: A challenge for science teacher preparation programs. *Science Education, 86*, 821–839.

Buehl, M. M., & Beck, J. S. (2015). The relationship between teachers' beliefs and teachers' practices. In H. Fives & M. Gregoire Hill (Eds.), *International handbook of research on teachers' beliefs* (pp. 66–84), London: Routledge.

Clarke, D. (2014, September 2). *Initiating students into mathematics discourse internationally.* Paper presented at EERA 2014 conference: The past, present and future of educational research in Europe. University of Porto, Portugal.

Cobb, P., Boufi, A., McClain, K., & Whitenack, J. (1997). Reflective discourse and collective reflection. *Journal for Research in Mathematics Education, 28*(3), 258–277.

Freudenthal, H. (1991). *Revisiting mathematics education.* Dordrecht, The Netherlands: Kluwer.

Government of Republic of Serbia. (2014). *Second national report on social inclusion and poverty reduction in the Republic of Serbia.* Government of Republic of Serbia.

Gregoire Hill, M., & Fives, H. (2015). Introduction In H. Fives & M. Gregoire Hill (Eds.), International handbook of research on teachers' beliefs (pp. 1–10). London: Routledge.

Hattie, J. A. C. (2009). *Visible learning: A synthesis of over 800 meta-analyses relating to achievement.* London: Routledge.

Hick, P., & Thomas, G. (Eds.). (2008). *Inclusion and diversity in education.* London: Sage.

Hmelo-Silver, C. E. (2006). Design principles for scaffolding technology based inquiry. In A. M. O'Donnell, C. E., Hmelo-Silver, & G Erkens (Eds.), *Collaborative reasoning, learning and technology* (pp. 147–170). Mahwah, NJ: Erlbaum.

Ing, M., Webb, N. M., Franke, M. L., Turrou, A. V., Wong, J., Shin, N., & Fernandez, C. H. (2015). Student participation in elementary mathematics classrooms: The missing link between teacher practices and student achievement? *Educational Studies in Mathematics, 90*(3), 341–356.

Jefferson, G. (2004). Glossary of transcript symbols with an introduction. In G. H. Lerner (Ed.), *Conversation analysis: Studies from the first generation* (pp. 13–31). Philadelphia, PA: Benjamins.

Jones, L. (2007). *The student-centered classroom.* Cambridge: Cambridge University Press.

Korthagen, F. A. J. (2004). In search of the essence of a good teacher: Towards a more holistic approach in teacher education. *Teaching and Teacher Education, 20*, 77–97.

Levin, B. B. (2015). The development of teachers' beliefs. In H. Fives & M. Gregoire Hill (Eds.), *International handbook of research on teachers' beliefs* (pp. 48–65), London: Routledge.

Natan, M. J., & Knuth, E. J (2003). A study of whole classroom mathematical discourse and teacher change. *Cognition and Instruction, 21*(2), 175–207.

Pajares, M. F. (1992). Teachers' beliefs and educational research. Cleaning up a messy construct. *Review of Educational Research, 62*, 307–332.

Sinclair J. M., & Coulthard, R. M. (1975). *Towards an analysis of discourse: The English used by teachers and pupils.* London: Oxford University Press.

Spasenović, V., & Matović, N. (2015). Preparedness of class and subject teachers for work with children with developmental difficulties. *Nastava i vaspitanje, 64*(2), 207–222.

Stigler, J., & Hiebert, J. (1999). *The teaching gap: Best ideas from the world's teachers for improving education in the classroom.* New York, NY: The Free Press.

Tschannen-Moran, M., & Woolfolk Hoy, A. (2001). Teacher efficacy: Capturing an elusive construct. *Teaching and Teacher Education, 17*, 783–805.

Vieluf, S., Kaplan, D., Klieme, E., & Bayer, S. (2012). *Teaching practices and pedagogical innovation evidence from TALIS.* Paris: OECD Publishing.

World Bank. (2012). *Country report, systems approach for better education results.* World Bank.

World Bank. (2015). *Project report development of comprehensive monitoring framework for inclusive education in serbia: Pilot study and assessment of inclusiveness of primary education.* Belgrade: UNICEF; Social Inclusion and Poverty Reduction Unit, Government of Republic of Serbia; Fund for Open Society Serbia and the Institute for Psychology, Faculty of Psychology, University of Belgrade.

Jelena Radišić
Department of Teacher Education and School Research
University of Oslo

Aleksander Baucal
Faculty of Philosophy
University of Belgrade

PART 4

FROM RESEARCH TO TEACHING

JANE HUGHES

13. FIGURED WORLDS AND IDENTITY DEVELOPMENT IN ACADEMIC ACCOUNTING

INTRODUCTION

This chapter explores the figured worlds and identity development of accounting postgraduates, studying in a university business school. Marshall and Case (2010) argue that study in higher education involves taking on a 'new identity in the world'.

Exploring student identity development offers a way to explore how learning takes place (Holland et al., 1998).

From a sociocultural perspective, individual student learning trajectories are the result of student enculturation in an educational setting and offer a way to explore the transformational and developmental aspect of learning.

A sociocultural perspective has not been common in accounting educational research to date and this chapter aims to contribute to the existing accounting education research on why accounting students focus on the procedural aspects of accounting and exclude conceptual aspects of accounting (Jackling, 2005; Umapathy, 1984).

This chapter uses student identity development to explore how accounting students change their actions and behaviours (seen in their identity development) in order to meet the teaching curriculum's requirements (contextual features). Different contexts produce different responses (Vagan, 2011; Boaler & Greeno, 2000). Ligorio et al. (2013) suggest that identity development is the result of contextual features and personal situations and note the 'uniqueness' of student learning trajectories. This chapter aims to explore two topics:

1. How do students come to focus on procedural aspects of accountancy, even when they are encouraged to do otherwise?
2. How do accounting students develop different study behaviours, even when they experience the same teaching and assessment context?

The focus of this chapter is the interaction of contextual features and personal situations in accounting students, using a figured world concept (Holland et al., 1998) to explore a university setting.

The chapter aims to contribute to the literature on how individual learning trajectories develop in university students, who have experienced the same teaching and assessment context.

A. Surian (Ed.), Open Spaces for Interactions and Learning Diversities, 179–192.

Theoretical Framework

. A figured world can be defined as:

> a socially and culturally constructed realm of interpretation in which particular characters and actors are recognized, significance is assigned to certain acts, and particular outcomes are valued over others. (Holland et al., 1998)

University lectures and seminars are social activities, established by the institution and its educators. How these events are experienced and interpreted by students can be seen in student behavior, for example, behavior in class as well as assessment performance. Students' narratives (self-report), as they engage in and reflect on such social activities as attending seminars or carrying out revision activities, indicate what students perceive as important. Such narratives highlight the characteristics of the university world that students see as valuable to their own learning and development. A figured world interpretation of an university educational setting helps show how students make sense of accounting in the classroom, that is, how students come to 'figure out' who they are as they participate in an educational world constructed by university educators.

Figured worlds show how individual identities develop, by exploring the contextual elements that influence the learning journey. Contextual elements are, for example, shown in the artifacts and discourse that students learn to value on their journey (Hatt, 2007). Discourse, as seen in narratives, or 'stories' (Sfard and Prusak, 2005) is also a way of explaining identity and identity development (Gee, 2000). Artifacts are:

> collectively developed, individually learned, and made socially and personally powerful. (Holland et al., 1998)

In an educational setting, artifacts are the objects that become meaningful to students through usage. Accounting problems, which require students to resolve a specific business issue, such as, deciding which project a business should invest in, are illustrated by teachers in lectures and seminars. How students respond to such problems and use them to develop their student identity is an important consideration for how students come to figure the academic accounting world in which they are located.

Ligorio et al. (2013) showed how the uniqueness of individual trajectories arose from the reaction of individual learning trajectories to both activities (contextual features) and to students' personal circumstances. Hence both contextual elements and personal situations (Dreier, 2003) require investigation in order to explore the uniqueness of trajectories.

When uniqueness arises from the differing circumstances of individuals, it suggests that individual circumstances (past histories and future ambitions) need to be considered when exploring learning outcomes of individuals. Individual student learning trajectories, or learning journeys, provide a way of relating individual circumstances with individual learning outcomes. Sfard and Prusak (2005) use the notion of a learning trajectory as an exploratory tool to explore identity development, by using learners' narratives, drawing on Gee (2000) and Holland et al. (1998). Sfard and Prusak (2005) argue that narratives can be illustrated by actual identities and designated identities. Actual identities are represented by actual states of being: 'I enjoy managerial accounting' or 'I am not good with numbers' might be statements from accounting postgraduates about a current situation. Designated identities focus on the expected state of being: 'I want to become an accountant' or 'I have to pass my accounting module.' Expected states of being might arise from previous learning experiences as well as current learning experiences.

Identity development is not pre-determined and may 'vary from individual to individual', even in highly prescriptive figured worlds (Urrieta, 2007). Vagan (2011) noted how 'multiple identities and different identification opportunities' existed for students studying medicine. Vagan (2011) suggested first and second year medical students experienced different figured worlds. Second year medical students gained medical skills that helped them make more sense of the problem-based clinical activities they were using. This professional medical knowledge was absent from first year medicine and without it, students created lay-figured worlds that were unsatisfying. In a similar way to medicine, accounting education at university is derived from a professional business practice (becoming a professional qualified accountant) external to the university. The challenge for students is how to make sense of accounting activities, shown as business management problems, in a classroom that lacks the real world practical accounting context.

From a sociocultural perspective, student identity development is an indication of both the learning journey of the individual student and the contextual influences of the educational setting. The contextual features of the educational setting (for example, the lectures, seminars, texts and teaching activities) provide ways for the learners to participate. How students participate, seen in their behaviour and actions, provides evidence of what has been learned and shows a growing competence in the academic skills, which are necessary in that setting. The learning journey, or learning trajectory, of a student at university is the result of their participation in the academic setting. An individual learning trajectory encompasses past histories and prior experiences, as well as current motives and future ambitions. In this way, what is learned, on a learning journey, is a way to bridge the 'gap' between where a student positions themselves on entry to university studies and where a student aims to be at graduation.

Methodology and Methods

This study took a case study approach (Yin, 2003). Student case studies were the main analytical focus. The three student cases, presented in this chapter, were part of a larger study and have been selected here for their diversity in identity development, despite experiencing the same teaching and assessment. The larger study had explored the effect of implementing seminar teaching using a problem-solving case study approach in the seminars. The larger study (not the focus of this chapter) evaluated how the seminar teaching affected student outcomes, in terms of their performance and satisfaction with their accounting experiences. Students had a positive reaction in terms of satisfaction to the seminar teaching and performance results were also satisfactory.

During the data analysis, of the larger study, the variety and uniqueness of student learning trajectories became apparent and an exploration student learning trajectories is presented below. In focusing on three student learning trajectories, the findings presented here aim to show the different ways in which students came to figure out how to participate in an academic accounting world. Student use of artifacts and narrative terms in their discourse illustrated the different student identity development.

Location, Students and Study Activities

This study took place in the business school of a UK university. The participants were postgraduate students studying accountancy as a core (mandatory) module on a generic management studies degree course. The participants studied 'accounting for managers' for one semester (twelve weeks). During the twelve weeks, each student was timetabled to attend a weekly lecture and a weekly seminar class. The size of each seminar group was limited to twenty-four students. The course leader delivered the lecture to the whole cohort (student numbers varied between sixty and one hundred and fifty). The teaching team members, comprising the course leader and seminar teachers, took the seminar classes. A number of seminar classes ran each semester, depending on the number of students enrolling for that semester. The accounting course focused on ten to twelve different, management accounting topics, for example, the topic of activity-based costing (a type of costing used in management accounting). Each weekly lecture focused on one topic and the seminar classes 'followed up' on the topic with a number of worked examples for the seminar class to review and discuss.

The seminar activities were designed around business management problems and students were asked to solve the problem. In deciding on a solution, students needed to identify and use the appropriate accounting techniques, in order to produce numerical evidence to support their decision. The seminar activities and solutions were presented to the students in a 'workbook'. The 'workbook' was available electronically; along with the lecture PowerPoint slides, on the university intranet. Students were required to download the documents and have access to them in the lectures and seminar classes. The 'workbook' activities were the artifacts that students came to value during their accounting studies.

Data Collection

Data are drawn from three sources: semi-structured student interviews (towards the end of the semester and after their accounting examination); seminar class and revision notes; and video observation of seminar classes.

Students were asked to volunteer to share their class notes and attend two interviews. In the larger study, fifty students (across six semesters) volunteered for an initial interview; eleven, of the fifty, students were able to return for a second interview and provide their notes. Three of the eleven students are presented below.

Data Analysis

Interviews were between thirty and forty minutes and were audiotaped and transcribed. Thematic analysis identified emerging themes and codes from the interviews. Thematic analysis used the narrative approach of Sfard and Prusak (2005) to identify self-reported actual and designate identity (see Table 1). The video recordings of class behaviour and a review of student notes allowed triangulation of themes from interview data. For example, one student, Abhay, described his enjoyment in accounting, partly due to his previous work experiences, and this enjoyment was also evidenced in video observation of his pleasure and his self-confidence in talking to the teacher at the end of each class about how to use the accounting technique in a business context. Abhay's class behaviour was distinctively different from other students.

'Pattern-matching' of themes from the student cases followed Yin (2003) and was organised around the defining elements of figured worlds: artifacts (how students used the seminar 'workbook' activities), discourse (the narrative terms used to describe what students thought was important for their accounting learning) and identity (how learning trajectories developed).

An 'explanation building' approach (Yin, 2003) explored how students perceived success in accounting and how students came to be successful, in their view, in accounting.

This chapter presents three case study students, Abhay, Mimi and Maor (Table 1). All three students attended the same lectures, seminar classes and sat the same examination. These students have been selected to show the different figured worlds for these different students, all of whom had the same teaching experiences.

Findings

The findings are in three parts, as follows.

The first part provides a snapshot of student behaviour, taken from the video observation of students in the seminar classes and summarises motivations and ambitions, taken from interview data.

The second part explores the contextual elements of accounting, in particular students' perceptions of the artifacts (accounting activities), as experienced by the students.

The third part explores student identity as evidenced in the students' learning trajectories. While the contextual features provoked some similarities in how student learning focused on the procedural aspects of accounting (in order to pass the examination), the student identity discussion shows how students had unique responses depending on their prior experiences and future ambitions.

Student Cases: Abhay, Maor and Mimi

Abhay was an active student. In the seminars, he participated in the class discussions, asked questions in plenary sessions (without waiting for a teacher prompt) and approached the teacher to 'chat' at the end of the class.

Although he did no class preparatory study work, he did not 'get stuck' and used his neighbours for checking results, rather than overcoming problems. He enjoyed accounting and the seminars, more so than the lectures, because he felt free, in particular, to ask questions whenever he wanted.

He was not worried about the calculations of management accounting; the examination was not 'scary' (Abhay; interview) and he developed his own technique for making the problems relevant to him. He thought that the accounting topics studied would be useful for his future career. He had already had some business experience running a family business, before commencing his postgraduate studies (see Table 1).

Maor was a highly visible student in class. He took a seat in the seminar class, usually an aisle seat, from which he could catch the teacher's attention when circulating round the class. He called out questions, interrupting the teacher. He could not articulate or explain what he found helpful or unhelpful when he was studying accounting. In the seminars, he did not want to interact with any other students. He just wanted to practise 'the drills' (his name for the calculations in the activities). Doing study work that is not assessed in the examination is a 'waste of time'.

Mimi was an invisible student in the seminars. She hid between, or by the side of, two friends of hers and kept her head over her desk; she looked as if she knew what she was doing. She did not like to interact with the teacher, by asking or replying to questions.

Mimi had never studied accountancy before and this, and her weak English language skills meant that she found herself 'lost' in the lectures and was not always clear about what she needed to do in the seminar classes. She was studying a postgraduate degree to satisfy parental expectations, rather than to satisfy her own career development needs.

Because of this, she just wanted a pass on her postgraduate qualification, as the level of pass mark did not matter.

However, Mimi did say that studying accounting had helped her understand some of the things her mother had talked about, with regard to the family business.

Table 1. Showing different motives for study, prior experiences of accounting and ambitions of the three case study students: Abhay, Maor and Mimi.

Student case	Motive for study	Prior experience of accounting	Ambition after graduation
Abhay	"My background is in engineering and I want to switch to the management side. I might actually go for an MBA later, but right now with my budget and time, I thought this would be the fastest way to switch to the management side"	None. Had worked in a family business. Undergraduate degree: Engineering	"I especially want to go into management consulting."
Maor	"I want to get more [qualifications], another degree, to put me in a better position, to get better work, but I also want to have the knowledge as well, business knowledge. It's a general degree and it touches a lot of areas, finance, marketing, accounting."	None: "I managed to avoid accounting (at undergraduate level.)" Undergraduate degree: International business with French	"I am not focused on anything at the moment."
Mimi	"I come to study here because [of] my Mum. She wants me to study, but I don't want to study […] I like to work, more than study. Because I think my relatives in Thailand, all the family, got MSc and PhD and my Mum wants me to have a proper degree to show off 'my daughter'."	None. Had worked in the family business for her mother. Undergraduate degree: Microbiology	"I am not sure."

Artifacts and Discourse

Artifacts are the objects valued by the participants and the practice in which they engage. Educational practice tends to be characterised by artifacts that indicate achievement or outcomes, for example, certificates of achievement accreditation. Hatt (2007) noted how some of the artifacts within high school were the grades, test scores and diplomas. These were evidence of achievement and were 'made socially and personally powerful' by all participants (Holland et al., 1998). For accounting students, artifacts are the accounting problems or activities, set out on pieces of paper, that are illustrated in seminars and assessed in the formal assessment, such as an examination.

For these accounting students, the accounting problems or activities particularly those experienced in the seminars, became personally powerful and meaningful as these seminar activities encouraged practising the accounting techniques. Students saw these techniques and their practise as being essential for examination success.

It was the practical aspect, practising the activities, of the seminars that the students valued. The word 'practise' was a constant theme in students' explanations of what made helped them become successful, when using the artifacts. The seminars provided an opportunity to practise the accounting techniques:

> the lecture was much more [about] explaining something and the seminar is more practical, (the seminar) gives you the practise of what you actually learn in the theory, in the lecture. Say it's like a car, yeah, in the lecture, the lecturer tells you how to drive a car, in the seminar, you actually drive a car. (Maor: interview)

Maor distinguished between other management subjects, such as marketing, that require 'discussion' rather than 'practise' as, in his view, these other disciplines require 'understanding' because they were of a more conceptual nature. For Maor, the 'practise' aspect of accountancy was important because it was necessary for examination success:

> it (the technique) sits down, it settles down in your brain when you are practising. I think the ideal position is to get in the exam when it's like automatic, doing the exercises. You don't have to think about it, so practising is the best, in this sort of subject, when you have to do exercises. (Maor: interview)

The practical aspect provided by the seminars was helpful for Mimi too:

> And what has made me successful is, first thing, that I attend seminar classes, every time, and I try to learn from the class because it is quite a new subject for me. And second thing, is the teacher, (they) teach me, teach me step by step in the class. (Mimi: interview)

However, 'practise', offered by the artifacts, was focused on examination success. The seminars provided the opportunity to experience the 'practise' that was viewed as necessary for examination success. Abhay was confident about his learned accounting skills ('it's not scary'), in particular the calculations required but went on to acknowledge how 'practise' had helped him in his examination preparation and helped him achieve a distinction-level mark in the examination:

> It was practise definitely. Everybody knows what the theory is and you read it once and remember it. It was the practise that really helped me, practising

more kinds of problems. There were several kinds of problems, we looked at many types of problems in the lectures and seminars and I think they were a great mix of all types of problems that can come in the examination. (Abhay: interview)

The accounting problems, as artifacts, figured academic accounting as a world where memorisation and practise were important. Student discourse was characterised in the terms that students used to describe the accounting activities. These terms associated the accounting activities with repetitive procedural activities (for example, the 'step by step' approach, as Mimi referred to it) where knowing the process was more important than having a conceptual understanding. To the question, 'how do you become a successful managerial accounting student?' Maor replied:

You have to revise a lot, practise the exercises 'the drills', there's no short way. If it's (revising) for the ratios, I was doing it everyday and there were some days I was focusing on something else and I didn't do the ratios and the next day, it took me longer to do it, because some ratios – it wasn't a natural thing… you have to memorise the moves. It's the same with ABC (activity-based costing), for example, every stage, you have to do it, you have to revise it, if you don't do it everyday, you go backwards.(Maor: interview)

Maor and Mimi emphasised the procedural aspect of accounting, although they had different, individual ways of making sense of the processes that they thought were essential for success. For Mimi, success comes from knowing the 'step by step' aspect of accounting and this is more important than either knowing the theory underpinning the accounting technique or how to apply the accounting technique to make a decision. The process subsumes any decision that will be made as a result of completing the seminar activity:

because it is about calculating and you have to have each step, step by step or you don't get a result from this step to that step your answer. I think it's very important to attend the seminar classes, it's more important to attend the seminar class than the lecture, because the lecture only tells you the meaning, the advantages, the disadvantages of this way (method) but when it's real, you have to practise by yourself and the seminars are very helpful. (Mimi: interview)

All three students were aware of the need to know the processes of accounting and for Mimi and Maor, the accounting processes, a procedural approach, dominated. However, Abhay described his aim to have an understanding of accounting that went beyond the 'steps' of the accounting process. He wanted to do more than just follow the 'steps' of the process. He said that he knew he had learnt something in accounting, when:

I can solve the problem without any help from anyone. If I can just solve the whole problem, and not just solve it because someone has already done it before but actually understood why I am doing this step and maybe this is the next step and then come to the right conclusion. (Abhay: interview)

Abhay went on to explain how the seminars helped him because they allowed him to interrogate the teacher; he felt 'free' to ask questions. Frequently, those questions were related to his work experiences. The seminar activities helped him to see the 'steps' but, at the same time, he used his prior experiences to make sense of the seminar accounting activities (see Table 1). In doing this, he found a personal relevance in the seminar activities, positioning himself as a student with a professional business manager outlook. For Abhay, seminars enabled a connection to be made between academic artifacts and the business world, as seminars:

really clarify the whole thing. After the lecture I am still lost, as in what was going on, but after seminars, it is very clear in my own head as to why we were doing that, why it is helpful for me, plus, I mean, I worked before, I had my own business, I can always relate managerial accounting to all the problems that I used to face, at that time. So seminars definitely make it a lot clearer and it gives a very clear picture of what's going on and how I can relate it to the real world. (Abhay: interview)

Abhay used his prior experiences to find a relevant conceptual understanding of accounting and this differentiated him from Maor and Mimi. Maor and Mimi were satisfied with finding a procedural understanding only. Both Maor and Mimi perceived a procedural understanding to be sufficient for the purpose of completing their postgraduate degree, which involved passing an accounting examination.

Actual and Designate Identities

'Student identities form as a result of day to-day activities undertaken in the name of a figured world' (Luttrell & Parker, 2001). The actual identity of these three students was differentiated according to their enjoyment and confidence in accounting. In Abhay's case, enjoyment in accounting was related to his 'real world ' experiences, prior to studying:

I am confident that I will do really well in this subject. I am not scared of it plus I really like it, this is probably the only subject that I really relate to the real world, (laughs). So it is very interesting to me – it is something I think I am definitely going to use later in life, so I just have this personal interest in the subject. So that's how I enjoy it more and that's why I am very confident in it. (Abhay: interview)

In contrast, Mimi was disenchanted with postgraduate study and did not think that it would add value to her life (Table 1). Maor found accounting frustrating and even boring. He had no prior experiences to draw on to make sense of accounting, from a managerial perspective and the accounting teaching curriculum was unable to help him find a personal relevance, other than that related to passing an examination. He described how he coped with an examination question that relied on a conceptual understanding of the accounting technique (activity-based costing). Even when a conceptual approach is required, Maor focused on the process of reading and note-making:

> You know what? What annoys me? The ABC (activity-based costing) examination questions. I read that huge (academic journal) article and now, when I think about it, it was a waste of time. I really made an effort to understand it, it's long and complex, I didn't get much out of it, maybe I should have summarised it instead, all the main points and just, maybe it would have been more useful. (Maor: interview)

Prior experiences influenced student learning trajectories. Like Abhay, Mimi has had some prior experience of business, at second hand via her mother, and tried to relate accounting, as experienced at university, to this experience:

> It (accounting) starts to give me an idea how to help me in daily life, help me to calculate about the money or something. I never managed my money. I used to work for my mother who used to say do you think the profit is good? I have to pay for electricity? air conditioning? When I study accounting, I see my Mum is right, she says, you have to include the fixed costs in your price. (Mimi: interview)

The difference between Mimi and Abhay is seen in how Abhay made a connection between his accounting experiences, his prior experiences and his designate identity of becoming a professional business manager (management consultant) (Table 1):

> It really helped me because whenever I read the problem, I have dealt with these problems before when I used to work in my family business and when it's a family business everyone is looking up to you – don't make a mistake (laughs). So I always used to look at it, ok, suppose this was given to me, should I invest in it or not and I always have that thing in my head and my father's looking at me, let's see how well you do in this. (Abhay: interview)

For Maor, this sort of interest in accounting is completely absent as he had no experience to draw on and no clear designate identity linked to a professional management career. He found the accounting topics, as experienced in the seminars, 'boring'. Both Maor and Mimi have a designate identity linked to getting a qualification. Mimi in order to fulfil parental expectations; Maor in order to 'get a better job' (see Table 1). For both Maor and Mimi, their designate identity focused on examination achievement, although examination achievement for both had a different motivation. Maor described how he would prepare for the examination, by using a rote learning approach:

> I am going to choose – I am going to go for the questions that are definitely going to be there …and then I want to know them as best as I can and probably – I want to practise them a lot. If you start thinking in exams, at least me, I will be doomed, believe me. (Maor: interview)

Maor and Mimi positioned themselves as individuals who can be successful in the examination, as long as the process has been memorised. Abhay has a less prescriptive approach. He acknowledged the value of practising accounting problems and techniques prior to the examination but put his examination success as being due to his ability to understand the conceptual aspects of accountancy due to his 'real world' experiences and his career aim:

> It kind of sounds childish, but I would look at the problem as my own problem, how I would deal with it. For example, if I am a manager or if I am a CEO (Chief Executive Officer) of a company and if I have to invest into something and it's my money, what would I look into. So I critique it in that way, so I really want to know, what other factors should I consider? Because first I used to approach it as a question and I always used to forget the [factors] that I should consider because it was like – I should do this, I should do that and that and then I talked to a lot of people and some of them told me "Consider it as your own money and then you won't forget any of the factors." That was my main way of approaching the problem. (Abhay: interview)

Further Discussion and Concluding Comments

'Discourse is one way that meanings of artifacts become collectively understood' (Hatt, 2007). In interviews, students talked about the need to 'practise' the accounting techniques, learn the layout and find the 'step by step' solution. This emphasised their view of academic accounting as embodying processes. The seminar activities required repetition and memorisation, as students prepared for the examination.

The identity development seen in the student cases in this chapter was shaped by the context in which the students participated (Vagan, 2011; Boaler & Greeno, 2000). Student identity development was seen in the move from actual to designate identity (Sfard & Prusak, 2005). The three students featured in this chapter experienced the same classroom setting but found different ways to participate, that developed from their different actual identity (comprising past histories) and different designate identity motives. Abhay's participation involved figuring a world of accounting where he could find a 'professional management' relevance in the accounting classroom problems. Abhay used his prior business experience and his motive for a designate identity to make sense of his study experiences. In doing so, he came to a conceptual understanding of accountancy.

Maor's participation involved figuring a world of accounting where the examination strategies dominated, so that designate identity focused on passing the examination and learning the 'drills'. His actual identity lacked any prior experience of accounting to draw on and he resorted to learning the 'bullet points'. Mimi's actual identity encompassed some limited business experience, with reference to accountancy, but she was unable to make the sort of personal 'professional management' connection, as Abhay did. This appeared to be due to her lack of personal study motive (designate identity) and her disenchantment with being at university (actual identity). Both Maor and Mimi remained limited to a procedural understanding of accountancy.

The sociocultural perspective of figured worlds and identity development suggests a further way to make sense of student dissatisfaction (and failure) with accounting studies. Gracia and Jenkins (2002) noted the different types of study behaviours associated with accounting success and failure/satisfaction and dissatisfaction but did not investigate how different study behaviours arose. Using a sociocultural perspective may contribute to an explanation of how heterogeneity in student study behaviours develops, despite the teaching curricula's assumption of student homogeneity. If the aim, in designing accounting curricula, is to prepare students for a post-graduation professional management life, then the role of a designate identity, in particular, may be an important consideration for accounting educators. Frequently, accounting educators' aims are to help students develop appropriate study behaviours. Consideration of how to help students envisage a personal accountancy 'designate identity', that encourages a conceptual understanding of accountancy, may be a useful addition to the aim of developing study behaviours.

This chapter showed how a sociocultural perspective might contribute to existing accounting education research. It aimed to make a contribution to the explanation of how unique individual learning trajectories arise. It supported the sociocultural view that university students find different contextual features relevant when experiencing the same teaching situations. In this chapter, the differences appeared to depend on students' individual situations, prior experiences and future ambitions. Further research from a sociocultural perspective is recommended (Haggis, 2009) in order to support accounting educators in helping students use their personal experiences using the ideas of actual and designate identities (Sfard & Prusak, 2005) in their learning.

REFERENCES

Boaler, J., & Greeno, J. G. (2000), Identity, agency, and knowing in mathematics worlds. *Multiple Perspectives on Mathematics Teaching and Learning*, 171–200.

Coetzee S. A., & Schmulian, A. (2012). A critical analysis of the pedagogical approach employed in an introductory course to IFRS. *Issues in Accounting Education*, *27*(1), 83–100.

Dreier, O. (2003). Learning in personal trajectories of participation. *Theoretical psychology: Critical contributions*, 20–29.

Garcia, L., & Jenkins, E. (2002). An exploration of student failure on an undergraduate accounting programme of study. *Accounting Education: An International Journal*, *11*(1), 93–107.

Gee, J. P. (2000). Identity as an analytic lens for research in education. Review of research in education, 99–125.

Haggis, T. (2009). What have we been thinking of? A critical overview of 40 years of student learning in higher education. *Studies in Higher Education, 34*(4), 377–390.

Hatt, B. (2007). Street smarts vs. book smarts: The figured world of smartness in the lives of marginalized, urban youth. *The Urban Review, 39*(2), 145–166.

Holland, D., Lachiotte, W. Jr., Skinner, D., & Cain, C. (1998) *Identity and agency in cultural worlds.* Cambridge: Harvard University Press.

Jackling, B. (2005). Perceptions of the learning context and learning approaches: Implications for quality learning outcomes in accounting. *Accounting Education: An International Journal, 14*(3), 271–291.

Ligorio, M. B., Loperfido, F. F., & Sansone, N. (2013). Dialogical positions as a method of understanding identity trajectories in a collaborative blended university course. *International Journal of Computer-Supported Collaborative Learning, 8*(3), 351–367.

Lucas, U., & Mladenovic, R. (2009). The identification of variation in students' understandings of disciplinary concepts: The application of the SOLO taxonomy within introductory accounting. *Higher Education, 58*, 257–283.

Luttrell, W., & Parker, C. (2001). High school students' literacy practices and identities, and the figured world of school. *Journal of Research in Reading, 24*(3), 235–247.

Marshall, D., & Case, J. (2010). Rethinking 'disadvantage' in higher education: A paradigmatic case study using narrative analysis. *Studies in Higher Education, 35*(5), 491–504.

Mladenovic, R. (2000). An investigation into ways of challenging introductory accounting students' negative perceptions in accounting. *Accounting Education: An International Journal, 9*(2), 135–155.

Sfard, A., & Prusak, A. (2005). Telling identities: In search of an analytical tool for investigating learning as a culturally shaped activity. *Educational Researcher, 34*(4), 14–223.

Umapathy, S. (1984). Algorithm-based accounting education: Opportunities and risks. *Issues in Accounting Education,* 136–143.

Urrieta Jr, L. (2007). Identity production in figured worlds: How some Mexican Americans become Chicana/o activist educators, *The Urban Review, 39*(2), 117–144.

Vagan, A. (2011). Towards a sociocultural perspective on identity formation in education, *Mind, Culture and Activity, 18*(1), 43–57.

Wenger, E. (1998). *Communities of practice: Learning, meaning and identity.* Cambridge: Cambridge University Press.

Yin, R. K. (2003). *Case study research: Design and methods.* London: Sage Publications Ltd.

Jane Ellen Hughes
Open University Business School
The Open University (UK)

ALFRED WEINBERGER AND JEAN-LUC PATRY

14. V*A*KE (VALUES *AND* KNOWLEDGE EDUCATION)

INTRODUCTION

The development of moral values is considered an important goal in education. Empirical studies from different countries show that there is widespread agreement among teachers about the significance of values education as an integral element of formal and professional education (e.g., Klaassen, 2002; Mahoney, 2009; Sockett & LePage, 2002; Tatto, Arellano, Uribe, Varella, & Rodriguez, 2001; Thornberg, 2008; Thornberg & Oguz, 2013; Veugelers & de Kat, 1999). These studies also reveal that despite the teachers' claim of the significance of values education they barely implement it in their lessons. If addressed at all, values education is done, to a high degree, in an unconscious, unplanned and unreflected way often emphasizing inappropriate strategies like rewards and punishments. A main obstacle for implementing values education arises from the overloaded curriculum with the focus mainly on subject matter and content knowledge (Gruber, 2009). Further, the teachers lack in theoretical and practical didactical and moral knowledge that would enable them to get involved explicitly with values education (e.g., Klaassen, 2002). They consider their preparation for the moral aspects of teaching and learning in teacher education to be insufficient. One can ask, then, whether it is possible to combine values education with teachers' curriculum goals in different subjects so that the teacher can address values without neglecting the academic requirements of the curriculum.

THEORETICAL BACKGROUND OF V*A*KE

The teaching and learning approach V*a*KE (Values *and* Knowledge Education) offers a possibility to integrate values or moral education with the teaching of subject matter (Patry, Weinberger, Weyringer, & Nussbaumer, 2013). V*a*KE is based on the constructivist learning theory, according to which cognitive concepts, such as moral judgment or content knowledge, are constructed by the learner rather than being conveyed through an external world (e.g., the teacher). Within the constructivist learning theory two main theoretical streams can be distinguished which both provide the basis for V*a*KE.

The cognitive constructivism in the tradition of Piaget (1985) highlights the individual construction of cognitive concepts whereas social constructivism in the tradition of Vygotsky (1978) emphasizes the co-construction of cognitive concepts through social interaction.

Piaget's (1985) constructivist theory of learning is based on the assumption that cognitive conflicts ("disequilibria") initiate the learning process. A cognitive conflict is defined as a problem situation in which the learner's current cognitive concepts prove to be inadequate to grasp some new phenomenon successfully. Because of this dissatisfaction the learner starts to integrate new concepts into the existing concepts ("assimilation" in the terms of Piaget) or to reorganize the existing concepts and adding new concepts ("accommodation"). According to the theory of socio-cognitive conflict (Mugny & Doise, 1978) such cognitive conflicts most likely emerge when learners interact with each other in order to solve a learning problem.

In addition to these knowledge-oriented theoretical frameworks, VaKE combines the morality-oriented constructivism (Kohlberg, 1984) with constructivist knowledge acquisition by using a content related moral dilemma as starting problem that triggers cognitive conflicts which lead to both moral discussions and content-related learning processes. A VaKE-dilemma triggers two questions, namely (1) how the moral problem should be solved (values education) and (2) which additional knowledge is necessary to come up with a satisfying solution (knowledge acquisition).

The first question arising from the dilemma refers to moral issues and initiates a moral dilemma discussion in the tradition of Kohlberg (Blatt & Kohlberg, 1975; Lind, 2002) which has been shown to stimulate the development of moral judgment competence (Schläfli, Rest, & Thoma, 1985). According to Kohlberg (1984) moral judgment develops along three levels, starting with an egocentric perspective emphasizing personal advantages, which is followed by a socio-centric view that highlights social welfare, and culminates in a universalistic perspective oriented towards the welfare of human mankind and the universe. Each of these levels is subdivided into two stages of moral judgment development. Not each person reaches the highest stages.

The second question arising from the dilemma refers to content knowledge and serves as a starting point for inquiry-based learning, which involves developing questions, collaboratively collecting, analyzing, and interpreting data or outlining possible explanations (Bell, Uhrhahne, Schanze, & Ploetzner, 2010; Loyens & Rikers, 2010; National Research Council, 2000).

Inquiry-based learning rests on the social constructivist theories of Vygotsky (1978) and Dewey (1938) among others; both emphasize that meaning is constructed from an experience and is influenced by social interaction. Inquiry-based learning promotes the acquisition of meaningful knowledge through authentic experiences, which addresses the higher levels of Bloom's taxonomy of learning (Bloom, Englehart, Furst, Hill, & Krathwohl, 1956; Anderson & Krathwohl, 2000), particularly *understanding, applying, analysing, evaluating*, and *creating knowledge.*

According to the constructivist assumption that knowledge is not a copy of reality rather an individual construction based on own experiences, the notion of objectivity as truth in the sense that knowledge reflects an ontologically real world is replaced by the notion of viability. According to Glasersfeld (1998, p. 23), "an action, operation, conceptual structure, or even a theory, is considered 'viable' as long as it is useful in accomplishing a task or in achieving a goal that one has set for oneself". In VaKE the learners perform viability checks (Patry, 2014) in order to assess the usability of their moral and content related constructions by asking questions like "Is my solution based on appropriate moral principles?"; "Is the acquired knowledge helpful for the dilemma discussion?"; "Is my solution, are my arguments compatible with solutions and arguments proposed by others?".

STEPS IN A PROTOTYPICAL VAKE-UNIT

A VaKE lesson consists in at least eleven steps (plus a preparation and clarification step) which are depicted in table 1 and described briefly:

1. Preparation and clarification: If it is the students' first experience with VaKE, they need to be prepared since most of them are not familiar with constructivist learning methods and the shift from teacher-centred to student-centred active learning. The learners are informed about the principles of VaKE (including the eleven steps), are introduced into the discussion rules (e.g. to let everyone finish, to respond to the argument and not to the person) and learn how to organize and to process necessary information (e.g. doing a literature search, using reading techniques, distinguishing important from not important information, excerpting).

2. Introducing the dilemma: The dilemma is presented in a form adequate for the target group. Consider the following content related moral dilemma which was used in a grade 7 class in the subject Biology:

A family named Lehman bought an expensive bio-farm not so long ago. Every week they sell their organic vegetables and fruits at the farmer's market in town but the expenditures are very high in organic cultivation. Shortly after having bought the farm, their youngest son Morton (10 years) comes down with a disease and he suffers from pain. The income is barely sufficient to cover their basic needs and the medicine for Morton is expensive and only partly covered by the health insurance. The Lehmans have tried everything to find additional money so far but all attempts to improve this situation were unsuccessful. If Mr. and Mrs. Lehman do not earn more money soon Morton's life is seriously threatened. One day a man advised the family to use chemical pesticides that would increase the production of vegetables and fruits. However, the Lehmans know that chemical pesticides are illegal in organic farming. What should the family do in this situation? Why?

After they have read the dilemma the students identify the problems (e.g. using pesticides in organic farming to save the life of Morton versus using no pesticides in organic farming because it is illegal) and analyse which values are at stake (e.g. life of Morton versus honesty, law-abidance, and organic farming).

3. First decision: The students are given some time to think about the best solution and then write down their arguments: what they think the protagonist should do and why. This decision is taken with minimal information to the students and based on their actual knowledge; it is the first opportunity to recognize that they need more facts for the decision.

4. First arguments (dilemma discussion): In small groups the students argue in favour and against the different solutions to the dilemma; this corresponds to the dilemma discussion in the tradition of Blatt and Kohlberg (1975).

5. Exchange of experiences and missing information: The group experiences concerning the results of the argumentation are exchanged, although the dilemma discussion may not be finished yet. More importantly, at this stage of learning, there is the exchange about what kind of knowledge they need to be able to discuss the dilemma more deeply. The students set their individual learning goals (e.g. dangers of chemical pesticides, advantages of organic farming) which may correspond to the curriculum goals by asking concrete questions.

6. Looking for evidence: The students organize themselves to answer the questions and to look for evidence, while the teacher is a manager and counsellor of the whole endeavour; if clearly stated, in this step, the teacher can also serve as source of information and respond to the students' content questions – as one expert among others.

7. Exchange of information: After the step of information acquisition, there is once again a step of exchange of information in the whole class so that all students have the same level of knowledge.

8. Second arguments (dilemma discussion): With this new knowledge in mind, the students turn back to the dilemma discussion in groups, as in step 3.

9. Synthesis of information: There then follows a general dilemma discussion with the presentation of the results (current state of the negotiations). This can be done in anticipation of the task to be performed in step 10. The teacher might ask challenging questions which address the moral legitimacy of the different solutions and thus guide the discussion and foster the moral development of the learners.

10. Repeat 4 through 8 if necessary: If the knowledge base is not yet sufficient, the steps 4 through 8 are repeated, with additional material and internet research and maybe with a new focus (e.g., to satisfy curricular needs); this can be done several times, depending on the time constraints of the course.

11. General synthesis: The final synthesis presents the solved problem or the current state of the solution (including, if appropriate, new problems) of the group. This can be done in didactically sophisticated ways such as through a

role-play, writing a newspaper, a mock trial etc., possibly proposed by the students themselves.

12. Generalization: The generalization consists in dealing with similar issues to broaden the perspective. Very often, this does not need to be conceived; rather the students do it spontaneously. Sometimes they decide to act in some way (e.g., writing letters to newspapers or politicians, initiating a petition against pesticides, interviewing a bio-farmer).

Table 1. Minimal steps in a VaKE lesson; italics: values education; underlined: knowledge acquisition (from Patry et al., 2013, p. 567)

	Step	Action	
0	Preparation and clarification	Abilities in the working techniques; rules of interaction	Class
1	Introduce dilemma	Understanding dilemma and values at stake	Class
2	*First decision*	Who is in favour, who against?	Group
3	*First arguments (dilemma discussion)*	Why are you in favour, why against? Do we agree with each other? (moral viability check)	Group
4	<u>Exchange experience and missing information</u>	Exchange of arguments; what more do I need to know to be able to argue further?	Class
5	<u>Looking for evidence</u>	Get the information, using any source available!	Group
6	<u>Exchange information</u>	Inform the other students about your constructions; is the information sufficient? (content related viability check)	Class
7	*Second arguments (dilemma discussion)*	Why are you in favour, why against? (moral viability check)	Group
8	*<u>Synthesis of information</u>*	Present your conclusions to the whole class (moral and content related viability check)	Class
9	*<u>Repeat 4 through 8 if necessary</u>*		Group/Class
10	*<u>General synthesis</u>*	Closing the sequence capitalizing on the whole process	Class
11	*<u>Generalization</u>*	Discussion about other but related issues	Group/Class

A typical VaKE process lasts several units but it can be adapted (e.g. shortening the steps) to the students' needs, the curriculum goals and the structure of the institution. We have used VaKE so far in different educational settings in primary and secondary school, vocational training, summer courses for high ability students, professional education and in-service teacher training.

RELATIONSHIP TO DIFFERENT THEORIES

VaKE is based on constructivist theories following Piaget (e.g., 1985), Kohlberg (1984), Vygotsky (1978) and Dewey (1938), but the approach also has close relationships with or capitalizes on other theories. VaKE is an element of the methodological pool of teaching; therefore all theories of learning and instruction as well as classroom management are involved, and VaKE can be analysed and further developed on their base. Some of the theories that go beyond traditional didactics will be addressed here briefly.

Most of these relevant theories are to be classified as non-constructivist, and they focus not only on issues related to learning and teaching, but additionally on technological, cultural, psychological and developmental aspects. Some of these issues are: problem based learning (e.g., Barrows & Tamblyn, 1980), learning in groups (e.g., Johnson & Johnson, 1991); critical thinking (e.g., Paul, 1993); individualized and web based learning (e.g., Hron & Friedrichs, 2003); the interaction between formal, non-formal and informal learning (e.g., Belle, 1982); subjective theories (e.g., Groeben, Wahl, Schlee, & Scheele, 1988; Gastager, Patry, & Gollackner, 2011); personal development and identity (e.g., Gurucharri & Selman, 1982; Blasi & Kimberly, 1995; Redmore & Loevinger, 1979; Kegan, 1982; Erikson, 1968); discourse ethics (e.g., Habermas, 1990); culture (e.g., Parsons, 1970); wisdom (e.g., Sternberg, 2003). We have not yet finished investigating the relevance of each of the above theories for the VaKE approach.

Most important are the studies which show that indeed VaKE does not inhibit (but rather improves) content learning compared to traditional teaching; this is important because a teaching tool which would hamper learning would not be accepted in the regular school system.

EMPIRICAL STUDIES

Several empirical studies examined the effectivity of VaKE in different educational settings. We will present two exemplary studies that explore whether it is possible to combine values education with knowledge construction using VaKE. For that purpose, VaKE is compared with traditional teaching which is characterized by the emphasis on instruction. The contexts of the exemplary studies are a secondary school and a teacher education institution. According to the constructivist theoretical framework of VaKE that is based on inquiry-based learning to foster applicable content knowledge and on the dilemma discussion method in the tradition of Kohlberg (Blatt & Kohlberg, 1975; Lind, 2002) to stimulate the moral judgment competence, further, discursive strategies are considered to be morally appropriate ways to solve interpersonal conflicts (Oser & Althof, 1993), the hypotheses are as follows: (1) Students in a VaKE course construct more applicable knowledge than with traditional teaching; and (2) pre-service teachers (a) increase their moral judgment competence and (b) apply discursive conflict solution strategies with V*a*KE more than in traditional teaching addressing the same contents.

The first set of studies, addressing the first hypothesis, was conducted in the regular classroom. In most studies the participants were secondary I pupils, but in some studies primary and secondary II pupils were the subjects. Results of these studies indicated that the pupils who were taught according to V*a*KE constructed at least as much knowledge as those who were taught traditionally. For instance, in the study conducted by Weinberger (2001; Patry & Weinberger, 2004) V*a*KE was evaluated in the subjects Chemistry, Biology, History and Religion in the 7th grade. A quasi-experimental cross-over design with experimental and control groups was used to test the hypothesis. This design comprises of two phases; in each phase a different topic was addressed. In the first phase class A (N = 23) was the experimental group taught according to V*a*KE and class B (N = 22) was the control group taught traditionally; the topic addressed in both classes was nuclear power plants. In the second phase class B was the experimental group taught according to V*a*KE and class A the control group taught traditionally; the topic was Jewish life and religion. Two instruments were used to assess the constructed knowledge. The first instrument was a teacher-made test with 30 items of different levels according to Bloom's taxonomy of learning (Bloom et al., 1956) used in the pre- and post-tests. The second instrument was the WALK ("W" assessment of latent knowledge), a summative assessment of constructivist teaching addressing the higher levels of Bloom's taxonomy (Patry & Weinberger, 2010) used for post-test only. The WALK consists of several pictures dealing with the topic of the V*a*KE lesson. "W" refers to the six "W"-questions (Who, What, Where, When, Why, How), that guide the pupils during the first WALK part, where they write down as many key-words as possible to each picture. In the second part they frame the key-words as questions, and in the last part they try to answer these questions. The achievement score is determined by the number of responses in each phase, after a content analysis based on a differentiated coding handbook. An analysis of variance with repeated measurement was performed to test differences between the two groups for each topic separately. The results of the teacher-made tests indicated a significant intervention effect and no interaction with teaching type in both phases. This means that the students acquired knowledge with both teaching methods, and they did not learn less with V*a*KE than with normal teaching. The results of the WALK indicated a significant effect of teaching type for the first part of the WALK (first phase: $F(1,44) = 24.02$, $p < .001$, part. $\eta^2 = .36$; second phase: $F(1,44) = 20.02$, $p < .001$; part. $\eta^2 = .30$), showing that the students constructed more applicable knowledge with V*a*KE (first phase: $M = 13.10$, $SD = 4.10$; second phase: $M = 12.42$, $SD = 4.14$) than with traditional teaching (first phase: $M = 11.30$, $SD = 5.03$; second phase: $M = 10.56$, $SD = 3.37$).

In the second set of studies to test hypothesis 2, V*a*KE was applied in teacher education. In one of them (Weinberger, 2014; Weinberger, Patry, & Weyringer, 2015) in a course called "Conflict solution strategies and social learning" which focussed on pedagogical knowledge and pedagogical content knowledge, the pre-service teachers analysed and discussed authentic dilemmas which arose from interpersonal conflict situations in their internship. In a quasi-experimental design with pre- and posttest VaKE (experimental group: N = 32) was compared with a traditional knowledge-centred learning approach (control group: N = 26). The course contents in both groups focused on types and emergence of conflicts in school, conflict solution strategies, and classroom management methods. Two instruments were used:

- The first instrument was the Moral Judgment Test MJT (Lind, 2008), which assesses the moral judgment competence. The MJT consists of two dilemmas and twelve arguments (six pro and six con arguments), representing the Kohlberg stages for each dilemma, which the participants have to rate on a nine-point Likert-scale (-4 = totally disagree, $+4$ = totally agree). Moral judgment competence is defined as the ability to apply certain moral orientations, which refer to Kohlberg's stages, in a consistent and differentiated manner in varying social situations (Lind, 2008).
- The second instrument were ten reflections (five for pretest and five for posttest), written by the pre-service teachers, focusing on their solution strategies in interpersonal conflict situations. The written reflections were content analysed according to Mayring's approach of qualitative content analysis (2014) which combines qualitative and quantitative steps of analysis. Interrater-reliability has proved to be very high (Krippendorff Alpha: .94).

The data were analysed using analyses of variance with repeated measurements.

The results concerning the MJT indicated a significant interaction between teaching type and intervention ($F(1,56) = 6.22$, $p < .05$, part. $\eta^2 = .10$). Further analysis of this effect with Bonferroni corrected Alpha-level showed that the moral judgment score (C-score) increased significantly with VaKE teaching from M = 18.5 (SD = 14.0) in the pretest to M = 35.7 (SD = 27.1) in the posttest ($p < .01$; d = .81), whereas with traditional teaching there was no significant difference found ($M_{pretest} = 24.8$, SD = 14.2; $M_{posttest} = 27.4$, SD = 15.0; ns). This confirms hypothesis 2a.

With regard to the application of discursive conflict solution strategies a significant interaction between teaching type and intervention was found ($F(1,56) = 16.67$, $p < .001$; part. $\eta^2 = .23$). Subsequent analysis of this effect with Bonferroni corrected Alpha-level revealed that the VaKE group increased significantly the application of discursive strategies to solve interpersonal conflicts from M = .23 (SD = .27) in the pretest to M = .72 (SD = .52) in the posttest ($p < .001$, d = 1.02), whereas in the control group no significant difference was found ($M_{pretest} = .27$, SD = .25; $M_{posttest} = .31$, SD = .44; ns). This confirms hypothesis 2b.

DISCUSSION

This article was guided by the question whether moral education can be integrated within teacher's curriculum goals. We introduced the teaching method VaKE that capitalizes on scientific theories (Piaget, Kohlberg, Vygotsky and Dewey) as an attempt to combine values education with knowledge construction. The studies reported show that it is possible and that VaKE might lead to both increased knowledge and increased moral competence and practice in teacher education.

The aim of our studies, however, is not to replace all traditional teaching in favour of VaKE but to combine different methods according to their appropriateness with regard to the learning goals and students' preferences. Although the evidence presented above suggests that VaKE can provide values education without neglecting knowledge construction, our experiences with VaKE in different educational settings reveal that teachers sometimes have problems and difficulties to implement VaKE. We want to address three of the main problems here.

First, teachers who prefer traditional methods might be afraid that they will lose control because the students abuse the freedom resulting in discipline problems. Our experience indicates, however, that discipline problems do not occur if VaKE is implemented carefully with a particular emphasis on the preparation and clarification step. The teacher's role in VaKE is not one of a professional "know-it-all" but an orchestrator of learning and co-constructor of knowledge and meaning in interaction with the learners. This implies that learning problems as well as social problems must be solved together, by the teacher *and* the students.

Second, the appropriate construction of a content-related moral dilemma fitting the learner's needs (e.g., their actual state of prior knowledge) turned out to be a challenging endeavour (e.g., Weinberger, 2006). The dilemma has to fulfil several criteria in order to serve as a learning problem that elicits cognitive conflicts. From the perspective of the learner, there must be a clear moral conflict between at least two equally important moral values *and* the story should trigger questions related to curriculum goals. Further requirements have shown that dilemma discussions are more effective if, among others, the learners can identify with the protagonists of the story, and if alternative dilemma solutions are excluded. Detailed instructions about how to construct moral dilemmas support teachers when implementing VaKE in their lessons (e.g., Weinberger, Patry, & Weyringer, 2008).

Third, it might happen that the teacher's beliefs about teaching and learning are incompatible with new constructivist approaches such as VaKE (e.g., Prawat, 1992). A large group of teachers still believe in the transmission model of teaching. According to this view there is one right answer and the teacher's aim should be to make sure that the pupils learn the correct answer. In order to implement VaKE successfully, we suggest that teachers make direct experience with VaKE in the role of learners and reflect their experiences based on their prior beliefs, which can contribute to change their existing beliefs.

Values education is considered as an important goal of formal and professional education. With VaKE, it is possible for teachers to overcome the problem of a trade-off between values education and knowledge acquisition – quite the opposite was found: The acquired knowledge is more applicable and the application is guided by responsibility.

REFERENCES

Anderson, L. W., & Krathwohl, D. (2001). *A taxonomy for learning, teaching, and assessing. A revision of Bloom's taxonomy of educational objectives.* New York, NY: Addison Wesley.

Barrows, H. S., & Tamblyn, R. M. (1980). *Problem-based learning: An approach to medical education.* New York, NY: Springer.

Bell, T., Urhahne, D., Schanze, S., & Ploetzner, R. (2010). Collaborative inquiry learning: Models, tools, and challenges. *International Journal of Science Education, 3*(1), 349–377.

Belle, T. J. (1982). Formal, non-formal and informal education: A holistic perspective on lifelong learning. *International Review of Education, 28*(2), 159–175.

Blatt, M., & Kohlberg, L. (1975). The effects of classroom moral discussion upon children's moral judgement. *Journal of Moral Education, 4,* 129–161.

Bloom, B. S., Englehart, M. B., Furst, E. J., Hill, W. H., & Krathwohl, D. R. (1956). *Taxonomy of educational objectives. The classification of educational goals. Handbook I: Cognitive domain.* New York, NY: Longmans Green.

Dewey, J. (1938). *Logic: The theory of inquiry.* New York, NY: Henry Holt and Company.

Gastager, A., Patry, J.-L., & Gollackner, K. (Eds.). (2011). *Subjektive Theorien über das eigene Tun in sozialen Handlungsfeldern* [Subjective theories about one's action in the social domain]. Innsbruck, Austria: StudienVerlag.

Glasersfeld, E. von. (1998). Why constructivism must be radical? In M. Larochelle, N. Bednarz, & J. Garrison (Eds.), *Constructivism in education* (pp. 23–28). Cambridge: Cambridge University Press.

Groeben, N., Wahl, D., Schlee, J., & Scheele, B. (1988). *Das Forschungsprogramm Subjektive Theorien. Eine Einführung in die Psychologie des reflexiven Subjekts* [The research programme subjective theories. An introduction into the psychology of the reflective individual]. Tübingen: Francke.

Gruber, M. (2009). Hindernisse schulischer Werteerziehung aus Lehrersicht [Obstacles to values education from the perspective of teachers]. In K. Zierer (Hrsg.), *Schulische Werteerziehung* [Values education in school] (pp. 231–237). Baltmannsweiler: Schneider Verlag Hohengehren.

Gurucharri, C., & Selman, R. L. (1982). The development of interpersonal understanding during childhood, preadolescence, and adolescence: A longitudinal follow-up study. *Child Development, 53*(4), 924–927.

Habermas, J. (1990). *Moral consciousness and communicative action.* Cambridge, MA: MIT Press.

Hron, A., & Friedrich, H. F. (2003). A review of web-based collaborative learning: Factors beyond technology. *Journal of Computer Assisted Learning, 19*(1), 70–79.

Johnson, D. W., & Johnson, R. T. (1991). *Cooperation in the classroom.* Edina, MN: Interaction Book Company.

Kegan, R. (1982). *The evolving self: Problem and process in human development.* Cambridge, MA: Harvard University Press.

Klaassen, C. A. (2002). Teacher pedagogical competence and sensibility. *Teaching and Teacher Education, 18,* 151–158.

Kohlberg, L. (1984). *Essays on moral development, Vol. 2: The psychology of moral development.* San Francisco, CA: Harper & Row.

Lind, G. (2002). *Mora list lernbar* [Morality can be learned]. Berlin: Logos.

Lind, G. (2008). The meaning and measurement of moral judgment competence revisited – A dual-aspect model. In D. Fasko & W. Willis (Eds.), *Contemporary philosophical and psychological perspectives on moral development and education* (pp. 185–220). Cresskill, NJ: Hampton Press.

Loyens, S. M. M., & Rikers, R. M. J. P. (2010). Instruction based on inquiry. In R. E. Mayer & P. A. Alexander (Eds.), *Handbook of research on learning and instruction. Educational psychology handbook series* (pp. 361–381). New York, NY & London: Routledge.

Mahoney, P. (2009). Should ought be taught. *Teaching and Teacher Education, 25,* 983–989.

Miller, M. (2006). *Dissens. Zur Theorie diskursiven und systemischen Lernens* [Dissent: A theory of discursive and systemic learning]. Bielefeld: transcript.

Mugny, G., & Doise, W. (1978). Socio-cognitive conflict and structure of individual and collective performances. *European Journal of Psychology, 8,* 181–192.

National Research Council. (2000). *Inquiry and the National Science Education Standards*. Washington, DC: National Academy Press. Retrieved December 20, 2015, from www.nap.edu/read/9596/chapter/1#ii

Oser, F., & Althof, W. (1993). Trust in advance: On the professional morality of teachers. *Journal of Moral Education, 22*(3), 253–276.

Parsons, T. (1970). *The social system*. London: Routledge & Kegan Paul Ltd.

Patry, J.-L. (2014). Die Viabilität und der Viabilitäts-Check von Antworten. In C. Giordano & J.-L. Patry (Hrsg.), *Fragen! Antworten? Interdisziplinäre Perspektiven* [Questions! Answers? Interdisciplinary perspectives]. Freiburger Sozialanthropologische Studien (pp. 11–35). Wien: Lit.

Patry, J.-L., & Weinberger, A. (2010) Leistungsmessung im konstruktivistischen Unterricht: WALK [Measurement of learning outcomes in constructivist teaching: WALK]. In K. Zierer (Hrsg.), *Schulische Werteerziehung* [Values education in school] (pp. 220–230). Hohengehren: Schneider.

Patry, J.-L., Weinberger, A., Weyringer, S., & Nussbaumer, M. (2013). Combining values and knowledge education. In B. J. Irby, G. Brown, R. Lara-Alecio, & S. Jackson (Eds.), *The handbook of educational theories* (pp. 565–579). Charlotte, NC: Information Age Publishing.

Paul, R. (1993). *Critical thinking. What every person needs to survive in a rapidly changing world*. Santa Rosa, CA: Foundation for Critical Thinking.

Piaget, J. (1985). *The equilibration of cognitive structures*. Chicago, IL: University of Chicago Press.

Prawat, R. S. (1992). Teacher's beliefs about teaching and learning: A constructivist perspective. *American Journal of Education, 100*(3), 354–395.

Redmore, C. D., & Loevinger, J. (1979). Ego development in adolescence: Longitudinal studies. *Journal of Youth and Adolescence, 8*(1), 1–20.

Schläfli, A., Rest, J. R., & Thoma, S. J. (1985). Does moral education improve moral judgment? A meta-analysis of intervention studies using the defining issues test. *Review of Educational Research, 55*(3), 319–352.

Sockett, H., & LePage, P. (2002). The missing language of the classroom. *Teaching and Teacher Education, 18*, 159–171.

Sternberg, R. J. (Ed.) (2003). *Wisdom. Its nature, origins, and development* (2nd ed.). New York, NY: Cambridge University Press.

Tatto, M. T., Arellano, L. A., Uribe, M. T., Varela, A. V., & Rodriguez, M. (2001). Examining Mexico's moral education in a globally dynamic context. *Journal of Moral Education, 30*(2), 173–198.

Thornberg, R. (2008). The lack of professional knowledge in moral education. *Teaching and Teacher Education, 24*, 1791–1798.

Thornberg, R., & Oğuz, E. (2013). Teachers' views on moral education: A qualitative study in Sweden and Turkey. *International Journal of Educational Research, 59*, 49–56.

Veugelers, W., & de Kat, E. (1999, April 19–23). *Moral development at home and at school: Division of moral tasks between parents and teachers in secondary school*. Paper presented at the Annual Meeting of the American Educational Research Association, Montreal, Canada. Retrieved December 20, 2015, from http://files.eric.ed.gov/fulltext/ED435490.pdf

Vygotsky, L. S. (1978). *Mind in society*. Cambridge, MA: Harvard University Press.

Weinberger, A. (2006). *Kombination von Werterziehung und Wissenserwerb. Evaluation des konstruktivistischen Unterrichtsmodells VaKE (Values and Knowledge Education) in der Sekundarstufe I [Combination of values education and knowledge construction. Evaluation of the learning method VaKE]*. Hamburg: Kovac.

Weinberger, A. (2014, June 25–28). *Promoting professional judgment in teacher education with moral case-analysis*. Paper presented at the EARLI Sig 13-conference in Verona, Italy.

Weinberger, A., Patry, J.-L., & Weyringer, S. (2008). *VaKE: Values and knowledge education. Handbuch für Lehrerinnen und Lehrer*. [VaKE: Values and Knowledge Education. Handbook for teachers]. Innsbruck: Studienverlag.

Weinberger, A., Patry, J.-L., & Weyringer, S. (2015). Improving professional moral practice through practitioner research: VaKE (Values *and* Knowledge Education) in university based teacher education. *Vocations and Learning*, 1–22. Retrieved December 20, 2015, from http://link.springer.com/article/10.1007/s12186-015-9141-4

A. WEINBERGER & J.-L. PATRY

Alfred Weinberger
Private University of Teacher Education of the Diocese of Linz

Jean-Luc Patry
Paris-Lodron University of Salzburg

15. DEVELOPING CROSS-CULTURAL AWARENESS IN HIGHER EDUCATION THROUGH THE USE OF VIDEO-LOGS FOCUSING ON CRITICAL INCIDENTS

INTRODUCTION

The attention for cross-cultural and intercultural awareness is gaining ground within education theory, as well as in educational policies while it remains little explored in practice (Baker, 2015). Higher Education institutions are promoting a variety of internationalization initiatives, including attracting foreign teachers and students, sending abroad their students for long periods, as well as offering face-to-face, on-line and blended teaching in a variety of languages – although English dominates this side of the internationalization process. Within Europe, the Erasmus Mundus university courses offer a significant amount of students the opportunity to complete their higher education degrees by attending more than one university. Worldwide, the number of colleges and universities offering study abroad programmes has dramatically increased (McAllister & Irvine, 2000). The development of students' intercultural competence plays a core role within such student mobility programmes (Anderson et al., 2006) and it is becoming a specific learning outcome. The immersion in a different environment in itself neither develops cross-cultural skills, nor it reduces stereotypical perceptions of otherness (Coleman, 1998; Shaules, 2007; Strong, 2011). In order to lead to the development of cross-cultural skills, experiencing diversity should be coupled with reflection and analysis (Alred, Byram, & Fleming, 2003; Jackson, 2010; Vande Berg, 2009). Recent handbooks offer targeted resources addressing these issues, an example being the recent IEREST manual which offers ten intercultural education teaching activities for students in higher education who are involved in the Erasmus programme. Exploring different cultures, learning new ways of thinking and behaving, improving cross-cultural knowledge and skills (Andrade, 2006; McClure, 2007) are listed among the potential learning achievements of student mobility programmes, although, so far students' cross-cultural learning outcomes are seldom assessed (Anderson et al., 2006; Gillespe, 2002). In order to address learning and assessment approaches in this field, at least three issues have to be taken into account. Firstly, international students develop specific requirements: when they are not acknowledged and met by host institutions students are prone to feel disappointed (Sherry et al., 2010). Secondly, as already mentioned, international mobility per se does not develop a greater cultural sensitivity: this requires the students (a) to experience cultural diversity and (b) to actively develop acknowledgement and understanding of cultural differences (Anderson et al., 2006). In addition, this is a relatively underexplored area in teachers' professional development in relation to educational practices addressing diversity. Exploring students' cross-cultural sensitivity during study abroad programmes provides interesting ground for a reflection on the efficacy of teaching practices in such contexts and support.

CRITICAL INCIDENTS AS TOOL TO ADDRESS CROSS-CULTURAL LEARNING

Through student mobility college and higher education students from a variety of countries come into continuous and first-hand contact with individuals of the host culture. There is still little evidence of teaching practice that acknowledges the dynamic ways cultures and languages are related in cross-cultural communication. Experiencing and reflecting upon cultural diversity has a core role in developing awareness and sensitivity in this field. Critical incidents offer one way of developing experience and reflection that might lead to enhanced cross-cultural awareness. Surian and Damini (2014) offer a short overview in relation to the use of critical incidents as educational tools in relation to cross-cultural learning. What is a critical incident?

> By an incident is meant any observable human activity that is sufficiently complete in itself to permit inferences and predictions to be made about the person performing the act. To be critical, an incident must occur in a situation where the purpose or intent of the act seems fairly clear to the observer and where its consequences are sufficiently definite to leave little doubt concerning its effects. (Flanagan, 1954)

Compared to case studies, critical incidents are shorter. From a cultural perspective, Wight (1995) summarises critical incidents as

> brief descriptions of situations in which there is a misunderstanding, problem or conflict arising from cultural differences between interacting parties or where there is a problem of cross-cultural adaptation.

They were introduced into intercultural training at the beginning of the 1960s (de Frankrijker, 1998). Although there are different approaches to critical incidents in training, their use typically implies providing short information in order to "set the stage", a snapshot of (the main facts concerning) the incident, and some comments about feelings and reactions by the involved parties. This short information should lead to question(s) encouraging participant(s) to provide their views on these facts and possibly to explain the portions that do not overlap across what is being taken for granted by the different par- ties, i.e. the cultural differences at stake.

Within cross-cultural critical incidents literature, cultural differences are understood mainly as implicit cultural standard and expectations. The critical incident approach does not make such cultural standard and expectations explicit. It rather encourages participants to identify them and to reflect upon them through the activity of finding viewpoints at work within the critical incident and generating potential operational scenarios in response to the incident (Wight, 1995).

According to most studies on intercultural competences (Deardorff, 2009), in order to develop intercultural competence it is crucial to learn to view the world, including "own" world including other viewpoints. This refers to the ability to learn how to "think about oneself" while at the same time one is observing the "other" and "oneself" (Fitzgerald, 2000), or, in other words, to observe the tensions across the relationships. This should contribute to develop an ability to analyse and find answers to what Spradley and McCurdy (1972) define as "cultural scenes", and Turner (1974) labels everyday life "social dramas". This implies an ability to make room and being ready to experience alterity within relationships as well as to conceive individuality as an evolutionary process.

Working with critical incidents can be instrumental in facilitating the development of self- reflection (Fitzgerald, Mullaveey-O"Bryne, Clemson, & Williamson, 1996; Fitzgerald, 2001) and to address and to de- construct cultural stereotypes. The communication misunderstanding at the core of the critical incident offers an opportunity to reflect in a critical way on the tensions that make the relationship difficult and therefore both on the "other" as well as on one's "own" culture. It is this potential "dis-oriented" position that offers an opportunity for a change of perspective (Glicszinski, 2007) when combined with reflective practices.

How can we introduce such reflective dimension in relation to critical incidents within higher education courses? The use of video-logs seems promising. Wired Magazine founder Kevin Kelly and Creative Commons founder and Stanford law professor Lawrence Lessig describe our cultural shift today as one from book literacy to screen fluency where video is the new vernacular—a "world beyond words".

The use of video-log has been proposed for fostering deliberate and scaffolded reflection on experiences that involve cultural diversity (Wong & Webster, 2012). A video-log is a form of blog in which the medium is the video. Its use in relation to the experience of students who study abroad is thus potentially interesting. In order to use video-logs on critical incidents to trigger reflection and to assess cultural awareness, it becomes crucial to explore tools for measuring acculturation and shifts in worldviews, i.e. cross-cultural sensitivity. The second part of this chapter explores first a tool to explore cross-cultural sensitivity and then tools to measure acculturation.

ASSESSING CROSS-CULTURAL SENSITIVITY

The Association of American Colleges and Universities (AAC&U) has produced a rubric to define Intercultural Knowledge learning outcomes. The rubric's definition of Intercultural Knowledge and Competence is based on the work by Bennett (2008). Intercultural Knowledge and Competence are spelled out as a set of cognitive, affective, and behavioural skills and characteristics that support effective and appropriate interaction in a variety of cultural contexts.

The rubric suggests a systematic way to measure the capacity to identify one's own cultural patterns, to compare and to contrast them with others, and to adapt empathically and flexibly to unfamiliar ways of being. Again, Bennett's (1993) work is referred to in order to inform the levels of the rubric consistently with the Developmental Model of Intercultural Sensitivity as well as with Deardorff's (2006) model of intercultural competence. Elaborated between 1986 and 1993, DMIS is not a model of attitude change or of skill acquisition. Rather, it is a model of the development of worldviews. It is structured into six stages: the first three stages are labelled "ethno-centric" and the later three stages are labelled "ethno-relative". In line with the dominant perception of the term, in Bennett's definition, ethno-centric means that one's own culture is experienced as central to reality in some way.

In Denial (stage 1), one's own culture is experienced as the only real one, and consideration of other cultures is avoided by maintaining psychological and/or physical isolation from differences.

In Defense (stage 2), one's own culture (or an adopted culture) is experienced as the only good one, and cultural difference is denigrated.

In Minimization (stage 3), elements of one's own cultural worldview are experienced as universal, so that despite acceptable surface differences with other cultures, deep down those cultures are seen as essentially similar to one's own.

The second three DMIS stages, i.e. the ethno-relative stage, indicate that one's own culture is experienced in the context of other cultures.

In Acceptance (stage 4), other cultures are experienced as equally complex but different constructions of reality.

In Adaptation (stage 5), one attains the ability to shift perspective in and out of another cultural worldview; thus, one's experience potentially includes the different cultural experience of someone from another culture.

In Integration (stage 6), one's experience of self is expanded to include the movement in and out of different cultural worldviews. This stage would be difficult to detect through a critical incident exercise.

Since the original version of Bennett's developmental model of intercultural sensitivity a few revisions have been made (Hammer, 2012): minimization is considered as a transition from ethnocentrism to ethnorelativism, and not a stage of the former mindset; Integration is not considered as a development of intercultural competence, but rather as the construction of an intercultural identity.

In summary the ethno-centric stages can be viewed as ways of avoiding cultural difference (by denying its existence, by raising defences against it, or by minimizing its importance) while the ethno-relative stages are ways of seeking cultural difference (by accepting its importance, by adapting one's perspective to take it into account, or by integrating the whole concept into a definition of one's identity). From an educational perspective it seems appropriate to refer to the DMIS (or similar models) more as potential intercultural strategies than as a rigid progression from one development stage to another in a linear way. Yet, the DMIS can be instrumental in referring people's attitudes towards cultural diversity to specific worldviews. DMIS can thus be a reference assessment tool for studies aimed at using qualitative tools such as critical incidents to identify students' viewpoints and competence in relation to cultural diversity.

As previously mentioned, through student mobility college and higher education students from a variety of countries come into continuous and first-hand contact with individuals of the host culture. Such process is defined as acculturation (Redfield, Linton, & Herskovits, 1936). It is a mutual process, in which individuals from different cultural backgrounds influence each other. Research has confirmed that acculturation occurs also for students who live temporarily in a foreign country (Pedersen et al., 2011). Risk factors for a dysfunctional adjustment that have been found are: differentiation between and host cultures; cultural distance; unsatisfying relations with host country individuals; weak host country identification; and poor language proficiency (Pedersen et al., 2011). How to assess the key components of such acculturation process? DMIS offers a grid to relate the qualitative assessment of critical incidents to the first five intercultural sensitivity stages. In addition, several instruments are available to assess students' acculturation. A significant proportion of such instruments include items assessing language proficiency, which is a relevant variable, although not always a variable that is adequately achieved during a few months mobility programme.

DEFINING ACCULTURATION

When there is a continuous and prolonged contact between two cultural groups, individual within the groups must adapt to the new cultural situation. (Huynh, Howell, & Benet-Martinez, 2009). This process has been called *culture shock*, *acculturation*, *cultural adaptation* or, finally, *cultural adjustment*. The first term, *culture shock*, was originally proposed by Oberg (Oberg, 1960), and referred to the anxiety resulting from losing all the familiar signs and symbols of social intercourse. The second term, *acculturation*, replaced the first one, to attribute to cultural contact a neutral connotation, as not necessarily all intercultural encounters have a negative outcome. Finally, *cultural adaptation* and *adjustment* refer to the behavioural and psychological changes that are mediated by technological artefacts (Inghilleri & Riva, 2009).

From Monodimensional to Bidimensional Models

Initially, the process of adapting to another culture was defined by a one-dimensional model, according to which the more time one individual spends in a host culture, the more oriented he or she becomes toward that culture and, at the same time, the more he or she relinquish their heritage culture (e.g., Cuellar, Harris, & Jasso,

1980). Thus, the acculturative process was represented as a line that starts from the origin culture and ends with the host culture: the more an individual detaches him- or herself from the origin values and behaviours to embrace the host values and behaviours, the more acculturated he or she can be considered (Inghilleri & Riva, 2009). However, one-dimensional models of acculturation fail in explaining situations that happen very frequently in cultural contacts, e.g. acculturative stress, inter-ethnic conflicts, and the like (Inghilleri & Riva, 2009). More recently, scholars working on the acculturation process have embraced the bi-dimensional model of acculturation, according to which individuals can have interdependent but separate orientations toward their origin and host cultures (Celenk & Van de Vijver, 2011; Heine, 2008; Huynh et al., 2009; Ward & Rana-Deuba, 1999). Berry (1974) was one of the first scholars who hypothesized a bi-dimensional model of cultural adaptation that take into consideration two cultural universes, the origin and host ones. Questionnaires should determine to what extent an individual wishes to remain who he or she was, rather than integrating to a wider social group, or what is the extent an individual wished to interact with people from another culture, rather than interacting with people of their own culture. If the position of an individual on the two dimensions is dichotomized, four different acculturative strategies are derived: integration, separation, assimilation, and marginalization. People with an integrative acculturative strategy value both cultural maintenance and intergroup relations. People with a separatist acculturative strategy value cultural maintenance but not intergroup relations. People with an assimilative acculturative strategy value intergroup relations but not cultural maintenance. Finally, people with a marginalization acculturative strategy do not value neither cultural maintenance nor intergroup relations (Berry, 2003). Such strategies would be relational (i.e., enacted in specific cultural contexts,) and not absolute to an individual. One individual might have a general integration strategy, but separate from the host culture in a certain circumstance (e.g., religious practices).

Acculturative strategies are considered significant predictors of acculturative stress. For instance, marginalization and separation were associated with higher levels of acculturative stress, integration was associated with lower level of stress, and assimilation was associated with an intermediate stress level (Berry, Kim, Minde, & Mok, 1987). It is thus fundamental to assess the levels of the identification with the origin and host cultures of individuals immersed in another culture, and the consequent acculturative strategy.

Assessment of Acculturation: Typological and Dimensional Approaches

Several bi-dimensional measures of acculturation have been developed in the past years, and they can be roughly categorized in *typological* and *dimensional* approaches, based on their approach to the assessment of the two cultural orientations (Kang, 2006). Following Berry's initial indications, acculturation research has mainly developed typological instruments including four separate scales for the measurement of Assimilation, Separation, Integration, and Marginalization (Ward & Rana-Deuba, 1999). For instance, an example of item to test individuals' level of assimilation strategy is "We're living in Canada, and that means giving up our traditional way of life and adopting a Canadian lifestyle, thinking and acting like Canadians." However, several authors criticized the use of four scales to measure acculturation (Ward & Rana-Deuba, 1999). From a theoretical perspective, measuring acculturation through four separate scales does not allow to compare directly students in term of the two core questions that Berry considered to underpinning acculturation strategies: "Is it considered to be of value to maintain one's identity and characteristics?" and "Is it considered to be of value to maintain relationships with the larger society?" (Berry, Kim, Power, Young, & Bujaki, 1989). The consequence of a typological approach then is a lack of independence among the scales, which can bring to results difficult to explain, e.g., the strong correlations between assimilation and separation scales, or between integration and assimilation scores (Berry et al., 1989). Moreover, most instruments measuring acculturation strategies through four scales include scale items that are lengthy and involve multiple concepts rather than simple, single-notion statements (Ward & Kennedy, 1994).

As an alternative, a few instrument have adopted a dimensional approach and assessed acculturation through two scales only, i.e., relationship to culture of origin and relationship to culture of contact, and have used a bipartite split to allow the investigation of the four acculturation strategies (see for instance the Vancouver Index of Acculturation by Ryder, Alden, & Paulhus, 2000, or the Acculturation Index by Ward & Rana-Deuba, 1999). For instance, an example of item testing students' attitudes towards the two cultures is "I often behave in ways that are typical of my *origin/host* culture." There are two approaches to splitting the identification scales, i.e. the scalar midpoint or the median score may be selected as the cut-off criterion. The first approach produces a result that allows cross-sample comparisons, whereas the second approach relies more on a within-sample classification scheme (Ward & Rana-Deuba, 1999).

Assessment of Acculturation: Limitations

Several open issues still limit a reliable use of acculturation scales. Firstly, most instruments have been developed for specific cultural context (e.g., The Acculturation Rating Scale for Mexican Americans, Cuellar, Arnold, & Maldonado, 1995). Conversely, other instruments have been developed for use with all cultural groups, but even so they have been originally tested on specific populations (e.g., Asian-Canadians for the Vancouver Index of Acculturation by Ryder et al., 2000, or international aid workers in Nepal for the Acculturation Index by Ward & Rana-Deuba, 1999). In both case, there are questions of cultural validity of the instruments when used with other populations (Celenk & Van de Vijver, 2011). Secondly, several instruments report a lack of independence among the sub-scales. Whereas we have already discussed this problem in relation to instruments including four separate scales to measure acculturation strategies, even some instrument using only two scales showed orthogonality between the heritage and the host scales. Kang (2006) suggested that the reason why certain acculturation scales have demonstrated the independence, whereas others did not might depend on scale formats. Acculturation indexes generally consist of paired questions to assess individuals' orientation towards the heritage versus host culture in multiple domains of life, but they do so with different formats of questions, i.e. frequency, proficiency, and endorsement. In the frequency format, people are asked to rate each item in terms of frequency of certain behaviours (e.g., "How much do you speak English/ Chinese at home?"). This format is often chosen to assess language use, but has been used for several other domains too (e.g., food, interpersonal network, and the like). In the proficiency format, people are asked to rate each item in terms of competence (e.g., "How well can you speak English/Chinese?"). This format is exclusively adopted to assess language proficiency. In the endorsement format, people are asked to rate each item in terms of agreement/disagreement with it (e.g., "I am proud of American/Chinese culture"). According to Kang (2006), the acculturation scales that showed independence between the two sub-scales used only endorsement format, rather than a mix of formats. The endorsement format appears then to be the most reliable way to assess acculturation, but implies renouncing to assess language proficiency, typically assessed through the proficiency format, a solution adopted by several instruments (e.g., the Vancouver Index of Acculturation by Ryder et al., 2000, or the Acculturation Index by Ward & Rana-Deuba, 1999). However, given the importance of language as the core element of acculturation, and its positive effect on adjustment, renouncing to assess people's language use and proficiency might lead to a partial view of their acculturation process (Kang, 2006).

DISCUSSION AND CONCLUSIONS

The increase of internationalization initiatives promoted by Higher Education institutions from all over the world, does not necessarily lead to greater intercultural sensitivity (Anderson et al., 2006), for a set of different reasons. For instance, gains in intercultural competence hardly ever assessed (Anderson et al., 2006), thus it is difficult for practitioners to know what is the level of acculturation of the students they are teaching too, and to set specific and attainable goals for them. In addition, students with different acculturation strategies, might have different needs, and different sources of cultural stress.

Thus, it is important to provide teachers and practitioners working in cross-cultural educational settings with tools to reflect on students' development of intercultural sensitivity and awareness. To this aim, and to foster theoretical advances about the nature of diversity understandings and strategies, we propose the combined use of video-logs to foster reflection on intercultural sensitivity, and acculturation scales to foster reflection on intercultural awareness.

Video-logs could help educational practitioners to explore whether students are increasing their cultural sensitivity (Anderson et al., 2006), what are their specific needs, and what are the sources of their acculturative stress (Sherry et al., 2010). Video-logs can help students to develop narratives about cultural incidents that have happened to them. Through narratives they can express, become aware of, and reflect *to be made about the person performing the act* (Flanagan, 1954).

In student mobility programmes, it is fundamental that students experience cultural unfamiliarity (Wong & Webster, 2012), and that teachers explicitly address it (Deardorff, 2009). Reflecting upon critical incidents through the use of video-logs cold be helpful in this sense. Video-logs could be used as an assessment instrument, to reveal students' worldviews, and as a training instrument, to have students reflect on their own cultural analysis of events. To do so, it seems promising to study students' narratives by using a combination of models and scales such as DMIS and acculturation scales. And narrative theory and analysis (as forthcoming) It also seems useful to have video-logs used in interaction with an analysis of students' identification with the host culture and the heritage culture. The most appropriate way to assess students' acculturation seems to be the dimensional approach (e.g., the Vancouver Index of Acculturation by Ryder et al., 2000, or the Acculturation Index by Ward & Rana-Deuba, 1999), as it helps to reflect on the fact that acculturation is not just the outcome of the encounter between two different cultures, but rather of an internal crisis between students' identification with values and practices of their original culture and their interest and openness towards values and practices of the host culture.

REFERENCES

Anderson, P. H., Lawton, L., Rexeisen, R. J., & Hubbard, A. C. (2006). Short-term study abroad and intercultural sensitivity: A pilot study. *International Journal of Intercultural Relations, 30*, 457–469. doi:10.1016/j.ijintrel.2005.10.004

Andrade, M. S. (2006). International students in English-speaking universities: Adjustment factors. *Journal of Research in International Education, 5*(2), 131–154.

Baker, W. (2015). Research into practice: Cultural and intercultural awareness. *Language Teaching, 48*, 130–141. doi:10.1017/S0261444814000287

Bennett, J. M. (2008). Transformative training: Designing programs for culture learning. In M. A. Moodian (Ed.), *Contemporary leadership and intercultural competence: Understanding and utilizing cultural diversity to build successful organizations* (pp. 95–110). Thousand Oaks, CA: Sage.

Bennett, M. J. (1993). Towards ethnorelativism: A developmental model of intercultural sensitivity. In R. M. Paige (Ed.), *Education for the intercultural experience* (pp. 21–71). Yarmouth, ME: Intercultural Press.

Berry, J. W. (1974). Psychological aspects of cultural pluralism: Unity and identity reconsidered. *Topics in Culture Learning, 2*, 17–22.

Berry, J. W. (2003). Conceptual approaches to acculturation. In K. M. Chun, P. Balls Organista, & G. Marìn (Eds.), *Acculturation: Advances in theory, measurement, and applied research* (pp. 17–37). Washington, DC: American Psychological Association. doi:10.1037/10472-004

Berry, J. W., Kim, U., Minde, T., & Mok, D. (1987). Comparative studies of acculturative stress. *The International Migration and Review, 21*, 491–511. doi:10.2307/2546607

Berry, J. W., Kim, U., Power, S., Young, M., & Bujaki, M. (1989). Acculturation studies in plural societies. *Applied Psychology: An International Review, 38*, 135–186.

Celenk, O., & Van de Vijver, F. J. R. (2011). Assessment of acculturation: Issues and overview of measures. *Online Readings in Psychology and Culture, 8*(1). doi:10.9707/2307-0919.1105

Cuellar, I., Harris, L., & Jasso, R. (1980). An acculturation scale for Mexican American normal and clinical populations. *Hispanic Journal of Behavioral Sciences, 2*, 199–217.

Cuellar, I., Arnold, B., & Maldonado, R. (1995). Acculturation rating scale for Mexican Americans-II: A revision of the original ARSMA Scale. *Hispanic Journal of Behavioral Sciences, 17*, 275–304. doi:10.1177/07399863950173001

Deardorff, D. (2009). *The sage handbook of intercultural competence*. London, UK: Sage.

Deardorff, D. K. (2006). The identification and assessment of intercultural competence as a student outcome of internationalization. *Journal of Studies in International Education, 10*(3): 241–266.

Gillespie, J. (2002). Colleges need better ways to assess study-abroad programs. *The Chronicle of Higher Education, 48*(43), B20.

Hammer, M. R., Bennett, M. J., & Wiseman, R. (2003). Measuring intercultural sensitivity: The intercultural development inventory. *International Journal of Intercultural Relations, 27*, 421–443. doi:10.1016/S0147-1767(03)00032-4

Heine, S. J. (2008). *Cultural psychology*. New York, NY: W. W. Norton & Company.

Huynh, Q.-L., Howell, R. T., & Benet-Martinez, V. (2009). Reliability of bidimensional acculturation scores: A meta-analysis. *Journal of Cross-Cultural Psychology, 40*(2), 256–274. doi:10.1177/0022022108328919

Inghilleri, P., & Riva, E. (2009). Il confronto fra culture e le dinamiche psicologiche (en. tr., Confrontation among cultures and psychological dynamics). In P. Inghilleri (Ed.), *Psicologia Culturale (en. tr., Cultural Psychology)* (pp. 49–88). Milano, IT: Raffaello Cortina Editore.

Kang, S.-M. (2006). Measurement of acculturation, scale formats, and language competence. Implications for adjustment. *Journal of Cross-Cultural Psychology, 37*, 669–693. doi:10.1177/0022022106292077

McClure, J. W. (2007). International graduates' cross-cultural adjustment: Experiences, coping strategies, and suggested programmatic responses. *Teaching in Higher Education, 12*(2), 199–217.

Oberg, K. (1960). Cultural shock: Adjustment to new cultural environments. *Practical Anthropology, 7*, 177–182.

Paigea, M., Jacobs-Cassuto, M., Yershova, Y. A., & DeJaeghere, J. (2003). Assessing intercultural sensitivity: An empirical analysis of the Hammer and Bennett intercultural development inventory. *International Journal of Intercultural Relations, 27*, 467–486. doi:10.1016/S0147- 1767(03)00034-8

Pedersen, E. R., Neighbors, C., Larimer, M. E., & Lee, C. L. (2011). Measuring sojourner adjustment among American students studying abroad. *International Journal of Intercultural Relations, 35*, 881–889. doi:10.1016/j.ijintrel.2011.06.003

Redfield, R., Linton, R., & Herskovits, M. J. (1936). Memorandum for the study of acculturation. *American Anthropologist, 38*, 149–152. doi:10.1525/aa.1936.38.1.02a00330

Russell, J., Rosenthal, D., & Thomson, G. (2010). The international student experience: Three styles of adaptation. *Higher Education, 60*(2), 235–249.

Ryder, A. G., Alden, L. E., & Paulhus, D. L. (2000). Is acculturation unidimensional or bidimensional? A head-to-head comparison in the prediction of personality, self-identity, and adjustment. *Journal of Personality and Social Psychology, 79*, 49–65. doi:10.1037/0022-3514.79.1.49

Segall, M. H. (1990). Acculturation. In M. H. Segall, P. R., Dasen, J. W. Berry, & Y. H. Poortinga (Eds.), *Human behavior in global perspective: An introduction to cross-cultural psychology* (pp. 299–320). New York, NY: Pergamon Press.

Sherry, M., Thomans, P., & Chui, W. H. (2010). International students: a vulnerable population. *Higher Education, 60*, 33–46.

Surian, A., & Damini, M. (2014). "Becoming" a cooperative learner-teacher. *Anales de Psicologia, 30*(3).

Taylor, E. (1994). Intercultural competency: A transformative learning process. *Adult Education Quarterly Spring, 44*, 154–174.

Ward, C., & Kennedy, A. (1994). Acculturation strategies, psychological adjustment, and sociocultural competence during cross-cultural transitions. *International Journal of Intercultural Relations, 18*(3), 329–343. doi:10.1016/0147-1767(94)90036-1

Ward, C., & Rana-Deuba, A. (1999). Acculturation and adaptation revisited. *Journal of Cross-Cultural Psychology, 30*(4), 422–442. doi:10.1177/0022022199030004003

Wong, E. D., & Webster, A. (2012, March). *Using digital video logs to promote global competency in study abroad programs.* Paper presented at the annual meeting of The Forum on Education Abroad, Denver, CO.

Christian Tarchi
Department of Education and Psychology
University of Florence

Alessio Surian
Department of Philosophy, Sociology, Education, and Applied Psychology (FISPPA)
University of Padova

Lightning Source UK Ltd.
Milton Keynes UK
UKOW06f1124300316

271173UK00001B/8/P